# Thomism and Aristotelianism

*A Study
of the Commentary by Thomas Aquinas
on the Nicomachean Ethics*

*By*

HARRY V. JAFFA

THE UNIVERSITY OF CHICAGO PRESS

The University of Chicago Press, Chicago 37
Cambridge University Press, London, N W 1, England
W J Gage & Co, Limited, Toronto 2B, Canada

*Copyright 1952 by The University of Chicago  All rights
reserved  Published 1952  Composed and printed by* The
University of Chicago Press, *Chicago, Illinois,* U S A

# Thomism and Aristotelianism

"*It is baffling to reflect that what men call honour does not correspond always to Christian ethics*"

WINSTON CHURCHILL

TO MY WIFE

# TABLE OF CONTENTS

# CHAPTER I

## INTRODUCTORY STATEMENT
## OF THE PROBLEM

THE problems to be discussed in this study will, perhaps, be more intelligible if they are first outlined within the broader context of the political situation from which their urgency is derived. Nearly everyone who is intelligently concerned with present-day political problems, and the moral problems which are in reality contingent features of the central political issues, is concerned to find a truly practical political or social science Yet, except for Marxism, there is virtually no large body of opinion that even claims to have a basis, that is both scientific and secular, for evaluating the claims of different groups and parties, and of rival ideologies and "isms." Modern social science is based on the absolute distinction between matters of "value" and matters of "fact,"[1] and attempts only to deal with the latter, or, rather, to deal with the former only in so far as the "values" people hold are themselves facts for the observation of the social scientist. But such a science is of little assistance where the problem concerns a choice between different systems of value. And, it might be added, nearly every practical question involves in some degree such a choice.[2] At most, this "value-free" social science can point out and describe the different systems, and perhaps ascertain whether certain values are based on correct or incorrect assumptions as to the facts All values, as such, are preferences, and all preferences are essentially part of the realm of "myth," and outside the ambit of science. Thus modern anthropology may deny the Nazis' assertions as to the inequality of races, by denying or criticizing any positive evidence that the Nazi "scientists" may bring forward in support of their doctrines But the anthropologists, qua anthropologists, cannot and do not contest the right of Nazis to be Nazis. They do not say that one ought not to be a Nazi, and that the Nazis' treatment of their enemies is morally wrong. To the anthropologist the principles of National Socialism are one of an unlimited number of possible sets of principles (along with those of all kinds and degrees of primitive peoples) And all such principles have an equal right to being accepted and followed, just because there is no demonstrable or "scientific" basis for preferring one to another.

Sometimes, however, a kind of liberal and democratic doctrine is made out of this position, from which many social scientists in this country infer that the condition of their discipline is really satisfactory. Because of this "equal right" of all systems of value, or to put it more simply, of all opinions, no one ought, on the basis of his opinions, to repress or, for that matter, to deny the equal validity of anyone else's opinions. From this point of view, the only "true" doctrine is the pragmatic one of trying to let everyone do as he pleases (and think as he pleases), while making the best practical adjustment toward this end in each situation as it arises.

This attempt at a solution of the value problem, which is quite generally accepted as a solution by liberally-minded social scientists today, leads, of course, to a very obvious paradox There can be no such thing as an "equal right" to every opinion on the purely negative basis that there is no demonstrable reason for preferring any opinion. Most opinions assert as a matter of course that they are superior to those with which they conflict, and assert a superior right in all important practical matters where power, wealth, honor, or duties and burdens must be divided or shared. Each of these opinions proposes to its adherents an end or goal—which, being a preference, cannot be criticized—and from this arises an obligation or "ought," the moral imperative sanctioning the steps taken toward the goal Furthermore, some opinions assert an absolute right, which leads to the consequence that the pragmatic social scientist can in reality grant equal right only to opinions

which concede the same equality to others This is clear, because the granting of any right to an absolutist doctrine results
automatically in the denial of any right to others And since
many claims are mutually exclusive, the pragmatic social scientist would seem to arrive at the formula, Justice is Equality,
meaning thereby that all claims asserting some kind or degree
of inequality must be, to that extent, denied.[3] And all systems
of value which assert an absolute right, of which the Catholic
Natural Law and the Marxist Classless Society are the two best
known today, must be absolutely denied Yet this very denial,
which is the life and substance of this social science, is itself
radically unscientific, even according to its own premise, that
values, as such, cannot be criticized by science. This pragmatic,
liberal-democratic doctrine does not, however, at least on the
basis of any scientific consideration, propose liberal democracy
as an end or goal carrying with it moral obligations. And from
this point of view liberal democracy, to the extent that it is
based on the above "solution," has no moral imperative of its
own, and thus is at an extreme disadvantage in competition
with creeds which bind their followers to them with elaborate
arguments, however spurious A merely pragmatic social science, therefore, is by its own principles prevented either from
laying any claim to the truth of the principles upon which its
practical teaching rests, or from effectively denying the truth
of the claims of any teaching to which it is opposed. The fact
that the practitioners of such a social science are passionate
believers in liberal democracy is, accordingly, of no consequence for the struggle in the political arena, that is, no credit
whatever attaches to their opinions and preferences from the
prestige of their science, because they themselves deny any scientific basis for those preferences. This certainly is the central
reason for the low estate of the social sciences in the Western
world, and explains why the opinions of the various social
scientists are only of the most subordinate and contingent inter-

est to those who must (or should) act responsibly within the
moral and political sphere.

Because of this central problem of the social sciences today,
great interest centers in any effort to bring "values" within
the compass of science. Now modern social science, like the
natural science which it attempts to imitate, has its origins in
the revolt against Aristotelian science in the sixteenth and seven-
teenth centuries. But Aristotle's moral and political teaching,
although it suffered a decline, has never suffered the total
eclipse, or virtual extinction, of his physical teachings. There
are a number of reasons for this. One is the contemporary interest in the history of ideas, and in particular what are now
called social ideas  The same impulse which led in the nine-
teenth century to the great efflorescence of historical studies,
and more recently to anthropology with its interest in primitive peoples, has led to a renewed interest in ancient societies.
And Aristotle, together with Plato, Herodotus, Thucydides,
and the great dramatists and poets, is a prime documentary
source for the study of the brilliant Athenian society of an-
tiquity. According to the current view, Aristotle's physical
teachings have been simply disproved by modern science, but
his moral and political teachings, being concerned primarily
with "values," which science cannot either prove or disprove,
retain their human interest. In fact the moral teaching of
Aristotle has been considered, along with Plato's dialogues,
the drama, and the relics of Hellenic art, as being primarily
of aesthetic interest. Yet this interest goes deeper than mere
aesthetic eclecticism. To quote Rackham's introduction to his
translation of the *Nicomachean Ethics:* "His review of the virtues and graces of character that the Greeks admired stands
in such striking contrast with Christian Ethics that this section
of the work [Books III and IV] is a document of primary importance for the student of the Pagan world. But it has more
than a historic value. Both in its likeness and its difference it

is a touchstone for that modern idea of the gentleman, which supplies or used to supply an important part of the English race with its working religion."[4] We see that although he seems hardly aware of the fact, Rackham rejects Aristotle's principles on their own ground as a matter of course That is, he does not reflect on the possibility that Aristotle's *Ethics* might be *the* true *Ethics*. It is of interest because it tells us something about the Greeks, who were very interesting people, and also because there is something extremely attractive in the things they admired But further, we are, it seems, still somehow compelled to admire what they admired And, Rackham finally confesses, in Aristotle's portrait of the perfect gentleman is embodied an important part of the "working religion" of the English race. Rackham takes it for granted that this cannot be part of formal religion, because (as it seems to him) it manifestly contradicts certain Christian principles Yet, although apparently he does not wonder why Aristotle's *Ethics* should have this compelling quality, he strongly implies that the English have been better people for allowing themselves to be influenced by it [5] And, if I am not mistaken, there is even a note of pride in Rackham's belief that the English gentleman has this element in his moral pedigree—as well as one of regret in the decline of this influence.

But another reason, and perhaps much the strongest one, why Aristotle's moral and political teaching has preserved at least a modicum of its former prestige has been its connection with the Roman Catholic doctrine of Natural Law This doctrine is, apart from revelation, the basis for all Catholic moral and political teaching, and the classic expression of Catholic Natural Law is to be found in the teachings of Thomas Aquinas But Thomas' teaching, although it culminates in purely theological doctrines, claims to have a foundation in natural reason independent of, and separable from, revealed doctrine. This foundation, upon which the Natural Law teaching (or, as we might say, the whole of Catholic social science) is said to rest, is, substantially, the moral and political philosophy of Aristotle.

It is from this direction that the most significant attempts are being made today to restore to social science some standard of moral and political judgment that is not merely arbitrary or dogmatic. The best known movement devoted to this aim is Neo-Thomism. It might better be described as secular Thomism, because within its ranks are some who accept the authority of Thomas' philosophy but do not necessarily adhere to his theological doctrines. Nevertheless it is important to remember that the movement is Catholic in inspiration. In a sense it is odd that it bears the name of Thomas rather than Aristotle, because just in so far as it is a secular teaching it is allegedly an Aristotelian teaching. In all moral and political matters that can be solved adequately by natural reason, to say nothing of theoretical subjects, Thomas is the disciple of Aristotle, and recognizes his authority as paramount. And the Neo-Thomists must presumably grant the same pre-eminence to the Philosopher. But a very grave problem exists as to whether the Aristotle that is seen wholly through the eyes of Thomas is the same as the one who composed the original treatises. This problem is not, and cannot be, disposed of merely by pointing out that the texts of Aristotle are readily available by themselves. The texts of Aristotle have never been studied in modern times as they were in the thirteenth century, with that philosophic passion which alone can produce the greatest possible care. The prepossessions of our contemporaries, as I have indicated above, and wholly apart from the competition Aristotle would have today from a thousand directions, would prevent his pages from being thus tirelessly searched for the Truth.[6] Accordingly, it is not unreasonable to assume that the Aristotelian teaching is more accessible in the pages of Thomas than in the original. Certainly no one in modern times, perhaps no one since Thomas, has possessed his mastery of the Aristotelian corpus, and his marvelous capacity for relating each point in that massive edifice to every other point. It is doubtful whether anyone today could possess his grasp of the whole of Aristotle's teaching, and it is almost certain that no one could attain his comprehensive knowledge. Why, then, should we not simply accept Thomas as interpreter and guide?

One fairly obvious answer is that, although no one since Thomas may have searched the pages of Aristotle with the same intelligence and care, there were a number of predecessors and contemporaries who did. To mention only two names, Averroes and Maimonides, the great Moslem and Jewish Aristotelians possess reputations not inferior to Thomas'. And it is notorious that the Averroists in the University of Paris had very different views of Aristotle's teaching from the Thomists. In the fourteenth century, a generation after Thomas' death, one of them, Marsilius of Padua, earned a reputation that was only overshadowed at a later day by Machiavelli. For this purely external reason we should at least exercise a certain caution in accepting Thomas as an interpreter of Aristotle. Surely it is worthy of note that the revival of interest in Aristotle stems primarily from one of at least two seriously divergent Aristotelian traditions. If it is true that there is some possibility that the desperate remedy needed by our present-day social science is to be found in Aristotle's moral and political philosophy, the fate of such a possible remedy should not be ventured uncritically. And to acknowledge the greatness of Thomas as an interpreter does not necessarily mean to accept his interpretations in every case. Thomas, whatever his merits as an original thinker, is certainly a very great teacher, and he has an unrivaled ability for clarifying difficulties without always obliging one to accept his solution of the difficulties. There is no doubt that Thomas brings us closer to Aristotle than any contemporary interpreter, but it is just on the basis of this better understanding that we must face the responsibility of determining to what extent the moral and political, as well as the theoretical philosophies of Aristotle and Thomas are in fact the same, and to what extent they are different. And if it is discovered that they are in some respects different it is necessary to try to discover the principles underlying these divergencies

The principal source for Thomas' moral and political teaching is the *Summa Theologica*. And, it should be added, this is the principal source for the Aristotelianism of Neo-Thomism. Yet there are certain disadvantages in relying on the *Summa Theologica* for the purposes we have outlined. It is, after all, a textbook addressed to beginning students in Christian theology.[7] The ultimate authority is revelation. Although Thomas assumes the impossibility of any real conflict between the teachings of right reason and revelation, this assumption cannot be made by anyone who does not accept his views either of natural reason or of revelation. If any actual conflict does exist, Thomas must of necessity have distorted one teaching or the other, or both.[8] Particularly in a theological work, Thomas would be under a certain temptation to correct Aristotle's "errors" without in every case pointing them out But if, for the moment, we overlook or minimize this issue, we would still have to assume that, inasmuch as revelation is said to go beyond natural reason, to complete and perfect it, the teachings of natural reason would at the very least have a different aspect, they would somehow look different in the greater light of revelation In other words, within the context of a book based mainly on the principles of revealed theology, Aristotle's principles, however great the authority they carry within their proper sphere, are bound to strike one differently than when they are considered in and by themselves. For this reason Thomas' commentaries on Aristotle, which apparently are intended simply and solely as enterprises in philosophic understanding, are of great importance for the difficulties with which we are faced.[9]

This point may be made clearer by illustration. There are, we all recognize, different ways of understanding the same phenomena (except those susceptible of purely demonstrative explanation). For example, an intelligent and well brought up child understands perfectly, in one sense, why he ought to obey his parents. He understands, that is, that it is for his good. And no amount of sophistication can really make that explanation, in itself, more complete. An intelligent adult, however, understands a great many things about children and parents which give him an insight and understanding hardly to be expected in the child. He realizes that children need to respect an authority which will bring the order and discipline to their lives that are an indispensable prerequisite for their future well-being Also, that to become a normal and well-balanced adult requires an accession of responsibility corresponding to the growth of the child, and that a proper habituation to parental authority is the means for saving the child from burdens which he cannot bear without harm This example, which is chosen advisedly, illustrates the difference between two levels of understanding of the same phenomena, each equally correct, yet somehow vastly different All the reasons in the adult's explanation are contained in the child's, although they are not visible to him. But if they were pointed out to the child they would seem utterly unreal to him, and they would supply him with no additional motive for being obedient Yet the practical test of the sufficiency of the explanation is its adequacy in supplying such a motive The other explanation, however superior in other respects, would be inferior in this, that it obscures, if it does not destroy, the best reason for prompting obedience in the child within the moral horizon of the child Thus in another sense the sophisticated explanation would be *wrong*, because it would not indicate correctly why the *child* should obey—but rather why others should make him obedient In other words, no reason not directly intelligible to the child could, strictly speaking, be the correct reason.

The parallel of the foregoing to the problem of Thomas' interpretation is easily drawn. Certainly it is not our intention to suggest that Aristotle's "natural" understanding is like a child's.

But it is suggested that explanation in the light of revealed truth, however consistent with any other explanation, is likely nevertheless to be a very different explanation, and may in fact be incorrect in the sense in which we indicated the sophisticated explanation above to be incorrect. One example from Thomas will suffice to conclude this discussion. In the famous case of the magnanimous or great-souled man to which we must recur at length later, Thomas is faced with the necessity of explaining why, according to Aristotle's account of him, the magnanimous man appears chargeable with the vice of ingratitude, as it is said that he "does not remember benefits received." In the *Summa Theologica*[10] Thomas merely states that, inasmuch as magnanimity implies the perfection of every virtue, it must also imply the perfection of gratitude, and the perfection of gratitude requires that one take more pleasure in being the author of benefits than the recipient of them In other words, starting from the Aristotelian premise that magnanimity is the virtue which implies the presence of every other moral virtue in its most perfect form, Thomas knows in advance that it is simply incompatible with ingratitude, and thus the alleged appearance of ingratitude is only indicative of the magnanimous man's greater concern with doing than with receiving benefits But in his commentary on the same passage,[11] Thomas gives a different kind of explanation, although one which in no way contradicts the other Here Thomas is much more concerned to explain the appearance of ingratitude This, he explains, is a quality which the magnanimous man does not *choose* to have (and hence cannot be a true vice), but is an unavoidable consequence of his virtuous disposition. Those things which are pleasant to us we think of more frequently, and hence remember better The unpleasant we think of less frequently, and hence forget more readily And thus it is natural that magnanimous people seem to remember better the benefits they have granted than those they have received This lucid exegesis, although it points the way to further difficulties, as we shall try

to show later, has the merit of explaining the moral phenomenon under consideration in a way that is intelligible within
the "frame of reference" of that phenomenon itself In the explanation in the *Summa*, the psychology of the situation is dis-
regarded or passed over, because the moral issue itself is so
decidedly settled by the higher principle involved It is for this
reason that Thomas' appreciation of Aristotle's moral and
political teaching ought not to rely solely on the *Summa Theologica*, and should be supplemented by careful examination of
the commentaries on the *Nicomachean Ethics* and the *Politics*

# CHAPTER II

## SCIENCE AND ETHICS

BEFORE proceeding, it may be well to repeat, in more specific terms, the motive and aims of this study. The motive is the necessity for ascertaining whether there is some basis in the Aristotelian moral and political philosophy for those "value judgments" without which any social science seems necessarily impotent, but which current scientific opinion asserts are, and of necessity must be, radically unscientific. According to present-day scientific opinion, all judgments concerning what "ought" to be done are, at bottom, arbitrary The question, then, of fundamental concern is whether, in the Aristotelian system, there is a basis for such judgments that is not arbitrary. The use of the word "arbitrary" however, requires clarification The difference between an arbitrary judgment and one that is not arbitrary is not necessarily identical with the difference between a "scientific" judgment and one that is unscientific, or at least not if our conception of science is the modern conception. If, that is to say, the canons of the exact sciences supply the criteria of what is or is not to be considered "scientific," then it may be that both the degree of assurance possible and that required for satisfactory value judgments will always fall far short of what would be in an exact sense scientific But for the very reason of that low order of requirement there may be no need for such a science, any more than the carpenter needs the geometer's knowledge of angles in order to do his work.[1] In the same way we may say that a science of value judgments involves different criteria from any of the exact sciences And, while there may be an absolute difference between scientific and unscientific statements in the exact sciences, there is not necessarily the same difference between statements about moral and political subjects that are arbitrary, and ones that are not arbitrary. This is illustrated in every-day parlance in the distinction between actions or opinions which are merely capricious, and those which, although no perfectly satisfactory explanation can be given for them, appear in some degree intelligible or sensible. From the standpoint of exact science all the degrees of difference between mere caprice and perfect responsibility, which yet fall short of scientific necessity, would be equally unscientific, and for that reason on the same level And yet, as everyone knows from every-day experience, these distinctions, which may be irrelevant to the scientist qua scientist, are of the greatest importance to everyone (including the scientist) in the practical business of life. One may hold the opinion that all opinions on moral worth are unscientific, and that there is no such thing as an "honest" man, because what is honest on the basis of one general premise is dishonest on the basis of another premise no more or less demonstrable. However, no one, for this reason, fails to distinguish or, rather, fails to try to distinguish between persons who are honest and those who are dishonest That is to say, whatever someone may think about the universal proposition, that there is or is not such a thing as honesty, or that there is or is not certain knowledge of what honesty is, we all nonetheless act on the supposition, or particular proposition, that in this or that instance we know what honesty is. And if it is possible to arrive at consistent opinions which satisfy the demands of what we all are familiar with as moral certainty, this moral certainty may be what is needed to supply the deficiency of modern social science.[2]

What we are seeking, therefore, is moral certainty concerning the principles of moral and political judgment, and in saying that we wish to replace merely arbitrary judgments with scientific ones, it is to be understood that the term "scientific" is so qualified. We do not, however, intend to prejudge the legitimate question as to whether there might not be *some* propositions concerning morals or politics about which knowledge of theoretical certainty is possible As we shall see, this question supplies one of the main problems to be considered in Thomas' interpretation of the *Nicomachean Ethics*

But we hasten to add that it is not our expectation to resolve within these pages the problem of the adequacy of the Aristotelian principles.[3] Such a resolution depends upon a much better understanding of those principles than is presently available But an understanding of Aristotle's teaching requires an interpretation of the texts of his works not vitiated by a prejudice against that premise of the Aristotelian system which distinguishes it from contemporary social science That premise is precisely this that intelligent inquiry into the subject matter of morals and politics may lead to the replacing of merely arbitrary opinions concerning what is good for man with opinions that are not arbitrary, and that such inquiry may, with some degree of practical assurance, show the basis upon which individuals and communities can attain happiness.[4] This premise, of course, leads to the presumption that an Aristotelian Ethics might be (although perhaps with errors of detail), the *true* Ethics Such a presumption, needless to say, is not a conclusion, and in no way binds one to accept any part of Aristotle's doctrine. It does, however, compel one to the most serious consideration of that doctrine, and it is not unimportant to consider exactly what is meant in this connection by the seriousness born of that "philosophic passion" mentioned above [5] Such seriousness arises from the belief that the inquirer's most important problem may have its solution in the investigation he is making, and an investigation of the meaning of Aristotle's *Ethics* is, indeed, motivated by a philosophic passion when it is believed that there is a real possibility (although, of course, no assurance) that the truth about the nature and importance of moral phenomena is contained in it In more personal terms, someone who believed that the means to his own happiness and, perhaps, that of his nearest friends depended upon his grasping the doctrine of the *Ethics* would certainly study it with a care which he would hardly exercise if he had any less pressing motive. It was in this spirit, generally, that the study of Aristotle's texts was approached in the Middle Ages, very much as the sacred texts were studied by theologians. This difference, however, was and is still to be recognized. The authority of a sacred text is always accepted by those who believe it to be sacred, the only question concerns the interpretation of the text. In the case of a philosophic text, the authority of the writing depends ultimately on the force of the arguments elucidated by the reader and interpreter In a sense, therefore, much more depends upon the interpretation of the philosophic text in the other case the light of reason is merely supplementary to the light of faith, much less value is attached to understanding the text than to believing it, in the case of the philosophic text no value can be ascribed to mere belief, and in this respect the philosophic passion is the greater of the two

We may thus distinguish the medieval commentator from almost all modern Aristotelian scholars, if only for the more or less accidental circumstance that, with few exceptions, practically the only road to philosophic or scientific truth for the former was through the Aristotelian texts The modern equivalent of the medieval scholar considering an Aristotelian text would be the exact scientist recording with infinite care the behavior of the physical data upon which all his research depends. But we may further distinguish the typical medieval commentator, and certainly Thomas, who was one of the great commentators, from all specifically modern interpreters who have not approached the problem of interpretation in this spirit What we here denominate "modern" interpretations are those which are motivated, implicitly or explicitly, by the assumption that the interpreter is already in possession of principles which are, in some decisive respect, superior to those of Aristotle This assumption, we believe, is indicated by any use in the interpretation of information which Aristotle himself has not evidently considered relevant to the exposition of his doctrine

This quite obviously excludes all information which Aristotle did not possess, so that all interpretations which in any way depend upon historical understanding not available to Aristotle (which also includes knowledge of doctrines unknown to him) would fall into this category It is clear that the use either of information unknown to Aristotle, or which he did not consider important, involves the assertion of a principle of selection different from Aristotle's principles, and the assertion of such a principle in the very interpretation of his works, as it implies the insufficiency of Aristotle's principles for explaining his own doctrines, certainly implies a depreciation of his principles But no one who already preferred another principle or principles could possibly be led to his study of Aristotle by the motives we have described For it is difficult to imagine that an intelligent person could bring himself to put forth the very considerable intellectual effort required for a sufficient understanding of Aristotle, when he knew in advance that the result of that effort would be the rejection of the only claim which would make such understanding supremely worth while One can hardly imagine an enterprising astronomer investing his serious effort on Aristotle's treatise *On the Heaven,* when he knew that a glance through the telescope would disprove the major conclusions of that work. In the same way, one can hardly imagine a serious moralist, or a present-day social scientist making the most intensive kind of study of the *Ethics,* when he knew in advance that its relevance to his actual problems was only slightly less indirect This is not to deny that there can be a serious interest in Aristotle's works on other grounds, indeed, the enormous literature would make such denial seem absurd But no other motive than that we have suggested appears to be sufficient to lead to the kind of understanding that will enable us to say whether Aristotle's teaching contains any solution to the dilemma of the social sciences. We cannot import into the interpretation of Aristotle any of the premises which lie at or near the bottom of present-day social science -without inevi-

tably reflecting in our version of Aristotle's teaching the difficulties for which we are seeking a solution. We may illustrate
this point briefly. If we take, for instance, the odious examples
of Aristotle's views of the natural inequality of the sexes, and
the existence of a class of natural slaves, we may say that this
merely reflects the prejudices of Greek society And this explanation may, of course, be correct. But whether or not it is
correct, the question may still be asked whether it constitutes
legitimate interpretation. Obviously, the explanation offered
cannot be one that Aristotle himself would admit. For, the moment he admitted it as correct, he would have abandoned the
views hence, as long as Aristotle held the views in question he
must have held them for other reasons, and the reasons cannot
be rejected without being examined. But to be examined they
must first be set forth However, the manner in which they are
set forth is all-important. For it is humanly impossible to expect that the arguments in favor of any proposition in which
our greatest interests are somehow involved will be set forth in
the same manner by one for whom the truth or falsity of the
proposition is already a closed matter, and by one whose decision depends, among other things, upon the light which he
hopes to gain from the correct elaboration of the argument he
is elucidating It is a different thing to seek confirmation of
one's own view, and to seek a correct view because one is dissatisfied with one's own. But presumably our whole motive for
studying Aristotle is dissatisfaction with our own views If we
close our minds to the possibility that any of the serious claims
raised as to the truth of Aristotle's moral and political teaching
might be valid, we approach the study of those doctrines with
a prejudice which practically precludes the possibility of our
making a full and just evaluation of the basis upon which such
claims are made. That some of those claims seem absurd to us
on the basis of our own typical modern premises is no longer
a sufficient reason for disregarding them It would, of course,
be absurd for someone to study those parts of Aristotle's phys-

ical theories that have been disproved by the empirical data of modern physical science, because he was dissatisfied with the hypotheses by which the physicists explain these data. The physicists do not need to place any special reliance on the "truth" of their hypotheses, so long as they treat them as hypotheses and not as truths The justification of an hypothesis in natural science is its ability to interpret the behavior of the physical data The truth that the physical scientist relies upon is not that of any given hypothesis as such, but that of the method by which hypotheses are tested The success of the physical sciences is a large justification for the confidence of its practitioners But no comparable success warrants a like confidence in the social scientist.

But the questioning of the premises upon which our thinking on moral and political subjects rests cannot be performed merely by the formal renunciation of all prejudices One of the peculiar characteristics of present-day liberal thought *is* its formal renunciation of all prejudices, and its determination to "tolerate" every possible point of view But, as has been shown, this very point of view has led to the impasse in which we find ourselves [6] A guide is needed to the very notion of detachment appropriate to the kind of understanding of which we are in need. In other words, before we can hope to make a critical evaluation of the Aristotelian position we must understand it fully, but to understand it means first to approach it divested of those prejudices which might lend an un-Aristotelian color to our interpretation. A critical distance from our own prejudices is what we may hope, at least, to gain in some measure from the study of Thomas' approach to the interpretation of Aristotle's *Ethics* That Thomas' own prejudices may be found to color his interpretation is, we might add, less of a danger for us, inasmuch as his errors, if they are found to exist, are less likely to affect our judgment But on the other hand, his freedom from our prejudices is likely to point the way to some, if not all, the advantages needed as a preliminary basis for a correct understanding of Aristotle's doctrine. One claim may certainly be raised for Thomas' interpretation of the *Ethics*, and it is a high claim indeed Thomas rarely, if ever, attempts to explain any statement of Aristotle except in terms of other of his statements. Nothing extraneous to the *Ethics* itself is, apparently, permitted to serve as the basis for the interpretation of the *Ethics* To this, only one evident exception need be noted other works of Aristotle *are* adduced by way of clarification or elaboration of the *Ethics*, and on some rare occasions are used to explain what Thomas considers otherwise unintelligible.

Of all the authors widely read today, Thomas is certainly the most important of those who may reasonably be called "sympathetic" interpreters of Aristotle in the sense affirmed above And, as has been said,[7] the movement to re-establish Aristotle's authority over the social sciences has been due largely to those whose understanding of Aristotle has been derived from Thomas In a sense, it is natural that this should be the case, because to anyone not prejudiced against the source from which they come, the Aristotelian arguments as presented by Thomas carry a force and conviction surpassing any contemporary presentation. Yet, just because of the forcefulness with which the Aristotelian position has been advanced by the present-day followers of Thomas, the prestige of that position may be said to be jeopardized, or, more accurately, the possibility of understanding it seems in one way rather to be further removed than brought nearer. This circumstance, paradoxical as it seems, may nevertheless be readily explained The objection raised in chapter 1 to Thomas as an interpreter of Aristotle, leads in a way to an objection to Aristotle himself To repeat, in Thomas' own system theology, or, more correctly, revealed theology, takes precedence over the teachings of natural reason And, although Thomas affirms the independence and the separability from revealed theology of the teachings of natural reason, those who dissent from his theology have the understandable suspicion that such "harmony" as Thomas finds between the teachings of reason and of revelation is primarily due to a corruption of the former. Such suspicion would in itself not be harmful if it led merely to an intensification of the search for the "uncorrupted" teaching. But it has also led to the further suspicion that the doctrine itself, to be susceptible to such "harmonization," must somehow be deficient. If it can be "harmonized" with a system of revealed theology which appears in all its vital aspects so manifestly opposed to it, how can it have any real inner core capable of providing independent practical guidance?

The suspicion cast over the whole philosophy of Aristotle by Thomas Hobbes, that what he wrote was "consonant to, and corroborative of" the pagan religion, and that he may have known it to be false, but wrote it nonetheless, "fearing the fate of Socrates,"[8] has both directly and indirectly affected the present-day attitude toward Aristotle. And the suspicion of Aristotle today, as in the case of Hobbes, has been largely fortified by the opinion that what is adaptable to one superstition must in all likelihood have been based originally on another superstition.[9]

This objection to Aristotle might, at first glance, appear unworthy of any truly fair-minded person. Hobbes, one might say, can be excused, because he had reason to believe that he had discovered a new basis for political and moral science, perfectly independent of the classics, which would prove of immensely greater practical value. But we today, who are the heirs of the method Hobbes laid down, having no reason for such complacency, have no such reason to dismiss Aristotle But upon reflection it would appear that there is in this objection something that Aristotle himself might consider sound. All Aristotle's moral and political reflections begin and end, as Aristotle never tires of repeating, with observations of the facts. We must consider our subject, Aristotle says,[10] "in the light not only of our conclusion and our premises, but also of what is commonly said about it, for with a true view the data har-

monize, but with a false one the facts soon clash." In other
words, the final test in moral matters is, for Aristotle, emphatically an empirical one  But moral facts have a twofold character, illustrated by the character of any moral action· the action
itself may be described in terms which let us know simply what
has happened, but inseparable from the action qua moral action
is its praiseworthy or blameworthy quality. And this quality of
the action is known as an opinion about it  And opinions about
morality are accordingly treated by Aristotle as among the
most important "facts" with which the student of moral science is concerned. The role of opinion in the determination of
true moral doctrine is explained perhaps most fully in the following passage [11] "We must, as in all other cases, set the observed facts before us and, after first discussing the difficulties,
go on to prove, if possible, the truth of all the common opinions
about these affections of the mind, or, failing this, of the greater
number and the most authoritative, for if we both refute the
objections and leave the common opinions undisturbed, we
shall have proved the case sufficiently " Rackham's comment
on this passage, in his translation of the *Nicomachean Ethics*,[12]
is excellent  "Aristotle holds that the opinions of the mass of
mankind, and of philosophers, on matters of conduct are likely
to be substantially true, although being stated from different
points of view, and sometimes in ambiguous language, they
often seem mutually contradictory. The business of Ethics is to
state them clearly, examine the apparent contradictions, discard
such parts of them as really refute each other, and elicit the
common residuum of truth " Thus it would seem that, although
there is a very great difference between common opinion, as
such, and philosophic opinion on what is the truth about morality, both share a common origin  The facts with which the
premises and conclusions of the philosopher must harmonize
are common, unphilosophical opinions, although not any and
all common opinions, but rather those which have not been
shown to be untenable on the basis of other such opinions
The ultimate justification of this method raises profound prob-

lems which cannot be dealt with here But it may be confidently asserted at the outset that it presents characteristics which in
no way contradict any intelligent preconceptions as to what
constitutes scientific method. Each step in the way is checked
by what might reasonably be called scientific observation of
what actually "is " It is just because Aristotle's method has this
radically empirical character that it recommends itself to us at
this critical juncture But for that same reason, the Aristotelian
teaching, subjected to its own test, appears, at least at first
glance, to be completely discredited If common opinion is to
be, in some sense, a final authority, then nothing can be more
evident, on the basis of common opinion, than the dissimilarity
of pagan and Christian ethics And to assert that the principles
underlying the two are in reality identical seems to fit, as
nearly as anything can fit it, the statement that "with a false
view the facts soon clash " Thus, the very success with which
Thomas has apparently shown—on the basis of Aristotle's own
principles—that there is no real contradiction between a pagan
ethics based on the true teaching of natural reason and a Christian ethics based on revelation, supplies a powerful argument
against giving serious consideration to Aristotle's *Ethics* We
are, therefore, faced with this difficulty Thomas is, of all the
authorities on the contemporary scene, the one who appears to
interpret Aristotle purely on an Aristotelian basis, and we may
confidently affirm that, at least in the commentaries, there are
scarcely any passages in which the authority for the interpretation is ascribed to any principle not presumed to be derived
from Aristotle himself Yet the net result of Thomas' interpretation is, apparently, the harmonization of pagan and Christian
ethics But the facts of observation, which Aristotle tells us
must always be the final test of the adequacy of a theory,
assert that there is a manifest and striking difference between
pagan and Christian ethics If this is true, how is it possible to
take Aristotle's *Ethics* seriously?

# CHAPTER III

# PAGAN VERSUS CHRISTIAN ETHICS

THE paradox involved in Thomas' interpretation of Aristotle's *Ethics* can be seen immediately, at least in a provisional way, by reflecting on the issue to which we have referred an issue which, furiously debated in Thomas' own day, is again becoming an important subject of discussion One need but refer to Augustine's famous dictum, that the virtues of the pagans were only splendid vices, to characterize the position Thomas opposed This fundamental lack of harmony between pagan and Christian ethics, also insisted upon by Machiavelli at the beginning of the modern era, and generally accepted by most modern moral philosophers (rather in the spirit of Machiavelli than of Augustine), has again been called into question by the present-day interpreters of Aristotle who are at the same time followers of Thomas They start from the assumption, properly grounded on the authority of their masters, that there is a natural morality, discerned by natural reason, and universally valid because of the unity of human nature This morality, they say, may be discerned in the characters of good men everywhere, that is, in all developed societies in which perverted customs have not thwarted natural capacities for moral action And, they further affirm, inasmuch as the Jewish-Christian revelation can in no sense be out of harmony with the nature of man, it can in no sense be said that there is a contradiction or conflict between pagan and Christian morality.

Now, there are several propositions in the position expressed above, and they must be distinguished, clarified, and their relevance to each other and to our problem made explicit. First there is the assumption as to the existence of a "natural morality." This assumption is, indeed, a legitimate inference from the

Aristotelian doctrine, and follows necessarily from the Aristotelian doctrine of species. If each species is one, and is properly defined by its form, which is its perfection, then each individual of the species attains its proper "good" in the realization of this perfection There is a human species, and the human good lies in the realization of man's perfection, which is reason. Moral perfection is the perfection and application of reason in the sphere of action Now this argument, although it has nothing in it which can be said to be incorrect as a statement of Aristotle's view, nevertheless is a doubtful statement of his moral doctrine It is doubtful because everything affirmed follows from a proposition derived from metaphysics and physics rather than from moral science The major premise of the reasoning represented is based upon the doctrine of species, but nothing is said of the grounds or proof of that doctrine. But even if one were to assume that adequate scientific grounds for it did exist (which, of course, almost no one would admit today), such proof would not constitute *moral* proof. One would naturally assume that, within Aristotle's system, if it were worthy of the name, there would have to be some sort of agreement between the metaphysical doctrine of species and the practical doctrine of human nature, and it may be the case that the latter could not be true if the former were not true. But such questions, although they may have a legitimate place in the full elaboration of the problem of morality, cannot be raised at a preliminary stage in the elaboration of that problem In the first place, whether the Aristotelian doctrine of species is true or false is of no immediate practical importance, because the problem of morality exists quite independently of it that is, the need for moral certainty exists and will continue to exist whether a metaphysical foundation for it can be found or not Furthermore, the metaphysical knowledge of the existence of a foundation for moral certainty is not a substitute, or even a basis for, a practical knowledge of the basis for moral certainty There is no a priori knowledge of the premises from which a practical doctrine of human nature

would have to be inferred, for the premises from which a sufficient knowledge of morality would have to be inferred are,
as Aristotle repeatedly says, a knowledge of the particular moral
facts,[1] and all general statements about morality are to be learned
from these facts, and must, as far as possible, be brought into
harmony with them  The statement that there is a natural morality may be admitted to be in itself a correct statement of Aristotle's opinion, or, rather, its correctness may be said to depend
upon how it is understood, and it is obviously susceptible of
much interpretation  One thing, however, is clear  it makes the
greatest difference whether, in the attempt to make clear the
moral problem, one treats such a statement as the starting point
of moral science, derived from the conclusions of metaphysics
or physics, or as a conclusion of moral science learned from the
facts of morality. Certainly it makes the greatest possible *practical* difference which way one begins  because to know that the
natural perfection of man may be read in the characters of good
men everywhere does not tell one what a good man is, and it is
only this latter knowledge which can become practical [2]

The second distinct proposition in the position represented
above is that concerning revelation. It is not necessary here to
elucidate the premises upon which such a statement is based, but
merely to point out that, such as they are, they form no part of
the subject matter of science. Obviously they form no part of
Aristotle's doctrine, as he seems to have known nothing of the
biblical revelation. Further, they have nothing to do with our
problem, which is not to prove Aristotle sound by Christian
principles, or vice versa  The point at which this proposition
touches our problem is in the gratuitous (as far as Aristotle is
concerned) assumption as to the harmony of pagan and Christian ethics. Now this assumption might, in fact, be made in different ways. Or, rather, it might actually be made only in one
way in a theoretical sense, and yet it might be made practically
in different ways. Theoretically, one would have to say, if one
accepted the authority of revelation, that the revealed doctrine

was in all respects the "truest" that the conviction carried by a doctrine based on natural reason was due to the reflection of the same truth exemplified in a higher degree by the revealed doctrine that both, therefore, are parts of the same truth, and that differences between the two must be apparent rather than real But because the truth exemplified in the revealed doctrine is truth in a higher degree, the apparent differences would, in principle at least, be resolved "in favor" of it. This, however, is not simply true, inasmuch as revealed doctrine itself needs to be interpreted, and to the extent that interpretation is a rational activity it proceeds along lines laid down by natural reason alone, that is, if the interpretation is not "inspired"—for then, of course, it is no longer interpretation but part of revelation—it must be guided by the principles of natural reason But just because there is in theory a necessary unity of the two kinds of doctrine, the assumption of their unity leads in practice to the assumption of their separability. And this assumption is also made by Thomas and his followers If, that is, the truth of natural reason is as much a part of *the truth* as the truth contained in the Bible, albeit a part inferior in dignity, it can be understood perfectly by itself. It would follow from the fact that Thomas considered Aristotle the highest authority in all things that could be understood by natural reason alone that he considered natural reason perfectly competent within its proper sphere It is no objection to this to say that Thomas on occasion criticized Aristotle, because, although natural reason may, in itself, be perfectly able to know all that it is proper for it to know, it does not follow that the reason of any one man is competent to know all that may be known. Nor does it follow that the lesser mind may not be able to correct errors of the greater mind Thomas' "corrections" of Aristotle do not, therefore, imply that he is correcting him in the light of what he knows from revealed authority In the commentaries, at least, all explicit corrections are based on Aristotelian principles [8] It would appear, therefore, that the assumption as to the "harmony" of the teachings of natural reason and of revelation could be the grounds for a perfect detachment in the consideration of the scientific doctrine. There is no need to correct a scientific doctrine, or even to be concerned in correcting it on the basis of any higher principles, if the reliability of its own principles can be confidently assumed This does not mean, of course, that any scientific doctrine is a true one, or that natural reason may not err within its proper sphere It means merely that natural reason possesses within itself the means for correcting its own errors and for arriving at that truth which is proper to it Quite obviously, there was no satisfactory philosophic teaching before there were philosophers —which was a long time even by biblical chronology—and yet there was natural reason From the Thomistic position there is, apparently, no necessary reason to introduce any element into the interpretation or criticism of a scientific doctrine which is not based exclusively on the findings of natural reason To say anything else would of course be to classify Thomas from the outset with the "modern" interpreters of Aristotle, who in some sense assume that they are already in possession of principles superior to his, and who could not be concerned simply to discover what Aristotle really meant In Thomas' case, we might say, the assumption that he was already in possession of superior principles does not seem, necessarily, to imply the disadvantage explained above, inasmuch as the superior principles are not taken to be different principles, but complementary parts of the same whole And it is important (although one could not quite say *as* important) to know each independently on its own basis

What makes it difficult to believe that this "solution" of the problem of how the principles of reason and revelation can exist side by side, without the latter inevitably serving as the basis of the former—which, if it were true, would discredit the scientific value of any such combination—is, again, the apparent contrast between pagan and Christian ethics And we must, accordingly, turn to a consideration of this contrast For it is a fact, a moral fact of the greatest significance, and one which has been particularly noted and commented upon since the Renaissance, that there is a manifest and striking difference between the meekness, submissiveness, and humility of the Ethics of the Sermon on the Mount, and the emphasis on "noble pride" which is the keynote of what is called pagan ethics. No one can fail to be impressed, in that now somewhat worn, but still overwhelming contrast between the heroes, respectively, of the theological and philosophical traditions, Jesus and Socrates, by the difference between the meekness and capacity for long-suffering of the one, and the proud indifference to suffering of the other. It is true that critics have claimed to find much evidence of spiritual pride in the former, and many have asserted that Socrates was superior only in his humility. But these points of view overlook the fact that Jesus' pride (if it be such) appeared, or at least was affirmed, only as instrumental to the purposes of a divine agency, while Socrates' alleged humility ("that he knew nothing") was precisely the basis for his superiority to all other men Jesus, standing silent before his judges, and Socrates demanding a state pension as "retribution" for his offense, present an irreducible difference in human types [4]

But what are the significant differences between the two types? One of the most striking differences has been represented as being the difference between a citizen morality and an otherworldly morality, in which the claims of citizenship have distinctly secondary status in the hierarchy of moral demands. This, of course, was the primary ground for the rejection of Christian morality by such great modern political philosophers as Machiavelli and Rousseau. For these men, as for the classics, human perfection (or whatever was the equivalent in their vocabularies) was possible only in and through the development of political society. However, political society, as they conceived it, was a limited or "closed" society, a society depending for its very existence upon the distinction between citizens and strangers. But, we may ask, how can this be reconciled with a morality which considers all men "brothers," and in which an absolute distinction is made between the things that are God's and the things that are Caesar's? For Thomas himself there is a perfectly clear distinction between the philosophic virtue of justice and the theological virtue of charity. But how, indeed, can a man imbued with the spirit of charity to all men strike down, not merely with a good conscience, but with a firm and resolute will, other men who are, by a mere accident of birth, citizens of another political community? In other words, how can the demands of justice, in which the demands of citizenship are paramount, be reconciled with charity?[5] This was the ground of Rousseau's attack on Christianity the Christian as citizen may go to war as a matter of duty, but he knows "better how to die than how to conquer "[6] Thus, even granting a dispensation which tells him to "render to Caesar the things that are Caesar's," and to "obey the powers that be," how can his moral intention be really identical with that of a man for whom the highest moral good is essentially a right relation between free and equal *fellow-citizens,* and for whom no obligations outside the bounds of political society are in the same degree moral obligations?[7]

Yet this objection to a harmonization of pagan and Christian ethics has been itself objected to on the grounds that, for the pagan philosophers, and above all Aristotle, the perfection of human nature is not moral perfection but intellectual perfection, and that the highest human type is not the citizen but the philosopher The example of Socrates would seem to bear this out. Socrates would, indeed, seem to be represented by Plato as the perfect citizen And the perfect citizen appears to be the one who, at all costs, obeys the laws. Socrates, apparently, preferred death to disobedience to the laws And, according to Plato's account in the dialogues *Laches* and *Symposium* (above all the famous drunken speech of Alcibiades), Socrates possessed in the very highest degree the virtues of the soldier. But a closer inspection even of Plato's portrait of Socrates in those dialogues which were designed to present a "popular" impression of his master, shows that this is not simply true. It is evident that no duty to the law could compel Socrates to cease philosophizing And, we may suspect, Socrates may have considered his death a sacrifice not so much to the cause of citizenship as to that of philosophy We may wonder if Socrates would have submitted to the same fate had it overtaken him before his great philosophic life-work had been entrusted to disciples who could carry it on [8] And in the portrait of Socrates the soldier, the truly remarkable feature is not merely his imperviousness to fear (which, of course, added to his personal safety as it did to that of the state), and to hunger, thirst, and fatigue, but his ability, just because of his perfect control of these affections, to continue philosophizing in the midst of the greatest rigors of a campaign. Thus, it may be said that, if there is, in fact, no conflict between the claims of citizenship and those of philosophy (a very large if), it is because of indifference to citizenship on the part of philosophers, or rather because of its recognition merely as an indispensable pre-condition to the attainment of a society in which philosophy can flourish. In this sense the philosopher, like the Christian, is merely rendering to Caesar his due, and his attachment to political society is a secondary attachment, so that to the philosopher the claims of political society are as subordinate in his hierarchy of values as the moral obligations to political society recognized by the Christian However, this important difference remains for the Christian secondary moral obligations are subordinated to primary ones, the philosophic virtues are subordinated to the theological ones, justice to charity But for the philosopher there would seem to be no moral horizon beyond the political horizon [9] That this is unqualifiedly true of Aristotle will, we hope, become quite clear in the course of our analysis of the commentary For the present it would seem to be a sufficient indication of his view that, in the famous chapter on natural right, in the fifth book of the *Ethics*,[10] Aristotle describes natural right (which, according to Thomas, includes within its scope all the principles of natural morality) as a *part of political right.*

But from this point of view classical morality would seem to be paradoxical Morality is admittedly a human good, and as such part of man's perfection otherwise how could it have an obligatory character? But if the highest moral virtue is a part of political excellence, then the essence of moral goodness would seem to be good citizenship [11] And yet, from another standpoint the ultimate standard of judgment would seem to be an a-moral intellectual perfection, implying a depreciation of morality That intellectual perfection is, in itself, a-moral is testified to by Thomas. In the *Summa Theologica*[12] he asks the question, whether there can be intellectual virtue without moral virtue The answer is that prudence, or practical wisdom cannot be, but the other intellectual virtues can be, without moral virtue But Thomas also says[13] that intellectual virtue is better than moral virtue, and again[14] that wisdom (i e , philosophic wisdom) is the greatest of the intellectual virtues Thus we see, by Thomas' own assertion, that according to the philosophic teaching the highest natural perfection of man is possible without moral virtue This clearly implies a grave depreciation of morality, a depreciation which is no longer present in Thomas' moral teaching because the addition of the theological virtues, dedicated to that perfection which has its fruition in another world, makes intellectual virtue without moral virtue impossible [15] But it remains true, as Thomas explicitly says, that as far as natural morality is concerned, the highest perfection is possible without moral virtue This further confirms the statement above that, according to Aristotle, the moral horizon is limited to the political horizon For if all the moral virtues are embodied in justice, and justice is essentially political, and if, further, practical wisdom, which supplies the rule and measure of moral virtue, is in substance the same virtue as political wisdom, as Aristotle also says,[16] then it is clear that there is no moral virtue which is not essentially a part of (or derivative from) the political relationship

But if it is true that the highest human good is possible without moral virtue, then there is no moral obligation to be morally virtuous binding on those who can attain the highest good without moral virtue  Moral virtue would then seem to be obligatory only to those who are capable of nothing more than moral virtue.[17] This, however, would in any case imply a double standard  one for philosophers and one for nonphilosophers. But if this dualism cannot be overcome, what becomes of the Thomistic position that the natural morality, based on the unity of human nature, is a single, universal standard?

In reply to the difficulty we have raised it might be alleged by Thomists that Aristotle's natural reason guided him to a conception of morality in every respect complete except for the insight, possible only on the basis of revelation, of the other-worldly end of man. The apparent contradiction may be said to be solved as follows  Aristotle reached the conclusion, on the basis of natural reason, that man's natural perfection and highest happiness was something trans-moral and trans-political (i.e , philosophy)  This, of course, might also be said to be affirmed by Christianity, but for Christianity the trans-political sphere could no longer be called trans-moral, or at least not in the same way  The brotherhood of man and the fatherhood of God suggest political relationships among all men, and moral distinctions which are in no way vitiated by ordinary political distinctions  But by the affirmation that perfect happiness is possible only in another world, and that moral perfection (on a universal, not narrowly political basis) is a necessary condition for this final and perfect happiness, Christianity affirms a function for morality that was unknown to Aristotle  Yet it may be said that, while Christian morality in this sense goes beyond Aristotle, it does not in any sense contradict him  Morality, of course, becomes vastly more important, yet the content and character of natural morality remain the same. The universality of the "true morality" (i.e , the natural morality completed by revelation) may be said to be pre-figured in Aristotle's implicit depreciation of morality, so long as it was essentially and merely an ingredient of the civic life Yet, as far as he went, it may be alleged, Aristotle's natural reason guided him truly to a true perception of those virtues inherent in a developed human nature.

Before criticizing the solution just proposed, it is necessary to point out a certain element of paradox in a proposition assumed for the purposes of that solution There is, as we have shown, an implied depreciation of morality in Aristotle's doctrine because, according to it, morality is not an integral part of the highest human good Morality becomes an integral part of the highest human good in the Thomistic system, because it is an indispensable prerequisite for that immortal felicity which is made known through revelation Yet from another point of view the revealed doctrine may be said to depreciate morality, and the philosophic doctrine to elevate it For in the philosophic doctrine morality is always treated as something good, although a good inferior to the highest good But it has the character of a final cause of moral action, that is, the good achievable by moral action is contained in the good action itself, "for good action itself is its end."[18] And for this reason those good actions which exhibit moral virtue in its highest degree according to the principles of the purely philosophic doctrine have quite different proportions from those which are considered the highest degree by theological standards. For however highly one regards the Christian martyr, one cannot help distinguishing him from the pagan who makes a virtuous sacrifice of his life, but who is motivated by no hope of reward beyond what he gains from the act of virtue itself. And thus, although morality may not have the exalted function of being instrumental in the attainment of eternal life, as in the Christian scheme, the moral action itself seems to attain a larger dimension. Thus, although morality may be said to be more important from the Christian standpoint, it does not seem possible to consider it "heroic" as in the actions of the great pagans It is not simply true therefore that morality is depreciated in Aristotle's doctrine, or that its status is en-

hanced by the addition of the other-worldly end in the revealed
doctrine  From this criticism of the premise upon which the
solution proposed above is based, a serious objection to the solution itself may be made

This objection may be directed at once to the conclusion  that
the content and character of morality remain the same in that
part of morality not touched directly by the theological virtues
How can the character of morality remain the same when the
motive for moral action is transformed? If it be replied that the
true motive for moral action is always one and the same, except
that it stands fully revealed only in the theological doctrine, we
can object on the grounds of the illustration offered in our introduction  the two ways of understanding the same thing are not
one because the object of understanding is the same  The pagan
who acts for the sake of virtue alone, not perceiving (as the
Christian theologian would say) the ultimate reason why moral
virtue is good, is for that reason acting from a different motive,
because, as with the child in our example,[19] if the "true" motive
for his action were explained to him it would be utterly unintelligible  And for that reason it cannot be said to be the same
motive

This brings us again to our initial observation on the difference between pagan and Christian virtue. The different *appearance* of the two kinds of virtue does not seem to be explained
away by any argument designed to show that the apparent difference is not a real difference, because within the sphere of
moral action there seems to be a peculiar identity of appearance
and reality. It is this difficulty which, at the outset, seems to constitute the most forceful objection both to any interpretation
which has as its conclusion the "harmonization" of the two kinds
of morality, and to the doctrine susceptible of such interpretation  And it is with this difficulty in mind that we must turn to
the commentary written by Thomas on the *Nicomachean
Ethics* [20]

# CHAPTER IV

## THE ORDER OF THE VIRTUES

WE WILL begin by considering Thomas' interpretation of those virtues in which the conflict of "appearances" between pagan and Christian virtue is most striking. Of these, courage, magnificence, and magnanimity are probably most noteworthy, and courage, as it comes first in the *Ethics*, will be taken up first here But, in order to discuss properly the specific problem of courage, or any of the individual virtues, it is necessary first to take up a more general problem presented by the commentary as a whole That problem concerns Thomas' method of dividing up the text of the *Ethics* These divisions might be compared to a modern analytical table of contents, yet their significance is much greater The very first words of the commentary, quoting a dictum of the *Metaphysics*, affirm the principle that "wisdom is the highest perfection of reason, whose distinguishing mark is the recognition of order For the sensitive faculties recognize some things absolutely, but the order [i e , relationship] of one thing to another is the work of intellect or reason alone."[1] This principle is, as we shall see, applicable to every aspect of the interpretation, but it is particularly important as a clue to the understanding of what might otherwise, at first glance, seem a relatively superficial matter. The outline that Thomas follows in the course of his interpretation is an integral part of that interpretation, or, stated somewhat differently, it is the form of the commentary, and is in itself an exemplification of the principles underlying the commentary as a whole In the divisions of the text, and the explanations accompanying them, Thomas sets forth his theory of the "order" of the *Ethics* Accordingly, it is only within the framework of this general theory of the "order" of the *Ethics* that his theory of the role of any individual virtue may be properly considered

His method of analysis illustrates his belief that every step in the argument of the *Ethics* has a purposeful character, that there is a reason not only for everything Aristotle says, but for his saying it in just that way and just that place. Thomas' attitude in this respect is the exact opposite of that modern opinion that considers the *Politics* a "conflation of five separate treatises."[2] Thomas evidently considers that there is an intellectual problem, not a mere textual problem, in the sequence of the exposition It would appear that the *Ethics* is, to Thomas, a book satisfying the literary standards set forth by Socrates in Plato's *Phaedrus*.[3] every statement serves a vital function, as in the body of an animal, where nothing is superfluous and every part stands in a necessary relation to every other part. In this sense, it would not be too much to say that the distinctions and explanations forming Thomas' analysis of the *Ethics* make up a kind of critical anatomy We hasten to add, however, that this analogy, although of preliminary usefulness, has limitations which will appear later [4]

In describing the general structure of this outline, and in showing how Thomas accounts for every step in the argument by means of it, it may be simpler to start by taking an individual section, and then an individual passage, and trace their position within the framework of the whole. We will therefore take as a starting point the section on courage, the initial subject of our detailed inquiry The account of courage occurs in Book III, chapters six through nine,[5] a bare seven pages in the modern English Oxford Aristotle. The whole section dealing with courage is divided by Thomas into three parts The first part, which Thomas calls the investigation of the "matter" of courage, establishes the definition of courage, what courage is about and what it really "is " The second part is called by Thomas the investigation of the *modum operationis*, the manner of action or, as we might say, the way in which courage functions. The way in which it functions may also be said to define its specific qualities, as distinct from its general definition; and to distinguish it both from the opposing vices which are germane to the same subject matter, and from the species of apparent courage which are not the true virtue itself. The third section, which is brief, is called by Thomas a "determination of the properties of courage, by which it is related to pleasure and pain."[6] This comprises a special discussion of those aspects of courage which present a problem for Aristotle's general theory of the relation of pleasure and pain to moral virtue.

The analysis of the first part of the section on courage is presented in Table 1.[7] The tabular form, however, is not part of the original, Thomas' divisions are only given verbally in the text, and the numeration and indentations are our addition. However, they correspond exactly to Thomas' divisions and seem to make them more easily intelligible Presumably an audience of medieval scholars was almost as familiar with the text of Aristotle as the professional expositor. However, such detail is almost intolerable to the modern reader unless simplified visually. Thomas mentions each of the major subdivisions that follow immediately upon each division Thus, in introducing I, the "matter" of courage, he states forthwith that this is divided into A and B And, as B is taken up after A, he identifies it by quoting the initial phrases of the passage with which it begins Thus, also, when he comes to B he begins by saying that this is divided into 1, 2, and 3 (each time using, not the numbers, which are our addition, but some phrase descriptive of the subject matter). As 2 and 3 are not taken up immediately these, again, are identified by the words with which each passage begins in the text of Aristotle. Under B, 1 contains only one passage and is not further subdivided But 2 is divided into a and b; and a into 1' and 2', and so forth. In each case the process of subdivision is carried out until a topical subdivision is reached that corresponds to an individual passage. These individual passages, which we have indicated in the table by the arabic numbers at the right in parentheses, are the units, comprising a single sentence or several sentences of the Latin text, which evidently signify to Thomas the smallest segments of "meaning" In the section represented in Table 1 there are thirteen such passages, (which occupy about one page of English text), together making up one "Lectio" or reading, the equivalent, in the commentary, of a chapter division There is no necessary correspondence between the "Lectiones" and the sections into which the

### TABLE 1

THOMAS' ANALYSIS OF THE FIRST PART OF THE SECTION ON COURAGE
I Investigat materiam fortitudinis
  A Primo resumit quod manifestum est ex praemissis de materia fortitudinis, scilicet circa quas passiones est (1)
  B Secundo, inquirit objecta illarum passionum, prout circa eas est fortitudo (2-13)
    1 Ostendit quae sint objecta timoris (2)
    2 Ostendit circa quod genus horum, sit fortitudo, quia circa timorem mortis (3-7)
      a Primo ostendit circa quae non sit (3-6)
        1' Primo proponit quod intendit, scilicet quod fortitudo non videtur esse circa timorem omnium malorum (3)
        2' Secundo, probat propositum (4-6)
          a' Primo, quod fortitudo non sit circa timorem infamiae (4)
          b' Secundo, quod fortitudo non est circa timorem paupertatis (5)
          c' Tertio, quod fortitudo non est circa quoscumque timores malorum personalium (6)
      b Ostendit circa quorum malorum timorem sit fortitudo (7)
    3 Ostendit in speciali circa cujus mortis timorem sit fortitudo (8-13)
      a Primo ostendit circa quod genus mortis sit fortitudo (8-10)
        1' Primo proponit quod intendit (8)
        2' Secundo, probat propositum dupliciter (9-10)
          a' (first proof) (9)
          b' (second proof) (10)
      b Secundo, ostendit quo ordine se habeat fortitudo circa omnia genera mortis (11-13)
        1' Primo quomodo se habeat in timendo mortem (11-12)
          a' Ostendit circa quam mortem principaliter sit fortitudo (11)
          b' Ostendit quomodo se habeat impavide fortis circa alias mortes (12)
        2' Secundo quomodo se habeat in audacia, quae fit circa hujusmodi pericula (13)

text is divided, each Lectio is merely of convenient length and generally corresponds to some important unit of the subject matter of the text In this particular instance the inquiry into the matter of courage occupies Lectio XIV of Book III.

The analysis of the inquiry into the "matter" of courage, as represented in Table 1, is divided into two parts A, consisting of passage one, recalling from the sketch of the virtues in Book II that courage is concerned with certain passions, "that it is a mean with regard to feelings of fear and confidence", and B, consisting of passages two to thirteen, investigating the objects of these passions, and how courage is concerned with them The B, in turn, is divided into three parts In the first, says Thomas, Aristotle shows what are the objects of fear (the passion with which courage is principally concerned, confidence being secondary). In the second Aristotle is said to show with which kind (*genus*) of fear courage is concerned (namely, with fear of death). Thirdly there emerges the specific fear within the genus, that is, the definition of the particular kind of death, fear of which it is said to be the special function of courage to overcome

Again, section B2, devoted to establishing the "genus" of the fear courage is especially related to, itself has two parts *a*, setting forth what fears courage is not particularly concerned with, and *b*, consisting of passage seven, which states the conclusion that courage must be concerned with the fear of death But *a*, dealing with the fears courage is not concerned with, is also subdivided into 1′ setting forth the proposition that courage is not concerned with fear of all things, and 2′ setting forth the proofs (*a′, b′, c′*) that it cannot be concerned with fear of disgrace, poverty and disease, or the "personal evils" (i.e, insult, envy, and the like).

The third section, 3 (passages eight to thirteen), elucidating the specific fear of the particular kind of death with which courage is concerned, is divided into *a*, showing what kind of death courage is related to, and *b*, showing in what order courage is related to all kinds of death. The former, *a*, is divided into 1′, containing the proposition that it is death in battle which is the special kind of death with which the brave man is concerned, and 2′, the two-fold proof, *a′* that these deaths take place in the greatest and noblest danger, and *b′* that they are correspondingly honored in political communities. In *b* (passages eleven to thirteen), where Aristotle is said to explain the relation of courage (which has been said to derive its specific character from its relation to the particular fear of a certain form of death) to other forms of death, there follows another two-fold division the first, 1′, contains the subsections *a′*, repeating the conclusion of the previous discussion, showing what kind of death is properly that of the brave man, and *b′*, showing how the brave man behaves when faced with other forms of death The second, 2′, shows how the brave man acts in situations calling for confidence.

We hope to make clear, by means of this painstaking detail, our former remark that Thomas tries to relate each and every statement in the *Ethics* to every other statement, and that he tries to account for each such statement as if it were a part of a vital organism To illustrate this point further, however, we propose to take a single passage, passage five, and show how its position is traced in relation to the structure of the entire *Ethics* It might be added, however, that any passage would do as well for this purpose, although our choice here, for other reasons, is not random.

Passage five can be located by a glance down the right side of Table 1 It contains the statement that courage is not concerned with fear of poverty. This, it will be noted, is the second of three proofs to the proposition that courage is not concerned with fear of all things. The proposition and the proofs together form the section designed to show what fears courage is not concerned with. This section, *a* (under 2, under B), together with *b*, which shows with what fear courage is concerned, makes up section 2, which contains the whole exposition

of the genus of fear with which courage is concerned. Section
2, again, is one of three making up the whole inquiry into the
objects of the passions with which courage is concerned, and
this, again, is joined with the résumé in passage one to make up
the whole inquiry into the matter of courage

But now let us proceed into the larger frame of reference. At
the bottom of Table 2 it will be noted that the investigation
of the "matter" of courage is the first of the three main subsections making up the whole treatment of courage. Courage,
however, is one of two moral virtues dealing with the passions
concerned with the preservation of life itself In the next step
up the table it will be seen that courage is grouped with temperance, the former being concerned with the passions arising
from the things which are destructive of life, while temperance
has to do with the passions arising from the things which preserve human life, namely, food and sexual intercourse. Together these form the group of moral virtues concerned with
the "principal passions."

Going another step up Table 2, we note that the moral virtues concerned with the principal passions are linked to a section on the moral virtues having to do with the secondary passions, which are the passions connected with "external goods,"
honor and wealth being the principal of these The virtues connected with the primary passions together with the virtues of
the secondary passions make up a unit consisting of all the virtues of the "interior passions " But again, the treatment of the interior passions is linked, in the next step up the ladder, with the
virtue of "exterior operations" or actions This refers to the famous discussion of justice, which occupies the whole of the fifth
book And the unit comprising the treatment of the virtues of
the "interior passions" and "exterior operations" makes up the
whole discussion of the "particular" moral virtues But the discussion of the particular moral virtues (i e , courage, temperance, liberality, magnificence, magnanimity, justice, etc.) is
preceded by the discussion of what is common to all the moral

TABLE 2

PROEMIUM (BOOK I, LECTIONES 1–3)
TRACTATUS (I 4–X)

    I De Felicitate (I 4–18), quae est summum inter humana bona perducens ad hoc, consideratione felicitatis, quod est operatio secundum virtutem
    II De Virtutibus (I 19–IX)
    III Complet suum tractatum de felicitate, ostendens qualis et quae virtutis operatio sit felicitas (X)
    II De Virtutibus
       A Determinat ea quae sunt praeambula ad virtutem (I 19–20)
       B De virtutibus
          1 De ipsis virtutibus (II–VI)
          2 De quibusdam, quae consequuntur ad virtutes, vel comitantur eas (VII–IX)
          1 De ipsis virtutibus
             a De virtutibus moralibus (II–V)
             b De virtutibus intellectualibus (VI)
             a De virtutibus moralibus
                1' Determinat ea quae pertinent ad virtutes morales in communi (II–III 13)
                2' De virtutibus moralibus in speciali (III 14–V)
                2' De virtutibus moralibus in speciali
                    a' De virtutibus quae sunt circa passiones interiores (III 14–IV)
                    b' De justitia et injustitia, quae est circa operationes exteriores (V)
                    a' De virtutibus quae sunt circa passiones interiores
                        1" De virtutibus moralibus quae sunt circa principales passiones, respicientes ipsam hominis vitam (III 14–22)
                        2" De virtutibus moralibus quae sunt circa quasdam secundarias passiones, respicientes exteriora hominis bona (IV)
                        1" De virtutibus moralibus quae sunt circa principales passiones
                          a" De fortitudine quae est circa passiones respicientes corruptiva humanae vitae (III 14–18)
                          b" De temperantia quae est circa passiones respicientes ea quibus humana vita conservatur, scilicet cibos et venerea
                        a" De fortitudine
                            1''' Investigat materiam fortitudinis
                            2''' Determinat modum operationis ipsius
                            3''' Determinat quasdam proprietates virtutis

virtues as such. And the discussion of what is common to all the moral virtues, when added to the investigation of what is particular to each moral virtue individually, makes up the discussion of moral virtue as a whole. But the discussion of moral virtue is then linked to the discussion of intellectual virtue (in Book VI) to form the whole of the treatment of what is proper to virtue as such But the completion of the discussion of virtue requires not only what is proper to virtue as such, but the discussion of what "is linked to it, or follows from it." Accordingly, there follows in books seven, eight, and nine the discussion of continence and friendship friendship, for example, is not considered a virtue, but an effect of virtue. Thus we see, proceeding further up the scale, that the treatment of the virtues themselves ("*De ipsis virtutibus*") together with those which are effects of the virtues, or linked to them ("*De quibusdam* etc.") makes up the whole of the treatment of the virtues, simply and unqualifiedly This, however, is preceded by a short section, described by Thomas as a preamble to the subject of virtue.

Yet the treatment of the virtues, although forming the main body of the *Ethics*, is nonetheless described by Thomas as the second of three main parts of the whole work The first of these is the discussion of happiness in Book I, in which the conclusion is reached that happiness is the highest of human goods, the mark at which all human action, qua human action, aims. It is further determined there that it is an *operatio secundum virtutem*, a virtuous activity Thus the universal principle of all human activity is defined, and this definition is seen to set in motion the discussion of the virtues which occupies the greater part of the *Ethics*. Moreover, this order is seen to be a necessary order, because the end of all human action must somehow be defined for that activity to be intelligible Thus happiness is shown to be the end in Book I, and is defined as virtuous activity But, although the intelligibility of human action, and of virtue, is thus made known, they cannot be fully understood until one knows what virtue is. And hence the discussion of virtue, occupying books two to nine, follows After virtue has been fully explained it is possible (but only then) to complete the discussion of happiness, that is, to speak about it with full understanding, knowing not only that it is virtuous activity, but what virtuous activity is. On this basis it is possible to discriminate the different kinds of virtuous activity, and to judge which kind constitutes the highest and most perfect form of happiness, and what the relationship is of this highest kind to inferior ones Finally, we call attention to the fact that, according to Thomas, these three main parts of the *Ethics* form the "*Tractatus*," which is preceded by a "*Proemium*" or preface. The significance of the preface may be briefly stated as setting in motion the discussion of happiness, in the same way that the discussion of happiness sets in motion the discussion of virtue all action is seen to aim at some good, and therefore the first question to be answered is, What is this good?

Some parenthetical remarks would seem in order here. We leave it to the reader's imagination to grasp the vastness of the detail by means of which Thomas makes it possible to trace every individual statement to an intelligible locus within the framework of the whole In tracing the structure of the outline upward from the passage in the section on courage, we have only indicated a few of the reasons by which Thomas connects up the various parts, but these should be sufficient to indicate in general that he has a perfectly clear conception of a necessary and intelligible relationship between all these parts There is a monumental impressiveness to the intellectual effort invested by Thomas in discovering a purpose in every step of the *Ethics*, and it is well that we appreciate the immense advantages which this method provides, before assaying it more critically By way of contrast, we again quote some of Rackham's remarks The following concerns one of the most discussed subjects of modern Aristotelian scholarship. In the introduction to his translation of the *Eudemian Ethics*,[8] Rackham

comments on the problem of whether books five, six, and seven
of the *Nicomachean Ethics* belong to the *Nicomachean* or *Eudemian* treatise "But all Aristotle's treatises are so loosely put
together that the arguments for neither view are convincing
It is probable that the three common books represent his final
doctrine, except insofar as they are modified by other parts of
his works—thus the excursus on the ethical value of pleasures
in E E. VI = N E. VII was doubtless superseded by the more
accurate treatment of the topic at the beginning of N.E. X."
These comments, which could be multiplied many-fold from
other sources with unimportant variations, illustrate the modern point of view to which objection has been made above The
superiority of Thomas' method can be sufficiently shown by a
single apposite example We do not know that Thomas ever
read or commented on the *Eudemian Ethics,* nor consequently
of his having remarked on the problem of the relationship of
these two treatises His analysis of the disputed books, however, leaves no doubt that he considered them integral parts of
the treatise before him. It is obvious that he would have dis-
sented vigorously from the notion that Aristotle's treatises are
loosely constructed. Where Rackham considers the two treat-
ments of pleasure in the *Nicomachean Ethics* as separate and
distinct—that in the seventh book he calls an "excursus"—
Thomas considers them as complementary parts of a single
whole In commenting on the introduction of the subject of
pleasure at the beginning of Book X, Thomas remarks upon
the fact that pleasure has already been discussed in Book VII.[9]
But there, he notes the subject was brought up because of its
connection with continence, and for that reason the discussion
turned mainly on the sensible and bodily pleasures. Here, he
says, Aristotle again considers pleasure, because of its connection with the theme of this section, happiness But in this context the discussion turns mainly on the mental and spiritual
pleasures.

Whether Thomas' explanation even of this point is perfectly

satisfactory there is no need to say here. He has offered a plausible hypothesis concerning the relation of the two discussions of pleasure, and it is indisputable that he has himself made a careful attempt to relate the two by grasping the thematic character of the context within which each occurs And any criticism of his hypothesis would first have to make the same or a similar attempt, an attempt apparently not even contemplated by Rackham.

### B CRITIQUE OF THE ANALYSIS OF THE "COMMENTARY"

But we must now inspect Thomas' design of the *Ethics* more closely. And upon closer inspection it will appear that the metaphor of an organism used above is not quite appropriate. We may at present try to describe its limitations by suggesting another metaphor that rather of an architectural structure The parts fit together in the manner of an edifice, built by placing one stone upon another. Let us take for example the treatise on the virtues. This has two parts (see Table 2) first the preamble (A), and second the treatise on the virtues proper (B). The treatise proper (B) has two parts the treatise on the virtues themselves (1), and a kind of "post-amble" (2). The treatise on the virtues themselves is divided into two first, the part consisting of the moral virtues (*a*), and second, the part consisting of the intellectual virtues (*b*). Thomas' explanation of the *ratio ordinis*, the reason for this sequence, is an important indication of his attitude toward the whole *Ethics* it is that the moral virtues are more known, and through them we are disposed toward the intellectual virtues. This explanation will perhaps be more understandable if we recall Aristotle's remarks at the beginning of the *Ethics* concerning the student of moral philosophy,[10] in which he says that young men are not fit auditors of lectures on such subjects, since they tend to follow their passions. In other words, according to Aristotle, the study of ethics presupposes moral virtue, for only because we are already disposed toward moral goodness is it intelligible that we should seek to become good, which is the end and aim of ethics.

And Thomas implies that Aristotle in taking up the moral virtues before the intellectual virtues is following the natural order of things, according to which one comes to us before the other, and is the means of leading us from the one to the other Similarly, in the next step in the outline, what is common to all the moral virtues is taken up before the individual virtues, because the natural way of perceiving anything is to proceed from the general to the particular. From the three parts of the treatise on courage, we may note the same conception of the "reason," i e., order, inherent in the subject matter, determining the "order" of the subjects taken up in the *Ethics*. The matter of courage contains the general definition, which is followed by the manner of action of courage defining its specific qualities, and finally from its specific qualities (the differentia) we are able to determine its peculiar properties Thus the *Ethics* becomes, from this point of view, less a book than an articulation of the subject matter, which reflects by its form no less than its content the character of that subject matter.

Coming to the moral virtues themselves (*a*), the problem of "order" becomes more complex Thomas' explanations, however, are always as simple as they can be. The moral virtues are, as we have seen, divided into those of the "interior passions" and justice, which is concerned with "exterior operations." This "order" is because it is by the passions that we are moved to action, and hence we must understand the virtues of the passions before we can understand the virtue of actions. But the virtues of the passions are also divided into those of the principal passions and those of the secondary passions. The principal passions are those concerned with the preservation of life, and of these the passions concerned with preservation from destruction, as they are the most powerful, are in a radical sense the primary passions And so courage, the virtue of these passions, comes first. Temperance, which is the virtue of the passions arising from the things that preserve life (food, drink, and sexual intercourse), comes next. Courage and temperance are grouped together, Thomas says, because they are both virtues of the irrational part of the soul  courage of the irascible, temperance of the concupiscible. However, by implication Thomas affirms that the passions arising from fear are stronger than those arising from pleasure and hence courage is more "primary" than temperance. That the virtues connected with wealth and honor are secondary is equally evident  wealth and honor *are* secondary to life itself in an obvious and most important sense, and it is clearly the natural mode of understanding that one understand the virtues of the naturally most powerful passions before attempting to explain those that are by nature less powerful.

And so Thomas' analytical outline proceeds, explaining that the general comes before the particular, the passions before the actions, the primary before the secondary  In each of these explanations it is clear that each step builds on the one before, and is necessary as a step leading to what comes next  And it is in this sense that we suggested that Thomas' conception of the "design" of the *Ethics* is rather of an architectural structure than an organism  But we must now call attention to an aspect of this outline which appears most strange, as soon as one reflects on it. And that is that it does not imply any notion of growth or ascent in the elaboration of Aristotle's moral doctrine. The architectural metaphor is a very exact one, we believe.[11] From the way in which we traced the place of an individual passage through the whole plan of the *Ethics,* as laid out by Thomas, it might be said that the individual passage is to him a kind of building block, bearing the same relation to the whole *Ethics* that the individual stones of which wall, buttress, or foundation are comprised, bear to the whole building. And as in each building that is built according to a single plan by a single architect, the whole building is implied in each of its parts, so each part can be understood as necessary to the whole building. And thus each part is intelligible as part of the whole, and implies the finished whole even in the course of construction, while the stones are being laid one upon the other. Thomas, similarly, seems to regard the *Ethics* as a whole of such character that each part implies the finished whole from the very beginning, like a building whose extent and weight may be inferred from the extent and depth of the foundation. But we may contrast this conception with another, and substitute for the metaphor of a building operation that of the growth of an organism. The very first step in the building operation implied a completed plan  but the early stages in the growth of an organism, whether of an acorn or an infant, disclose relatively little of the fully matured being  indeed, the acorn or infant, unlike the cornerstone, is not a part of the completed whole, except through the intermediation of successive stages of growth  What is here suggested is that Aristotle's *Ethics* may be rather like the organism, disclosing its intention and meaning through successive stages of growth, rather than through the fitting together of its parts [12]

The difficulty to which we are pointing may now be stated more simply  Thomas does not in his outline show that Aristotle, in his review of the virtues, constantly proceeds from lower to higher. There is, in his plan of the *Ethics*, no real conception of *development*, although there may, in a sense, be one of progress [13] And it is, in a way, astonishing that this striking fact about the *Ethics* is not brought out by Thomas  Looking at the treatise on the virtues, it is evident that moral virtue is, absolutely, something lower than intellectual virtue. Furthermore, justice, the virtue of "exterior operations," comes after the virtues of the passions, not only because the passions cause the actions, but because justice is the highest and greatest of the moral virtues. Turning to the virtues of the passions, the thesis we have proposed becomes less obvious, but it can be easily proved as to the main order of the subject matter, even if it may not be demonstrable as to each detail. There are four main virtues treated in books three and four  courage and temperance are the first two, liberality and magnificence we group together as the third, and magnanimity and proper pride as the fourth Now the "order" of the first two virtues is problematical, that of the first two groups of virtues is ambiguous, but there can be no doubt as to the standing of the last main virtue magnanimity implies the perfection of every virtue, certainly every moral virtue, and hence must, itself, be the greatest of the virtues considered up to this point. But if we consider magnanimity and proper pride on the one hand, and liberality and magnificence on the other, it is evident that the virtues concerned with honor are "higher" than those concerned with wealth Wealth is something material and merely instrumental, honor is an immaterial good, and is loved for its own sake Yet, as regards magnificence, wealth is not merely material and instrumental "the magnificent man is like an artist," and wealth, although still intrinsically something instrumental, yet is seen in its highest function not as serving to relieve human wants, but as a medium for the reflection of that nobility of soul which is part of human perfection From this consideration, we see the appropriateness of grouping the virtues concerned with wealth together with those concerned with honor, and the sense in which together they represent a progress beyond the virtues concerned with mere life itself Thus, although it may be true that the virtues concerned with life itself are primary, they are not for that reason "higher" or "better "[14] The virtues concerned with wealth and honor have more to do with the good life, than with mere life, and hence, from Aristotle's point of view, reveal more of that human perfection which is the guiding conception of his whole moral and political philosophy From this point of view we can understand why the discussion of the social graces comes at the very end of Book IV It seems absurd to speak of a good sense of humor as a greater virtue than courage, yet it is not absurd to say that the constellation of personal qualities, of which good humor is an integral part, is the attribute of a character which is something rarer and finer than one which is merely courageous

There is, therefore, a fairly clear scheme within the treatise on the virtues of the passions, showing a development to progressively "higher" things. The virtues of the secondary passions reveal more of human perfection than those of the primary passions, the virtues concerned with honor, which occupy the second half of the treatise on the secondary passions, are higher than those concerned with wealth, which occupy the first half  The discussion of the social graces, which comes near the very end of Book IV, concerns the nicest refinements of human personality, and for that reason is a fitting sequel to, and, in a sense, an adornment of, the description of the magnanimous man  There are, however, some apparent exceptions to this general rule of "development" we have suggested  the development proceeds uninterruptedly from liberality to magnificence, and then to magnanimity. There follows, however, the subject of "proper pride," the virtue for which there is, actually, no name, but which is related to magnanimity, in the sphere of honor, as liberality is related to magnificence in the sphere of wealth  It might at first seem sufficient to say that this is an exception to the rule, that Aristotle does not follow a hard and fast scheme  But the exception is not merely fortuitous  For magnificence and magnanimity together comprise a kind of unit, as is indicated by the prefix they share, which occurs in both the Latin and Greek, as well as in the English [15]  But there is another reason for treating them together, and for this we can, admittedly, offer not proof, but only testimony  The descriptions of the magnificent and magnanimous man together form one of several peaks of the *Ethics*, points which somehow sum up certain vital aspects of the notion of human perfection  This is indicated not merely by the formal character of the argument, and by the structure of the *Ethics*, but by the particular fulness of the descriptions of these human types, and by the subdued, but no less intense, passion with which Aristotle's writing becomes charged in these passages  This is equally true of parts of Book V, on justice, and is even more true of the rapturous description of the philosophic life in Book X, which is, both from a literary and logical point of view, the climax of the entire *Ethics*. I need not here refute the objection that this is merely a "subjective impression": because this has, I believe, been the impression of discerning readers throughout the ages, and is visible through the medium of any tolerable translation It would therefore, on sound Aristotelian grounds, constitute a "moral fact," and hence ought not to be left out of any moral discussion It is significant that Thomas takes no account of such considerations. It also serves to explain what would otherwise be a mere deviation from the rule we laid down The summing up of the two forms of "greatness" would have been disturbed by a pedantic insistence on the same sequence in treating the virtues of honor as was followed in treating the virtues of wealth There is, of course, a still simpler explanation, but one which we have reserved for the last because, although sufficient in itself, it does not emphasize what has been implied concerning Aristotle's deeper motivation. This explanation is that the equivalent of liberality, "proper pride or ambition," is actually a virtue without a name, and it is more intelligible to begin with magnanimity, the virtue concerned with honor which can be identified by name. It should be clear, however, that this "exception" does not reflect on the validity of the general rule of "development"

There is one difficulty, however, of a different degree from that dealt with immediately above. It concerns the "order" of courage and temperance Here we are confronted with a flat contradiction of our rule by Thomas according to his interpretation temperance is distinctly lower in dignity than courage. Thomas' view is based on Aristotle's observation that pleasure is easier to resist than pain, for the one tends to destroy our nature, while the other preserves and perfects it,[16] and, furthermore, the opportunities of becoming temperate by acting temperately occur frequently in daily life, and involve no risk, whereas the chance of becoming brave is much rarer, and is always dangerous.[17] Now there can be no gainsaying the soundness of this argument, nor denying that, on these grounds, Thomas is right. It may be asked, however, whether these are the grounds on which Aristotle ranks the virtues.

In the first place, we must now call attention to the circumstance that there are, in the *Ethics*, two distinct (although not unrelated) treatises on moral virtue, and that these are not really recognized as such by Thomas Books VII through IX, of which the main subjects are, apparently, continence and friendship, are described by Thomas as a section devoted, not to moral virtue as such, but to certain things that are effects of virtue, or are linked to virtue [18] He does not take full cognizance of the fact that Aristotle says, at the beginning of Book VII, that he is now making a "fresh beginning," and that he does, in fact, proceed to re-discuss the whole subject of moral virtue, although from a different point of view, a point of view for which everything that has preceded is, in some way or other, a preparation Aristotle begins Book VII as follows [19] "Let us now make a fresh beginning and point out that of moral states to be avoided there are three kinds  vice, incontinence, brutishness  The contraries of two of these are evident  one we call virtue, the other continence, to brutishness it would be most fitting to oppose superhuman virtue, a heroic and divine kind of virtue, as Homer has represented Priam saying of Hector that he was very good,

> For he seemed not, he,
> The child of a mortal man, but as one that of God's seed came.

Therefore if, as they say, men become gods by excess of virtue, of this kind must evidently be the state opposed to the brutish state, for as a brute has no virtue or vice, so neither has a god, his state is higher than virtue, and that of a brute is a different kind of state from vice " As the guiding conception throughout the *Ethics* is that of human perfection, it is not inappropriate to say that the principal theme of the section introduced by the passage just quoted is heroic virtue, notwithstanding the fact that, in Book VII at least, the principal subject actually discussed is continence and incontinence From a broader point of view, the entire subject of moral virtue is rediscussed in Books VII through IX Up to this point the moral problem has appeared simply as the problem of virtue versus vice Here it is shown that this is only one part, albeit the practically most important part, of the moral problem Yet the range and variety of moral possibilities is now shown to be much greater than has heretofore been considered This becomes manifest if we consider courage and temperance Immediate evidence of this re-discussion is presented by the apparent contradiction, in Book IX, of Aristotle's statement in Book III that the exercise of the virtue of courage is painful.[20] The statement in Book III is presented as a refinement and qualification of his general remarks about the character of moral virtue in Book II, where[21] he had said that the sign of moral states is the pleasure or pain that accompanies our actions, "and he who stands his ground against things that are terrible and delights in this or at least is not pained is brave, while the man who is pained is a coward " The statement in Book III has all the appearance of finality, and is a decisive qualification "And so, if the case of courage is similar [to that of the boxer, who suffers painful blows for the sake of the garland of victory] death and wounds will be painful to the brave man and against his will, but he will face them because it is noble to do so or because it is base not to do so And the more he is possessed of virtue in its entirety and the happier he is, the more he will be pained at the thought of death, for life is best worth living for such a man, for he is knowingly losing the greatest of goods, and this is painful  .. It is not the case, then, with all the virtues that the exercise of each of them is pleasant, except in so far as it reaches its end " Now this must be compared with the following remarks in Book IX "It is true of the good man too that he does many actions for the sake of his friends and his country, and if necessary dies for them, for he will throw away both wealth and honors and in general the goods that are the objects of competition, gaining for himself nobility, since he would prefer a short period of intense pleasure to a long one of mild enjoyment, a twelvemonth of noble life to many years of humdrum existence, and one great and noble action to many trivial ones Now those who die for others doubtless attain this result, it is therefore a great prize that they choose for themselves "[22] The only point at which these latter two quotations would appear reconcilable is in the qualification at the end of the former, that the exercise of courage is painful, "except in so far as it reaches its end." In the context of the passage, however, this would simply mean, "except in so far as the brave man conquers, rather than dies", as the action of the boxer, which is painful throughout the conflict, is partially redeemed by pleasure in receiving the laurel of victory—that is, if he happens to be victorious One might, of course, treat this exception to mean, "except in the case in which the bravery of the brave man is finally consummated in action " The true end of courage is, indeed, the brave or courageous action And it may have been Aristotle's aim to indicate, even here, that the brave action is, in itself, always pleasant This may in a sense be the true commentary on the passage in Book III, but it is significant that it is not suggested by the passage itself, but can only be read retrospectively into it on the basis of the passage in Book IX. But reading an interpretation into one passage, on the basis of a later one, however it may be justified as showing the relevance of Aristotle's ultimate intention at a preliminary point, does not disclose his immediate aim in concealing that ultimate intention, or presenting it in an equivocal or ambiguous form, at the particular preliminary point. The striking, though perhaps superficial, contradiction between the two passages is, we believe, at this point a more reliable guide to Aristotle's real intention than any statement of that intention which is not based on the solution of the difficulties presented by the apparent contradiction.

The contradiction between the passages concerning courage in Books III and IX is sufficient to show that there are, at the least, two different contexts within which courage may be discussed, and, for immediate practical purposes, two different kinds of courage  Thomas does not recognize this distinction and, consequently, his ranking of courage over temperance is of necessity ambiguous. For, while it may be correct to say that heroic courage is greater than temperance, it is not nearly so evident that the ordinary species of courage, analyzed in Book III, is higher  There are a number of signs that the reverse is, in fact, the case  In the first place, there is the circumstance, already noted, that ordinary courage has something imperfect about it, namely, that its exercise is painful, whereas, from the point of view of the general theory of virtue, the perfection of each virtue is accompanied by, and indeed made possible by, pleasure.[23] Another striking fact about courage, or rather about Aristotle's account of it in Book III, is that it is, apparently, the most easily imitated of the virtues. Nearly half the treatise on courage is taken up by the discussion of five specious forms of courage, in the case of none of the other virtues does Aristotle enter into any similar discussion. The only possible exception is temperance, if we wish to consider continence as a specious form of temperance. But Aristotle, strangely, never mentioned continence in his original treatment of temperance in Book III, but rather takes it up in the context of heroic virtue in Book VII  Now it is possible that there are sufficient reasons[24] for this, wholly apart from the question of the order of the virtues, nonetheless, the effect of this procedure, i e , emphasizing the "imitable" quality of courage, together with its "painfulness," is to reinforce the impression that courage is, in a sophisticated sense, lower in the scale of virtues than temperance  But we must inquire further into this "separation" of temperance and continence.

A reason why the discussion of continence is placed in the latter section, while that of the specious forms of courage is in the former, is that the understanding of the various specious forms of courage is primarily of practical importance It is of practical significance because, although the motive for a specious kind of courage may be different from that of the true kind, its practical consequence may be the same. In fact, as Aristotle observes, the action of certain kinds of false courage may for some purposes be better than that of the true variety "But it is quite possible that the best soldiers may be not men of this sort [i.e , truly brave] but those who are less brave but have no other good, for these are ready to face danger, and they sell their lives for trifling gain."[25] Now, although it is Aristotle's aim throughout the *Ethics* to be "practical," it is nonetheless true that the most eminently practical questions are dealt with in the earlier books What we have to know, in the broadest sense, in order to become brave and temperate, we are told by the end of Book III. What we learn about these virtues in Books VII to IX does not add much to this knowledge, what we gain from these books is rather a deeper knowledge of the character of morality itself, and a capacity to appreciate the conclusion of the whole *Ethics*, in Book X, which places the highest good not in morality, but in theoretical wisdom In other words, the discrimination of temperance and continence is, in the crude sense, less of a practical question than the discrimination of the true and specious forms of courage. Ultimately, of course, it may be said to be more practical, in that it more nearly approaches to the heart of the central question of the *Ethics*, the question of what constitutes the highest good Yet from either point of view, it has more to do with the "highest" ethical considerations, and for that reason belongs to the later section.

A comparison of continence and the specious forms of courage suggests some other points that may supply the clue to Aristotle's criteria for ranking courage and temperance Both are "good" states of character, yet neither is a virtue. Taking the first and highest form of specious courage, that of the citizen-soldier, we may note that it is, at its best, induced by the love of honor This falls short of true courage, which is due not to the love of honor, but to the nobility or moral goodness intrinsic in the brave action itself. Honor is the just reward of such goodness, but this reward is not itself the proper motive for the action of the true virtue The defect of this form of courage is a kind of rational defect it is no lack of control of the affections which detracts from its virtue, as the action in itself is no less difficult.[26] It is a defect in the opinion which governs the action In the case of the continent man, the opinion governing the action is the same as that which governs the action of the temperate man. Here the defect is in the affections, as the continent man, being of the opinion that to act temperately is good, must nonetheless overcome intemperate desires in order to act continently And the overcoming of contrary desires is itself a painful process This brings us to a suggestive reflection continence bears a certain resemblance to true courage, in that the action of each is painful, albeit for different reasons The action of the truly brave man, indeed, is more painful than that of the man possessed of less virtue, just because the consciousness of his goodness makes the prospect of death more painful. Yet how can this "consciousness" be painful, unless it is, in some sense, a desire for life somehow in conflict with the choice of a noble death? According to the notion of heroic virtue in Book IX[27] there is no such pain accompanying the choice of a noble death What we suggest is that in Book III Aristotle is still dealing with the conception of courage in its popular form, and it would be too paradoxical to suggest that a noble death could actually be pleasant. It requires the whole development of his doctrine between Books III and IX to make this appear intelligible, and even sensible Yet, in retrospect, it is clear that the courage described in Book III is an imperfect kind of virtue, having, in certain respects, more in common with continence, an imperfection of temperance, than temperance itself, and for this reason also it may be said to be ranked lower than temperance

Another reflection is prompted by the old problem[28] as to whether continence or temperance is the greater virtue Aristotle's answer to this admits of no doubt  continence is not even called a virtue, and temperance is obviously the higher moral state  Yet the arguments are of some relevance to us whether it is better, i e , more virtuous, to overcome bad desires, or to be so constituted as not to have them, or have them only weakly. The actions of the temperate man and of the continent man, it will be remembered, are the same, only the one takes pleasure in acting temperately, while the other painfully overcomes his bad desires.

There is no real problem for Aristotle as to which is better, primarily because for him moral virtue is so decidedly "second best" among the goods achievable by man  For if morality were to be considered the highest good, it is possible, in a sense, to consider continence better than temperance  We may illustrate this from Aristotle's point of view by a remark in Book X concerning the absurdity of attributing moral virtue to the gods. "And what would their temperate acts be? Is not such praise tasteless, since they have no bad desires?"[29] The gods do not have bad desires, but neither does the temperate man. It is only the continent man, of those who are good, who has bad desires  Yet, from Aristotle's observation, it would seem that we are not to attribute moral virtue to a being who is without bad desires  But this is absurd, for then temperance would no longer be a moral virtue. Aristotle means, of course, that the gods are not capable of bad desires, and for that reason are no more capable of temperance than of intemperance. The temperate man was capable of intemperance, and for that reason may be described as morally virtuous  In becoming temperate, he had to go through the various stages of moral education in which he imitated the actions of temperance without being temperate  At first he probably imitated these actions under the direct discipline of those in charge of his education, later, more indirectly, under the fear of the bad opinion of others There must have been an intermediate stage, however, in which the opinion that to act temperately was good became his own opinion, but before his inclinations were thoroughly accommodated to this opinion That is, he must have become continent before becoming temperate. The decisive moment in his moral education must have occurred when his bad desires were mastered by his will-power, not under the direct or in-direct influence of any external discipline, but solely under the influence of the opinion that to act temperately was good The discipline of continence, then, would have to be the necessary condition for the actualization of temperance Yet at the mo-ment that a man became temperate, it would be more pleasant for him to act temperately than otherwise There would be no difficulty in acting temperately The power of continence, therefore, in mastering powerful desires, is, in a sense, the greater power and hence the greater virtue In other words, from a point of view in which morality is the highest good, to over-come temptation is a kind of triumph of morality, and such is the case with the action of the continent man But in the action of the temperate man there is no moral issue whatever This is, of course, the vein of the theological tradition, as represented in the saying "that there is more rejoicing in heaven    ."[30] But from Aristotle's point of view, the triumph of morality is not valued so much because of the value of morality, but because it makes possible the attainment of non-moral goods. This is, in our opinion, the deepest reason for his valuing temperance. And it is also a reason for believing that Aristotle must have ranked temperance higher than courage For courage—even heroic bravery—although it may represent the highest consum-mation of morality, cannot be said to be instrumental to any end higher than morality [31] In the case of temperance, this is not simply true the actions of temperance are not, indeed, the greatest triumphs of morality, but they are, as is suggested by

Aristotle's remarks about the gods, the means of an emancipation from those desires which are an impediment to the attainment of a higher good than the moral good

We have shown with some conclusiveness, we believe, the senses in which temperance as a virtue is to be ranked higher than ordinary courage We have just suggested that temperance may also be higher than heroic bravery It is, indeed, questionable whether it is proper to distinguish courage and temperance as we have done, when speaking of heroic virtue. We will not try to answer the propriety of this manner of distinction here, as the problem of heroic virtue must be taken up in greater detail later. It is not inappropriate, however, to ask what, in some sense, would be the equivalent, in the sphere of temperance, of heroic bravery. This presents something of a problem because, as we have shown, there is a clear basis for a distinction between ordinary courage, as described in Book III, and heroic courage, as described in Book IX  Heroic temperance—the very name has an absurd sound—cannot be the sphere of superhuman temptations, because then the action of the temperate man would be reduced to that of the continent man Certainly, from Aristotle's point of view, temperance assumes heroic proportions only in the case of the man who is a philosopher. Alcibiades' portrait of Socrates, in Plato's *Symposium*, would seem to be what Aristotle had in mind  the conception of a man who was not merely temperate, but was completely emancipated from the sphere of the desires commonly subject to temperance.[32] In fact, upon reflection it would seem that heroic bravery might actually be only a special instance of this highest form of temperance, or moderation, whose universal effect is to preserve its possessor from any and all passions that might disrupt the free exercise of reason  From the example of Socrates, certainly a model of heroic virtue, the aspect of temperance clearly predominates over that of courage. This is symbolized in the *Symposium* by the fact that, in Alcibiades' account of Socrates, the story of his phenomenal bravery is

only the prelude to the true climax of the tale, namely Socrates'
perfect freedom from temptation in what Alcibiades (and
the company present) evidently considered a more remarkable
trial of virtue [33] Finally, we may say that the very arguments
used by Thomas (albeit, apparently, Aristotle's own) to show
that courage is a greater virtue than temperance—that the occasions for courage are fewer and more dangerous—may be used,
on the basis of deeper reflection, to indicate the opposite of
what at first they seemed to indicate. For they may be turned
around it may with equal truth be pointed out that the occasions for intemperance are more frequent, and less dangerous
It must be remembered (from the discussion of the specious
forms of courage) that the laws generally make cowardice very
unsafe Also, where, on the basis of such adventitious helps as
the laws, almost everyone is somehow made capable of the actions of courage, a fairly large proportion of those who thus
imitate true courage may become brave for it is by habituation
to the action of each virtue that we acquire the virtue [34] The
absence of any discussion of specious forms of temperance in
Book III thus enforces the impression that it was Aristotle's
opinion that courage was a much more common and widely
diffused virtue than temperance Indeed, on the basis of the discussion of continence in Book VII we are persuaded that temperance is actually of rare occurrence there must be many more
people who act temperately, but are by no means free from
contrary desires, than those who actually take pleasure in acting temperately But the step from at least the highest form of
specious courage, that of the citizen-soldier, to true courage,
must be relatively easier and of more common occurrence than
the step from continence to temperance The courage of the
citizen-soldier Aristotle calls "most like to that which we described earlier [i e , true courage], because it is due to virtue,
for it is due to shame and to desire of a noble object [i e.,
honor] and avoidance of disgrace, which is ignoble "[35] What is
needed then to make the citizen-soldier truly brave is a correc-

tion of the opinion that places in honor the motive for his
action  Although we may be assured that it is a difficult and
rare thing to act bravely solely for virtue's sake, it is still no
great distance that separates the citizen-soldier from the truly
brave man  for if the true citizen-soldier, for whom acting dishonorably was more painful than any brave action, once found
himself in a situation in which no honor was to be anticipated
from his brave action, he might readily perceive the value of
the honorable action itself, and suddenly realize that the true
motive for brave action had always been virtue itself. The continent man, however, although he has a correct opinion of the
value of temperate action, does not have the same control of his
affections as the citizen-soldier. Although acting temperately
over a considerable period of time may insensibly transform
him into a truly temperate person, it is nonetheless a longer
process, and of more uncertain issue  We may apply to the continent man something of the censure that Aristotle directs to
the incontinent man [36] "But to the incontinent man may be
applied the proverb 'when water chokes, what is one to wash it
down with?' If he had been persuaded of the rightness of what
he does, he would have desisted when he was persuaded to
change his mind, but now he acts in spite of his being persuaded
of something quite different " The continent man acts rightly,
persuaded of the rightness of temperate action, but he does not
take pleasure in it  But of such a man one may ask, if, having a
right opinion, and having even the will to compel himself to act
on it, he is still incapable of disciplining his affections to desire the
temperate action, what will enable him to become temperate?
The answer to this question is not, we believe, simply the one
already suggested  that habituation will eventually effect the
result. In a sense the merely continent man has little real incen-
tive for the extremely difficult moral discipline of rooting out
intemperate desires. The whole trend of Aristotle's argument
leads us to believe that the most serious reason for the difficulty
of acquiring true temperance, as well as the real justification

for its superiority, is that it requires for its most perfect consummation an end beyond moral virtue, the motive of an
emancipation from the disturbance of wayward desires for the
sake of the life of reason.

### C SUMMARY

In concluding this section we will review briefly the evidence for the thesis concerning the "development" of the
*Ethics,* and show the problems this raises for investigation in
the next section. That there is a development in the broad
structure of the *Ethics* is proved, we believe, by a mere
glance  the superiority of intellectual virtue to moral virtue
and of justice to all other moral virtues is granted by Thomas,
and, indeed, is undeniably the Aristotelian doctrine. That this
broad scheme of development is more difficult to maintain
when descending to particulars we granted at the outset.
Nevertheless, it has been sufficiently shown that, although the
virtues concerned with honor and wealth may not be greater
than courage and temperance in every sense, they are so in
certain senses, and that these latter are the criteria that Aristotle uses in the ranking of the virtues Finally, we have tried
to show that courage, at least as described in Book III, was
the lowest of the moral virtues on the basis of these criteria
In order to give evidence on this point it was necessary to
show that Aristotle's last word on courage, and, indeed, on
moral virtue altogether, was not to be found in that part of
the *Ethics* which Thomas describes as the treatise on moral
virtue proper, but rather in a later section described by
Thomas as a treatise on certain effects or concomitants of
virtue. In certain remarks which evidently refer to the character of courage, in Book IX, it was seen that Aristotle in this
later section refines the whole conception of moral virtue
Furthermore, there appear to be certain statements in this
later section which, superficially at least, contradict statements
in the earlier section This leads to the difficulty, not merely

of finding the principle on which such apparent contradictions may be reconciled, but of discovering why the *appearance* of these contradictions is preserved by Aristotle in the course of the development of his doctrine. Recurring to the problem formulated above,[37] it is necessary again to insist on the importance of knowing why at each point morality appears as it does, because it is by the form in which morality appears to us that we are prompted to act, and therefore moral values can only be judged properly in the light of these appearances. Certainly sound judgment on moral matters can only be reached on the basis of full consideration of the role played by conflicting appearances, and the opinions to which they give rise. Aristotle, we venture to say (and proof will be offered shortly), has deliberately preserved certain of these conflicts of appearances, because they are symptomatic of a deeper ambiguity in his attitude toward the whole moral problem—an ambiguity which does not of necessity imply a fundamental ambivalence in his attitude toward morality, but which reflects certain difficulties inherent (according to his view) in the subject matter itself

Thomas, we might say, reflects in his analytical outline the notion of a perfectly unambiguous conception of the moral phenomena. There is, in this outline, no apparent room for the possibility that Aristotle's treatment of courage is incomplete in Book III, albeit apparently complete, and that judgment on the character of courage (and, indeed, on the character of morality as a whole) must be revised in the light of an enlarged moral horizon which emerges only in Books VII to IX In the metaphor of the building operation we said that the steps in the outline were comparable to building blocks, each a unit of the whole, and that each block is a "perfect" unit, in that it is an integral part of a larger whole The conception of the *Ethics* we have adduced, however, is different it would appear that the "unit" on courage, in Book III, for instance, is not a complete whole in the sense that Thomas would make it appear The treatment of courage there is essentially incomplete, although it may be said to be complete in the sense that it contains all that can be said about courage at that point In fact, it may be, as with the two explanations of the reasons for the obedience of a well-behaved child, that only the "incomplete" account of courage can be correct at that point, because only such an account can accurately portray the courage which ordinarily motivates moral action in the ordinary business of life The heroic courage portrayed in Book IX may, perhaps, be said to be unintelligible as a motive for moral action, except in a moral stratosphere visible only in the most advanced stages of moral perceptiveness.

# CHAPTER V

## HEROIC VIRTUE

### A INTRODUCTORY

IT HAS been explained in the preceding chapter[1] in what sense Thomas seems to conceive of the *Ethics* as a book which renders by its form, as well as by its content, the phenomena of morality  The main body of the *Ethics* is "set in motion," we might say, from Thomas' point of view, in the following manner  The observation of all activity, and particularly moral action, reveals that all action is intelligible only as action for the sake of some good, as Aristotle affirms in the very opening words of the *Ethics*  Accordingly, we must know what is the good or goods at which each thing aims in order to understand its activities, and, indeed, we must understand the activity of each thing in order to know what the thing itself really is  In the case of man, we must know what is the good achievable by action at which man aims  And this is the end which determines the character of morality  Aristotle is therefore compelled to say first what this summum bonum is, and he finds it to be happiness. But, as Aristotle himself indicates,[2] happiness thus defined is only a kind of verbal agreement testifying to the fact that everyone somehow divines that there is one final end and aim to all human action  It is an agreement forced upon us by the observation of the universal character of the quest for the good  But Aristotle's next step is, by a refinement of the argument, to say what happiness is, and it is found to be, or to consist in, virtuous action  Thus a quest for the meaning of morality is resolved into an inquiry into the nature of virtue and virtuous action  We are thus led to the treatise on the general character of moral virtue, then to the moral virtues themselves, the intellectual virtues, and so forth

As has been said, Thomas implies that this is the way in which we are led naturally, and hence reasonably, by the intrinsic order of the subject matter.

But Thomas, equating nature with reason, and the *Ethics* with the nature of moral phenomena, is led to make the following further inference concerning the design or plan of the *Ethics*. For it is a further inference from the notion that a thing is reasonable, that it is free from ambiguity and paradox. That is, to the extent that a paradox may be called reasonable, the two apparently conflicting opinions are reconciled by a third, and to the extent that an ambiguous statement is reasonable, the ambiguity can be resolved in the light of further evidence. Thomas' conception of the "order" in which Aristotle's natural reason discovers the truth about moral phenomena implies that as much of the truth as has been elaborated up to a given point has been elaborated unambiguously and unparadoxically. A given topical heading in his analytical outline may indicate a part of a subject which in its entirety has not as yet been made fully intelligible yet it will be presumed, by Thomas' interpretation, to make that portion of the subject fully intelligible. Thus, the subject of happiness is taken up in Book I, although we do not actually learn what happiness is until Book X. Yet we do learn, first, that happiness is the summum bonum, and that it is virtuous action, and we learn these things clearly and unambiguously Similarly, we do not know what moral virtue is from the general treatment we must go on and learn about each individual moral virtue. Yet the general character of moral virtue *is* sufficiently indicated in the general treatment. It might be objected, of course, on Aristotelian grounds, that a general treatment of the character of moral virtue presupposes a knowledge of the particular moral virtues. But it may be replied that this presupposes no more than what Aristotle expected of all his auditors,[3] that is, good character and experience of life· and there is nothing paradoxical in Thomas' expecting that in the natural mode of understanding (which presupposes maturity), the general precedes the particular and can be complete in itself, although not with respect to the whole. There is, of course, a sense in which no part can be fully intelligible, except in so far as the whole is known It is in this sense that the building block, although a "perfect" and self-contained unit, is nonetheless un-intelligible, except to the extent that we can from its form and position infer the plan of a whole building of which it is to be a part Thus the explanation of the part, qua part, must include an explanation of the whole sufficient for rendering the part, in itself, intelligible But one need not know all the properties of circles and triangles in order to understand what a radius or hypotenuse is, although one must know what the definition of a circle is, and what the definition of a right triangle is. In the same way Thomas takes it for granted that the general account of happiness in Book I is a sufficient framework for the general account of virtue which follows, and the general account of virtue is sufficient for the account of the particular moral virtues To conclude, we may say that Thomas supposes that, within the framework of the account of the particular moral virtues, that is, in the treatment of courage, magnanimity, justice, etc, the last word on courage, etc, has been said. Or, to put it more cautiously, Thomas seems certainly to suppose that, in the section on courage, the nature of courage has been clearly and unambiguously set forth. Yet, as we shall try to prove,[4] the last word on courage, as well as that on justice (and hence, necessarily, on moral virtue as a whole), is not pronounced by Aristotle in the treatises proper to those virtues. And, moreover, the account of courage in Book III is far from being unambiguous Its ambiguity, as we shall undertake to prove, not only cannot be cleared up within the context of the account of courage, but is *necessary* to the clarity of that account Furthermore, we shall attempt to prove that real paradoxes in the nature of courage, and of moral virtue generally, cannot be, or at least are not by Aristotle, resolved, except in terms of considerations which lie outside the dimension of morality [5]

We turn first to the necessary preliminary task of proving, in terms of his interpretive principles, our assertion concerning Thomas' conception of the "wholeness" or unambiguousness of each topical subdivision of the *Ethics*, as set forth in the analytical outline, and particularly with respect to courage

### B THE PRINCIPLE OF THE "ULTIMATE"

We remind the reader[6] that the account of courage is divided by Thomas into three parts  first, concerning the matter of courage, second, its manner of operation or action, third, its properties  In accordance with the analysis of the first section, as presented in Table 1, we may note the following  The section is divided into two parts, consisting of A, passage one, and B, passages two through thirteen  Passage one summarizes what had been made clear in a preceding passage, namely, of what passions courage is a mean  Part B is divided into three additional parts  1, showing what are the objects of fear, 2, showing what kind of fear is the special object of courage, and 3, showing the special kind of death, fear of which is said to be the special object of courage  We may summarize the analysis of 2 and 3 by saying that they consist of a process of elimination, narrowing down the possibilities until a final statement on the subject matter can be made  Thus, the whole purpose of section 2, as announced in the topical heading for that section, is to establish the proposition that fear of death is the kind (*genus*) of fear which courage serves to overcome  The steps leading up to the assertion of this proposition consist of the statement of the kinds of fear with which courage cannot be said to be properly concerned, and the proofs of these rejections  The whole purpose of section 3, as announced in the topical heading for that section, is to establish the proposition that fear of death in battle is the special object of courage  Here the sequence is somewhat different, in that the proposition is presented at the outset, and the proofs follow  This, however, is not exactly the case, as passage eight, denominated by Thomas in the outline merely as the "proposition," actually contains a statement of, and rejection of,

alternative possibilities, preceding the proposition One may ask
why Thomas, who never spares any pains in making nice dis-
criminations, fails to note this The answer would seem to be
that Aristotle merely passes over these possibilities, without considering the reasons for rejecting them—as if that were hardly
necessary Therefore, it may be said that they form no real part
of the argument In any case, Aristotle returns to consider the
relation of the brave man to death in disease and at sea a few
passages later, and Thomas may for that reason have thought
that the real "place" for the consideration of these "non-essen-
tial" forms of death was in these later passages, and made his
topical allocation accordingly By the strict logic of Thomas'
outline, there is no room for these extraneous remarks, and he
lightly passes over what might appear as a superfluity. From
Thomas' own point of view, however, it is clear that the most
important statements in sections 2 and 3 are contained in passages seven and eight This is curious, because the former is the
last passage in the earlier section, and the latter is the first passage in the later section. Moreover, a cursory reading of the two
passages shows that together they form a kind of "natural unit,"
and the arguments adduced above[7] to account for the unity of
the treatment of magnificence and magnanimity would, we believe, apply here on a minor scale But, more important than
calling attention to the difficulty that Thomas has in containing
Aristotle's highly elastic procedure, is the fact that these two
passages together contain what is, in all essentials, the definition
of courage The brave man is there said to be the man who can,
above all, meet and overcome the terror inspired by death, the
most terrible of all things, but the specific quality of bravery
relates not merely to the magnitude of the terror, but also to
the nobility of the end for which it is suffered thus courage
is defined as the ability fearlessly to meet a noble death in
battle Hence, from the interpretation of these two key passages, we may seek the starting point for Thomas' interpretation
of courage

That these are the key passages in the definition of courage is confirmed by Thomas in his initial comments on passage seven [8] Aristotle here, says Thomas, says what a simply (i.e., absolutely) brave man is, from the fact that he is fearless in the face of those things that are terrible in the highest degree. Then Thomas introduces his central interpretive principle a virtue, he says, is determined by the highest degree of power, as Aristotle says in the first book of *On the Heaven*.[9] This dictum occurs again and again in the *Summa Theologica*,[10] and is the cornerstone of the theory of virtue there set forth For a full appreciation of its meaning and significance, we had best quote in full the original passage in *On the Heaven*.[11] "Now when we speak of a power to move or lift weights, we refer always to the maximum. We speak, for instance, of a power to lift a hundred talents or walk a hundred stades—though a power to effect the maximum is also a power to effect any part of the maximum—since we feel obliged in defining the power to give the limit or maximum A thing, then, which is capable of a certain amount as maximum must also be capable of that which lies within it If, for example, a man can lift a hundred talents, he can also lift two, and if he can walk a hundred stades, he can also walk two. But the power is of the maximum, and a thing said, with reference to its maximum, to be incapable of so much is also incapable of any greater amount It is, for instance, clear that a person who cannot walk a thousand stades will also be unable to walk a thousand and one This point need not trouble us, for we may take it as settled that what is, in the strict sense, possible is determined by a limiting maximum." Aristotle's explanation, both as the original for and the commentary on Thomas' dictum, is clear. It is a perfectly mechanical conception, or, rather, an explanation of the "maximum" applied to mechanical power We are thus faced with the fact that Thomas explains moral "power" in terms of physical or mechanical power, and this would confirm the main points of the interpretation advanced above the mechanical conception of the "ultimate" is precise and unambiguous, for the power of a man to lift a weight is a measurable quantity. Moreover, it is clear that no power greater than that described in the "ultimate" can be ascribed to any virtue. Thomas, applying the notion of the ultimate to the courage here described, implies that the present account of courage must be definitive. The possibility that there is a higher kind of courage than that here described is thus precluded by the very principle used to explain the present definition of courage. This also sheds light on the problem of why Thomas fails to note that, at the beginning of Book VII, Aristotle says, not that he is going to treat certain "effects and concomitants" of virtue, but that he is making a "fresh beginning" of the whole subject. According to the principle of the "ultimate," the limits of each virtue have been described already in the appropriate sections, and a really new treatment of the whole subject of morality would, from Thomas' point of view, be illogical.

But the theory of the ultimate, apart from the evidence against it already adduced, would seem to violate the following Aristotelian injunctions against attempting to deal too precisely with morality "We must be content, then, in speaking of such subjects and with such premises to indicate the truth roughly and in outline, and in speaking about things which are only for the most part true and with premises of the same kind to reach conclusions that are no better "[12] And again "But this must be agreed beforehand, that the whole account of matters of conduct must be given in outline and not precisely, as we said at the very beginning that the accounts we demand must be in accordance with the subject matter, matters concerned with conduct and questions of what is good for us have *no fixity*, any more than matters of health."[13] It is just this excess of preciseness, imparted to Thomas' interpretation by the mechanical conception of an "ultimate," that cuts off from his interpretation much of the subtlety and depth of the moral horizon of the *Ethics* The different relation of the highest degree of courage to pleasure and pain in Book IX has already been pointed out.[14] But that this is merely a particular instance of a general conception which regards all of moral virtue from a "higher" point of view may now also be shown. The perfection of justice implies the perfection of every moral virtue,[15] yet, says Aristotle, "when men are friends they have no need of justice, while when they are just they need friendship as well, and the truest form of justice is thought to be a friendly quality."[16] But a quality which makes the greatest moral virtue superfluous, or rather raises moral virtue to a higher degree than it would otherwise attain, is evidently not contained in the "ultimate" ascribed to moral virtue apart from it  This difficulty may, of course, be resolved by saying that the "true ultimate" of moral virtue is that taken together with friendship, in the sense in which Aristotle speaks of the "truest form" of justice being a "friendly quality." But the problem remains  why does Aristotle speak of the "truest form" of justice only after he apparently has said the last word on justice itself, in Book V? In any case, it seems clear that Thomas is wrong in simply ascribing the *ultimum in potentia* to each or any moral virtue described in Books II to V, if the truest form of justice is described, not in Book V, but in Book VIII. Obviously, only the latest and greatest "ultimate" can be the correct one

### C  THE LOWEST FORM OF COURAGE

The last criticism, however, is a criticism in terms of Thomas' own premise, namely, that the criterion of the "ultimate" is applicable to the definition of a moral virtue  But if, as Aristotle says, there is no fixity in the subject matter of morality, then it is not, strictly speaking, correct to define a virtue in terms of such a fixed criterion  The relevance of Aristotle's warning becomes apparent when we consider again the statement that was the occasion for Thomas' introducing his interpretive principle, that "death is the most terrible of all things, for it is the end, and nothing is thought to be any longer either good or bad for the dead " Although, within the context of the first section of the treatise on courage, this statement has all the air of finality, we are immediately confronted, at the beginning of the next section, with the remark that "what is terrible is not the same for all men "[17] Thomas himself illustrates Aristotle's point by an oblique remark showing clearly the problematical character of all generalizations concerning matters of conduct. The reason why death is the most terrible of all things, Thomas says,[18] is that it deprives us of everything good *in the present life* He implies that it may not, in fact, deprive us of the greatest good, in another life, but that it nonetheless deprives us of the "visible" good, which is the basis for our present fears and desires A little later[19] Thomas notes that to some men, the hope of a future life may make death desirable—and this is (albeit unintentionally) one of the best comments on Aristotle's statement that what is terrible is not the same for all men For it is clear that the terribleness of death must vary in inverse proportion to the degree in which a man has hope of a future life, or, more correctly, to the degree in which he has hope of another life better than his present one. Aristotle's statement that "nothing is thought to be any longer either good or bad for the dead" is based upon a particular opinion concerning the mortality of the soul Thomas' observation that "what pertains to the state of the soul after death is not visible to us," implying that it has no practical moral bearing, loses its force in his own admission that some men may consider death actually desirable [20]

This brings us to the primary difficulty connected with the problem of defining courage Thomas' interpretation to this point has been as follows [21] courage is the virtue that overcomes fear, not any or all fears, but the fear of what is simply terrible. This is death but, the argument continues, fearlessness in the face of death is not yet the definition of courage, we must consider the different forms of death. Death at sea or by disease, for example, would not necessarily prove the bravery of a man. Death in the noblest circumstances provides the only adequate test And such a death is that which occurs in battle. Aristotle's definition of courage would then seem to be complete in the

following passage "Properly, then, he will be called brave who
is fearless in face of a noble death, and of all emergencies that
involve death, and the emergencies of war are in the highest
degree of this kind."[22] We must see how Thomas interprets the
statements leading up to this apparent definition. Aristotle says,
in passage eight, following his seemingly final statement of the
terribleness of death, that the brave man cannot be concerned
with death in all circumstances, but only with the noblest, and
the noblest are those deaths which occur in battle. Thomas comments  courage is not concerned with the death someone may
suffer in any mishap or in any circumstance, as at sea or in disease, but is concerned with the death which is suffered for the
sake of the best (i e., noblest) things (*pro optimis rebus*), as
when someone dies in war for the defense of his fatherland
And the same reasoning applies to any other kind of death,
which is suffered for the good of virtue. But particular mention
is made of death in battle, because on such occasions it more
frequently happens that men suffer death for the sake of what
is good [23]

Now the bare essentials of Aristotle's statement are these two
assertions  courage is concerned only with the noblest deaths,
and, secondly, these occur in battle  Thomas thus seems to interpret Aristotle's statement that deaths in battle are the noblest,
as merely illustrative of the highest degree of courage. Yet there
would seem to be a difference between considering death in
battle as the commonest example of a noble death, and considering it as the *noblest* noble death  Thomas says here that
the argument applying to death in battle applies equally to any
death suffered for the sake of virtue  He thus implies that the
perception of the "ultimate" of courage has a basis independent
of the perception of the moral greatness of death in battle. In
so doing, we might add, Thomas gives evidence of a reservation
in favor of the religious martyr's death, which, in his own moral
teaching, is illustrative of the highest degree of courage.[24] But
Thomas' interpretation inevitably raises the following question

if the perception of the moral nobility of death in battle is not
the real basis of the knowledge of courage, then what is?

The answer to this would appear to be given in Thomas' interpretation of the very next passage in the *Ethics*, the statement
explaining why deaths in battle are the noblest. The reason, Aristotle says, is that "these take place in the greatest and noblest
danger" That they take place in the greatest danger means,
Thomas properly explains,[25] that in the circumstances of battle
a man can most easily lose his life But that they take place in
the noblest danger, Thomas further explains, means that they
take place amid dangers that are suffered for the sake of the
common good, which is the best or noblest And, Thomas concludes, as virtue is concerned with what is greatest and noblest
(*maximum et optimum*), courage is above all concerned with
death in war Thomas, therefore, seems now to shift his ground,
saying not that death in battle is an example of a noble death,
but that it actually is *the* noblest

Thomas however is seldom, if ever, guilty of simple contradictions The perception that death in battle is the noblest is not,
according to Thomas, the ground for the formulation of the
conception of courage This becomes apparent when we examine Thomas' comment on the very next passage in the *Ethics*,
and compare it with the comment discussed above According
to Thomas' division of the text, the statement that deaths in
battle are the noblest has a twofold proof first, the passage just
noted, that such deaths take place in the greatest and noblest
danger, and secondly, the statement that "these are correspondingly honored in city-states and at the courts of monarchs "[26]
This "proof," Thomas says, may be regarded in the following
light [27] those who sacrifice their lives in battle, or expose themselves to death, are honored during their lives or after death
This, moreover, is true both in cities and monarchies (i e , under
different forms of government) The reason, Thomas explains,
is that honor is the premium of virtue, and it is to the virtue of

courage that honor is paid in the case of those who either risk death in battle, or actually suffer it

But we must make a distinction with respect to Thomas' terminology Strictly speaking, the evidence offered above cannot be called a proof. It is rather what would be called a "probability," i e , what most men know to be true for the most part.[28] Honor is, indeed, the "premium" of virtue, its proper reward or due And, *in general,* the fact that a given action, or a given type of person is honored, is indicative of virtue in the action or type of person But the fact that virtue ought always to be honored, and vice never, does not mean that virtue is, in fact, always, or even almost always honored, and that vice is never honored There is no necessary connection between what is honorable and what is, in fact, honored Therefore the fact that deaths in battle are honored as the noblest and bravest is in no sense a demonstrative proof. There is no doubt, however, that it is proof of a kind, and that it is of great importance to Aristotle's presentation From the way in which Thomas introduces it, this so-called proof can really be intelligible, not as demonstrative proof proper, but only as an indication of a probable connection between honor and virtue The question is, whether Aristotle means to indicate anything more than this probability, which rests merely on the generally accepted opinion connecting honor and virtue This brings us to a point made previously, that Thomas seems to know what courage is independently of the evidence for it contained in Aristotle's statements in the first part of the treatise on courage. What Thomas implies is that Aristotle's actual basis for his conception of courage is the *argument* that, as the common good is the greatest good (which, presumably, could be demonstrated),[29] and inasmuch as virtue is a power to do good, those show the noblest kind (i e , highest degree) of courage, who meet death in defense of the common good. If this *argument* is the real ground for the conception of courage, then it will be seen that Thomas was not guilty of inconsistency in affirming, first, that a noble death in battle was merely the commonest example of a noble death, and secondly, that it was the noblest noble death If the basis for the conception of a noble death is independent of any mere perception (i e , if it is demonstrative argument), then the example may be a perfect example of the rationale of the conception, without in any sense being identical with the conception of which it is an example That is, death in battle may be both the commonest example, and a perfect example, and yet there may be still *other* perfect examples.[30]

But we are still confronted with the problem as to why Aristotle did not present the conception of courage in these terms Why, that is, did Aristotle not embody his presentation of the conception of courage in the form of a conclusion deduced from evident premises, which Thomas implies is the actual embodiment of such conception? Following Thomas' own view of Aristotle's procedure, we must suppose that he deliberately avoided such presentation But if he deliberately avoided it, there must have been something wrong with it, according to Aristotle's understanding of the subject matter. The most striking thing about Aristotle's actual presentation of his conception of courage is that it is drawn from life. From the standpoint of the "scientific" character of Aristotle's *Ethics*, we might say that it is "empirically" known In every-day language, it might be said that Aristotle's first formulation of the conception of courage is essentially the same as that of every schoolboy It may not carry demonstration with it, but it carries immense conviction Aristotle's intention at this point would seem rather to be to find a formulation of courage that was testified to by a well-nigh universal experience, rather than by flawless logic Indeed, it might seem that he was prepared to sacrifice the consistency of logic to a much more unsophisticated kind of consistency Actually, as we shall try to show, Aristotle is thoroughly consistent throughout, but his consistency is intelligible only when it is seen that the conception of courage is subjected to a *development*, starting from a relatively crude beginning. The ultimate conception is only intelligible if it is reached through the intermediate stages But just because the succeeding stages go beyond the preceding stages, certain inconsistencies seem to appear if everything that is true of the one is premised as being equally true of the other Thomas, as we have already seen, does not take account of the process of development going on within the *Ethics,* and accordingly treats all cases of courage as approximately on the same level From this point of view, a number of inconsistencies do appear in Aristotle's account of courage, and Thomas would seem to be attempting to resolve these by casting the definition of courage offered at the outset in a rigorous and demonstrative form

To repeat, Aristotle, when he first formulates the conception of courage, has reached a point in his analysis where it has been determined that courage is the virtue which enables a man to overcome the greatest fears in the noblest circumstances Presumably, he might then have deduced from this that the brave man is above all concerned with death in battle, and this is what Thomas suggests that he does do [31] But according to our view Aristotle does not do this instead he perceives that, on the basis of the actual practice of political communities of all kinds, deaths in battle are honored as the bravest Now the inadequacy of this conception of courage becomes apparent when it is realized that it is virtually identical with the opinion that patriotism is an example of perfect virtue It arises from the generally-held opinion, according to which a man who sacrifices himself in war for the sake of the common good, as established by the laws of his native land, is brave. The common good, as established by the laws, is legal justice,[32] and this kind of courage is undoubtedly a part of legal justice [33] However, the legal justice of one community is different from that of another community, and different kinds of legal justice evidently cannot be equally good, if there is, as Aristotle says in Book V, but one political order which is everywhere by nature best.[34] Those communities which more nearly approach the best must be better than those which are further removed from it And the legal justice of perverted social and political orders must be in principle the very contrary of all good orders But what are we to say of the brave actions commanded by the legal justice of perverted communities? Let us, for example, consider the case of a gang of robbers, or of a community of the predatory character of a gang of robbers Such a community could hardly be called just, inasmuch as the end and aim of its laws would be the doing of injustice Yet the laws, as such, would not be simply unjust, inasmuch as they would include in their end the maintenance of relationships among the members of the community which, in themselves, would represent a kind of justice [35] This is obviously true because, unless there is some honor even among thieves, the thieves, as an organized group, cannot survive [36] Thus there must also be courage in the robber gang Moreover, the brave action of the member of the robber community in defense of his group is in a way the same as the action of the truly good man in defense of the truly good and just social order But let us for a moment consider the case of the "average" brave man, that is, one who is brought up to regard death for the sake of his community as the noblest of actions, but who is incapable of thinking critically of his community, of realizing that "patriotism is not enough" How different is he, in fact, from the member of the robber gang, or of a robber community? There clearly is a difference between the brigand who knows he is a brigand and the one who simply believes that he has the highest moral obligation to defend the laws of his community, and to attempt to obtain their fulfilment in action The latter type is, we must concede, not so very different from the member of the good community who, acting bravely in defense of his community, does so without, necessarily, any more understanding than the innocent member of the society of the brigands [37] Moreover, the case of the innocent bandit is not the same as that of the man who is fearless in the face of disgrace, or a flogging, or the prospect of the loss of money, although such a man might, as Aristotle says, be called brave "by a transference of the word to a new meaning, for he has something in him which is like the brave man, since the brave man is also a fearless person "[38] The courage of the innocent brigand is in reality substantially identical with that of the average brave citizen in the good community. His motive is really the same, that is, he acts for the sake of being brave in the service of the common good, and the fears and dangers that he encounters are the same.[39] Aristotle would seem to imply this by identifying courage, in his initial formulation, with the brave actions of brave men everywhere, that is, in all forms of political communities, which would mean irrespective of the goodness of those communities. But for this very reason Aristotle must have regarded this kind of courage, although truly courage, as nevertheless the lowest kind of courage, and indeed of moral virtue generally That it is truly courage may be affirmed because it is evidently a part of legal justice, and legal justice is evidently present even in the most unjust communities.[40]

### D  THE DIFFFRENT LEVELS OF COURAGE AND VIRTUE

Now the paradox which emerges from the foregoing considerations is due to the fact that we have considered moral virtue apart from intellectual virtue Yet, it might be alleged, Aristotle does not believe that moral virtue can exist apart from the intellectual virtue of prudence, or practical wisdom At the end of Book VI[41] Aristotle clearly states that it is impossible to be good in the strict sense without practical wisdom, any more than it is possible to be practically wise without moral virtue Aristotle says, furthermore, that the virtues do not exist in separation from each other, for without practical wisdom, there is no virtue proper, and the presence of practical wisdom implies the presence of all the virtues From this point of view we could not speak of a brave man who was not fully aware of the end of his brave action The "innocent bandit" would be an impossibility, and it would be impossible to call a citizen truly brave if he was fighting for a bad cause in an unjust war Thomas, because he starts from a definition of virtue which refers to perfect virtue, implies that any definition of courage relates to perfect courage. Accordingly, from Thomas' point of view the definition of courage implies the presence of prudence and hence, simultaneously, of the other moral virtues Yet from this fact, namely, that Thomas' definition implies prudence, as well as temperance, justice, and the other virtues, we can see its impossibility Thomas may be correct in his conception of that courage which *is* a part of perfect virtue, but in implying thereby that this is *the* definition of courage, it would follow that what falls short of the "maximum" is not courage. But it is evident from the foregoing that many, if not most, of those who suffer death on the field of battle for the sake of the common good are not possessed of anything like perfect virtue But it would be absurd, for this reason, to deny them the character of courage [42] Aristotle avoids these paradoxes because he makes no attempt to present a final or "ultimate" definition of courage, but rather to observe it in its natural context that is, the context in which everyone observes it, without that reflection which leads to a realization of its inadequacies as a virtue Thomas forces upon us a reflection that would be ultimately destructive of common bravery as a motive for moral action within a political sphere in which it seems peculiarly necessary That is, Thomas' definition of courage leads to the conclusion that to be truly brave a man has also to meet the requirements of virtue in its entirety. But such a demand would be much too much for the greater part of mankind. Confronted with such realization most people would despair of ever attaining virtue. But Aristotle's aim is always eminently practical.[43]

We may conclude, then, that bravery in Aristotle's initial formulation of this virtue, as it applies equally to just and unjust communities, to men who may be nothing but brave in the vulgar sense, cannot be a part of perfect virtue. But this interpretation is, we believe, borne out by Aristotle's explicit remarks about courage near the end of the account in Book III In the passage in which the relation of courage to pleasure and pain is discussed, it is said of the brave man that "the more he is possessed of virtue in its entirety and the happier he is, the more he will be pained at the thought of death, for life is best worth living for such a man, and he is knowingly losing the greatest goods, and this is painful "[44] Aristotle here explicitly refers to degrees of virtue, and explicitly distinguishes the courage of the man who is merely brave, from that of the man who is possessed of virtue in its entirety This would confirm our view that, although strict virtue implies all the moral virtues and prudence, Aristotle's description of virtue does not start with strict virtue Moreover, a "sign" of the difference between the two is the suggestion of the intellectual quality of strict virtue This may be gathered from the reflectiveness which appears to characterize the truly brave man In the account of the relation of the brave man to the terrible, at the beginning of the treatise on courage, Aristotle said that death was the most terrible of all things because "it is the end " Later, however, in the context of an account of courage more nearly related to perfect virtue, Aristotle considers not merely the terror itself, but the terror for the truly brave man It becomes evident that the latter suffers greater pain than ordinarily brave men for two reasons  first, because a virtuous life, being happier, is better, and in losing such a life the truly brave man is losing a greater good, which is painful, and secondly, because he is more pained "at the thought of death" because "he is knowingly losing the greatest of goods " Thus it is not merely the greatness of the good that makes death more terrible for the truly good man, but his consciousness of the greatness of such a loss This is why we say that Aristotle attributes a more thoughtful or reflective character to the man who is more nearly possessed of virtue in its entirety

Aristotle's notion of what the fear of death means to the

truly virtuous man may be further clarified by reflection on a
passage in the *Ethics* that comes only a few lines after the one
last quoted. At the beginning of the section on temperance
Aristotle remarks that courage and temperance are both virtues
of the irrational parts of the soul. Thomas, in the *Commentary*,[45]
explains that courage is concerned with the passions of fear
and confidence, which are in the irascible, while temperance is
concerned with the passions of pleasure and pain, which are in
the concupiscible part of the soul. But all these passions are
common to us and to the brutes, he says, and so are their objects.
This means that fear of death, which is the principal passion
controlled by courage, would be shared by human beings with
the brutes, just as desire for food, drink, and sexual intercourse.
Yet, however one may understand the notion that animals fear
death—and it is difficult to conceive of it in terms other than
fear of the pain associated with the things that cause death—
it is clear that there is a distinctively human fear of death. The
fear of death because "it is the end," certainly distinguishes
the human fear from the merely animal fear. But we must remember that animals, like children,[46] are incapable of happiness. Therefore they are incapable of the goods of which happiness is comprised. But the human fear of death is not really of
death itself—death itself can hold no terrors for those who really
believe that it is simply the end—but rather fear of the loss of
those good things of which death deprives us. This fear, and
the pain associated with it, Thomas tells us[47] is heightened by
two factors  first, when we are deprived of a good of which
we are worthy, and secondly, when we are deprived of a great
good. Now, the better a man is, the more worthy he is of living,
i e., of living happily. Moreover, the better he is, the greater
is his loss in dying, because in death he is deprived both of a
good life and of the virtues which he has acquired. And this is
painful It thus becomes clear that progress in virtue makes virtue
more difficult, at least in one respect The action of courage, in-
volving the possible loss of life, requires ever more virtue just be-

cause a virtuous sacrifice is a greater sacrifice. At the end of
the section on courage in Book III Aristotle really leaves us
with this paradox, which is formally resolved only in Book IX,
as has been shown above.[48] But this paradox emphasizes again
how impossible it is to assume a final "ultimate" giving the true
definition of courage, in connection with the courage described
in Book III.

It seems clear then, that even in the account of courage in
Book III, Aristotle indicates the problem of the different levels
of virtue. This, of course, is overtly suggested in the discussion
of the five specious forms of courage, but it is more subtly
suggested with regard to "true" courage in the discussion of
the difference between ordinary bravery and the bravery more
nearly allied to perfect virtue  The distinction between the
different levels of "true" virtue, as has been shown in the foregoing, hinges on two conceptions  the conception of fear and
the conception of nobility  The courage of the man more nearly
possessed of virtue in its entirety is greater than that of ordinary
virtue because his fear of death is greater. It is a greater fear
because death is more painful for such a man, and it is more
painful because death threatens him with a far greater loss.
But Aristotle has to make clear that such a man "is nonetheless
brave, and perhaps all the more so, because he chooses noble
deeds of war at that cost."[49] He acts more nobly than the
merely brave man because, in the consciousness of the magnitude of his own sacrifice, he is more aware of the nobility of
the moral good that motivates his action. Hence it is for a
more noble end that he acts  But it is never unimportant to
reflect on what might lie behind Aristotle's "perhaps."[50] A
possible reason for it here may be a suggestion made shortly
afterward, that "it is possible that the best soldiers may not be
men of this sort but those who are less brave but have no other
goods "[51] This is paradoxical, for if bravery is ability to overcome fear of death in battle, and those who do this most readily
are those who fear death least because they value life least,

then the growth of virtue would appear to be accompanied by a kind of incapacity for virtuous action. Now, although this may be absurd in a strict sense, there would seem nevertheless to be an important element of truth in it. For example, it is a commonplace that those who "think too much" are not as qualified for taking action, at least on the lowest level on which action takes place, as those for whom taking action is a simple matter [52] This would be confirmed by our previous discussion, in which it appeared that common bravery was, at least in principle, equally characteristic of just and unjust communities, that is, it did not "take thought of" justice But we may now view this characteristic of common bravery in an advantageous light if it is inconceivable that civil society can survive without military virtue, and if military virtue is handicapped without that promptitude which we find in the lowest form of bravery, this lowest form is an indispensable ingredient of civil society Thus it is, if not a part of perfect virtue, an indispensable condition for perfect virtue. Yet the quality of the more sophisticated kind of virtue, which in one sense unfits it for the task of common virtue, is in another sense the justification for that virtue That is, as common bravery is undiscriminating, it may serve bad ends. Hence common bravery is only truly legitimate when guided by the virtue of truly virtuous men Nevertheless, there is a sense in which it may be said that common bravery has its own "ultimate," a peak of efficiency proper to it within its own sphere, in which its virtuousness is unsurpassed even by the higher kind of virtue [53]

The last point of the preceding paragraph requires considerable amplification and clarification, and we must, accordingly, go back several steps in our argument We have shown how Thomas begins his analysis of courage by relating Aristotle's formulation of that virtue to the principle of the ultimate,[54] but that this principle is contradicted on the broadest ground by the fact that Aristotle explicitly speaks of a higher kind of justice, and hence of all moral virtue, when he introduces the subject of friendship in Book VIII. It has been further shown that Aristotle's initial account of courage is drawn, not from the demonstrable nature of courage, but from the observed behavior of those who are called brave. Our analysis, however, of what was involved in the virtue thus perceived, i e , perceived on the mere basis of common opinion, led apparently to an awareness of the insufficiency of courage as a virtue Now such an analysis as we made, leading to the conclusion that courage is a defective virtue, is nowhere obtruded upon the reader by the text of the *Nicomachean Ethics*. To have done so, would, as was remarked above, have been contrary to Aristotle's practical intention. Nevertheless it is, we believe, borne out by the text, in particular by the distinction between ordinary courage and courage more nearly allied with perfect virtue. But this distinction forces us to reconsider the relationship between moral virtue and intellectual virtue It was noted above[55] that Thomas' principle of the ultimate resulted in a definition of courage that led to the identification of the ultimate of courage with perfect virtue, and that this involved practical wisdom, according to what Aristotle says at the end of Book VI. We also showed, from our analysis of the insufficiency of courage as a virtue, in Aristotle's actual presentation, that he could not have meant this as an example of perfect virtue. This, to repeat, was explicitly confirmed in the distinction made at the end of the account of courage in Book III. But if it is the Aristotelian doctrine that every moral virtue *does* imply the presence of prudence, then what exactly is the status of the moral virtue which does *not* seem to involve prudence? Moreover, if Aristotle's account of moral virtue starts, as we have maintained, from the imperfect virtue that is without prudence, how can he infer the nature of perfect virtue from the imperfect? Thomas presents a consistent interpretation of the virtues and their relationships. Its very consistency, however, is inconsistent with a number of Aristotle's explicit statements, and still more of his implications, as we believe we have shown.

Yet it could be alleged that Thomas' interpretation is the most consistent possible, unless we can offer an interpretation of these difficulties more consistent than Thomas', stating the relationship of these two kinds of moral virtue

Let us examine more closely what Aristotle says about the relation of moral virtue to prudence or practical wisdom at the end of Book VI. There it is said[56] that the perfection of each virtue implies the presence of practical wisdom, that practical wisdom implies the presence of all the moral virtues, and that these do not exist in separation from each other. Now there might seem to be some ambiguity in the word "presence," because practical wisdom might be thought to be present in moral virtue the way rationality is present in the activities of intelligent, but nonrational animals. Ants and bees, for example, act in a highly intelligent manner without being themselves rational Aristotle however in this context excludes this interpretation "All men, then, seem somehow to divine that this kind of state is virtue [i e., moral virtue], viz that which is in accordance with practical wisdom. But we must go a little further For it is not merely the state in accordance with the right rule, but the state that implies the *presence* of the right rule, that is virtue, and practical wisdom is a right rule about such matters " Aristotle thus distinguishes between actions "in accordance with" practical wisdom, and those which imply its "presence." The truly virtuous man must be not merely passively obedient to prudence in his virtuousness, but must possess prudence as a conscious and active element within himself. It is clear then that it is the Aristotelian doctrine that moral virtue in the strict sense implies the presence of practical wisdom. But we must be well advised in the use of the adjective "Aristotelian " Let us pay especial attention, in the last quotation, to the brief sentence "But we must go a little further " The Latin text used by Thomas[57] might be literally translated, "One should [or ought to] go a little further." Whether the personal pronoun is implied or not the force of the statement remains the same Aristotle makes a small but important distinction on the basis of his own authority. Now Aristotle's typical procedure in the *Ethics* is to work through the opinions of others, or the opinions generally held It is unusual for him to distinguish what "all men" say or divine from what "we" say. It may be easier to appreciate the weight of this expression by recalling the "methodological" passage in the first chapter of Book VII, in which Aristotle explained his procedure as that of discovering the common element of truth in all common opinions, or if not all, then "the greater number and the most authoritative "[58] What is remarkable about the present passage is that Aristotle goes beyond this, and distinguishes his own position from that divined by "all men", and thereby indicates that in his strict doctrine he goes beyond the dimension of common opinion Therefore the point to which we have called attention is indicative of Aristotle's position in a peculiarly emphatic sense. For the most part, it is sufficient for Aristotle to describe the position which combines the elements of truth in most common opinions Now, however, it would appear that the final Aristotelian position transcends even this.

In the light of the foregoing we may reconsider the last chapter of Book VI It begins with the statement, "We must therefore consider virtue [i e , moral virtue] once more."[59] This suggests the opening of Book VII, "Let us now make a fresh beginning . . ," the significance of which has been discussed at some length.[60] It is important to add to these comments the observation that the last chapter of Book VI contains Aristotle's final résumé on the subject of moral virtue before the "fresh beginning" of Book VII And thus it is not unreasonable to suspect that it might contain what, at least from the point of view of non-heroic virtue, and apart from the conclusions of Book X, might be Aristotle's last word on the subject of morality It is in such context that Aristotle briefly and cautiously indicates a final viewpoint from which moral virtue in the strict sense can be identified only with a state or condition in which practical wisdom is fully present. But before Aristotle does this he introduces another important distinction that between "strict virtue" and "natural virtue." "Therefore, as in the part of us which forms opinions there are two types, cleverness and practical wisdom, so too in the moral part there are two types, natural virtue and virtue in the strict sense, and of these the latter involves practical wisdom."[61] But if Aristotle speaks here for the first time of natural virtue, as contrasted with strict virtue, we are compelled to raise the question, Which kind of virtue has he been speaking of in the preceding books, and in particular in the descriptions of the moral virtues, beginning with courage and ending with justice? This question is particularly relevant in the context of the present discussion, because we must compare the distinction between natural virtue and strict virtue with that between ordinary courage and the courage related to complete virtue. The answer, we believe, is not too difficult in the light of our whole analysis. If we can take literally what Aristotle says at the end of Book VI, as we can if he is really speaking rather more conclusively here than elsewhere, then we may accept as a dictum the statement that "This is possible [that the virtues exist in separation from each other] in respect of the natural virtues, but not in respect of those in respect of which a man is called without qualification good, for with the presence of the one quality, practical wisdom, will be given all the virtues."[62] Now, as it has been shown that Aristotle's account of courage is, at least in the beginning, oriented about a conception of courage unenlightened by practical wisdom, then it would seem to follow that he is speaking about natural courage rather than strict courage in Book III Or, to state this somewhat more cautiously Aristotle for the most part speaks of natural courage, rather than strict or true courage, in the account in Book III. It does not follow that he never refers to the higher kind of virtue inasmuch as the distinction between the two kinds of virtue has not been explicitly made—and as both have the same name—it is possible for him to refer to now one, now the other. Explicit discrimination may not be necessary for the level on which virtue is treated in Book III although, since the distinction is clear in Aristotle's own mind, we may justly apprehend that any "confounding" of the two kinds of virtue will be purposeful and intelligible.

Difficulties, however, remain. Is natural virtue simply equivalent to the common form of bravery described at the beginning of the section on courage in Book III? This would seem to be to take too low a view of ordinary courage. Aristotle says that "both children and brutes have the natural disposition to these qualities "[63] Yet in Book III he explicitly distinguishes true courage (meaning thereby ordinary courage) from the courage due to mere passion, or ignorance—two principal conditions of the courage of children and brutes Again, in a passage in Book VII where he repeats the distinction made for the first time at the end of Book VI, he speaks of "virtue either natural or produced by habituation "[64] Yet the common or ordinary variety of courage, which we held to be without practical wisdom, was evidently virtue produced by habituation, and thus may be contrasted with natural virtue [65] How, then, is it possible to identify the two? The solution, we believe, is somewhat as follows  Aristotle's distinctions are not always of the kind that is laid down to provide absolute dividing lines. These distinctions partake of the inexactitude that he ascribes to the whole of ethical science.[66] Rather, they are signposts, or poles, so that at one extreme (of those things that can be called moral virtues at all) we have natural virtue, and at the other strict virtue (implying practical wisdom). Natural virtue is not really virtue at all, is only a particular kind of propensity toward virtue (or, in the case of brutes, a resemblance of a propensity toward virtue). The virtue produced by habituation is a development of the natural potentiality for virtue, in the direction of true virtue. It becomes true virtue in the strict sense only at the moment when practical wisdom is added  At that moment, however, the distinction of the virtues becomes irrelevant, at least for the possessor of practical wisdom because, given that one quality, he is *ipso facto* the possessor of all the moral virtues. However, on the other hand, it is important to remember that he would never have become the possessor of practical wisdom if he had not had moral virtue. That natural virtue is not the only kind of virtue deficient in practical wisdom is shown by a phrase in Book II, where Aristotle remarks that "as a condition of the possession of the virtues knowledge has little or no weight."[67] Now it is evident that Aristotle could not be speaking here of strict virtue, because, as a condition of the possession of strict virtue, practical wisdom, an intellectual virtue, has the greatest weight The only reasonable interpretation of the passage in Book II, it would seem, is that it refers to the moral virtues in their merely moral character, that is, as they involve the formation of character by habituation on the basis of correct principles, but not on the basis of the intellectual apprehension of those principles. We would then interpret Aristotle's pronouncements at the beginning of Book II that "moral virtue comes about as a result of habit," and "none of the moral virtues arise in us by nature" to imply the distinction between moral virtue and natural virtue [68] There would then be a threefold distinction within the virtue-vice horizon of Books I through VI. the lowest would be natural virtue, next moral virtue (habituation without wisdom), and highest strict virtue (implying the presence of practical wisdom). However, as we have said, the lowest kind is not really virtue at all, but is called virtue "by a transference of the word to a new meaning," because of the similarity of natural virtue to moral virtue. With respect to courage this is very clearly shown to be the case in the discussion of the specious form of courage due to passion [69] The true dividing line remains that between merely moral virtue and strict virtue. However, as opposed to strict virtue, natural virtue and moral virtue may be nominally identified This identification, however, is made by Aristotle not merely because it is justifiable on the basis of the

foregoing reasoning The identification is part of the "natural"
mode of referring to the phenomena in question, and it would
be destructive of the phenomena, on the level on which they
present themselves to us in every-day life, to make distinctions
possible only on the basis of reflection. What we mean may be
made clearer by referring to the contrary procedure in Plato
In the dialogue *Laches*, Nicias attempts to define courage in
terms of the Socratic dictum identifying virtue with wisdom [70]
As a consequence he must admit that "a lion, a stag, a bull, and
a monkey have all an equal share of courage in their nature",[71]
that is, as he is forced to deny courage to brute animals he must
acquiesce in the assertion that they all have an equal share of
courage, in other words, none at all To Laches, the man of mere
common sense, this is simply absurd Now Aristotle, we might
say, approaches the subject of courage, and virtue generally,
rather from the point of view of Laches. That is, things that
look alike are called by the same name Paradoxes such as Plato
delights in, as in the situation represented in the *Laches*, he
avoids by not looking any more closely, at first, at the things
called by the same name, than we are wont to do in actual life.
Eventually, of course, he distinguishes everything that is distinguishable, but only in the context in which such distinction
does not seem absurd, as it does to Laches, but when it makes
sense on the basis of a development in his whole account of
virtue. Such is the case in the final chapter of Book VI, both
with respect to the distinction of natural and moral virtue, moral
virtue and strict virtue, and the ultimate identity of all strict
virtue in practical wisdom

In the light of the foregoing let us review the relation of
moral virtue to prudence, as revealed in Books I to VI of the
*Nicomachean Ethics*, with particular regard to the interpretation of courage We will attempt to express this relationship
in a metaphor Moral perfection might be compared to a sun,
emanating rays in different directions The rays of the sun are
the several virtues At their center they are united with practical

wisdom. The nearer the rays are to the sun, the more they partake of its light and heat, the more they resemble each other,
and the less distinguishable they are. Courage and temperance,
for example, are scarcely distinguishable in their higher forms.
In Plato's dialogue *Laches,* which provides many illustrations of
this point, the basic reason why the attempt to define courage
fails is that Socrates forces the discussion onto too high ground,
with the end result that it is found that an account has been
given of the whole of virtue, rather than of the part called
courage.[72] Laches attempts at the outset to define courage very
much as Aristotle does in his first formulation, with respect to
bravery in war But Socrates insists[73] that he wants an account
of the "courageous not only in war but in the perils of the sea,
and all who in disease and poverty, or again in public affairs, are
courageous, and further, all who are not merely courageous
against pain or fear, but doughty fighters against desires and
pleasures " We will not attempt to discuss all the numerous contrasts with Aristotle's procedure that this passage presents, it is
clear, however, that what Socrates asks for has almost as much
to do with temperance as with courage If Socrates had inquired
in like manner into temperance he would as surely have come
to the conclusion that the temperate man was safeguarded by
his temperance as much against the bad effects of fear and pain
as against those of bodily pleasure. The rays of the sun, as separate and distinct, are defined with reference to the regions they
illuminate The light itself has a different aspect according to
the atmosphere through which it passes. Yet as we trace the
light to its source (which is one, although the atmospheres and
regions it illumines are many and different) the differences in
atmosphere are assimilated to the one atmosphere which sur-
rounds the sun, and ultimately the quality of the rays is identical
in their common source The ranking of the virtues might be
explained by saying that the regions illumined by some virtues
are nearer the source of light than others temperance, for example, being nearer than courage. The most significant point

of our metaphor, however, is this that the virtues, qua separate and distinct virtues, are defined with reference to their *distance* from the sun, not their proximity to it. Their virtuousness, to be sure, is due to their being emanations from the sun, but their definitions, that by which they are known as individual virtues, and not as Virtue, are due to their acquiring, from the surrounding atmosphere, characteristics not derived from the source of virtue itself. In non-metaphoric language we might say that it is the imperfections of the individual virtues which give them their individuality. It is significant, in viewing the *Ethics* as a whole, that from Book VII on, where the dominant theme is heroic virtue, rather than ordinary virtue, the distinction of the virtues drops almost entirely into the background. In the passages in Book IX referred to previously[74] as exemplifying heroic bravery, it is noteworthy that Aristotle does not actually mention courage. What he is speaking of is the action of friendship, which contains a higher perfection than any discussed in the earlier books. It is irrelevant, from the point of view of friendship, whether the friendly action takes place within the sphere commonly identified with courage. The friendly action might, of course, be described as brave, but to call it brave is to fall very much short of indicating the actual degree of moral perfection that it represents.

But the converse of what we have just said is also, in a peculiar sense, true The brave action which is also an act of friendship is not fully measured when described in terms of bravery, but neither can the merely brave action, that is not part of a higher virtue, be accurately described in terms of perfect virtue Reverting to our metaphor, we may say that the ray called courage emanating from the sun of practical wisdom is insufficiently identified as a virtue by tracing it to its source It must, rather, be identified from the peculiar modifications it undergoes in the atmosphere of the region in which the actions of courage take place. In other words, that by reason of which it is called *courage*, and not *Virtue*, is due above all to the circumstances in which the action of the named virtue takes place. Of course, it also remains true that the reason why the named virtue is *a* virtue, even if not *Virtue*, is that it is an emanation from practical wisdom (i e , Virtue). But if there is some sense in which each individual, named virtue has a kind of individual "ultimate," it would follow that that ultimate would not be identical with practical wisdom. For if it were the latter it would not be the ultimate of the individual virtue, the ultimate containing the essence of the individual virtue qua individual virtue, but the ultimate of *Virtue*, in which the distinction of the individual virtue is lost.

Now, from the slight but important indication Aristotle has given us concerning the peculiar character of the lowest kind of courage, namely, that it is more capable of taking action at the lowest level (that of the soldier) than a higher kind of virtue would be, we may gather that the ultimate of common bravery is not simply contained in the higher ultimate of more perfect virtue. This ultimate (of common bravery) is rather determined by the peculiarities of the circumstances in which the brave action takes place, and which give it its peculiar color These circumstances may cause a distortion of the illumination coming from Virtue, so that the individual virtue may be a corrupted or degenerate kind of virtue, from the standpoint of the pure original Yet, being a practical virtue, it may be superior to Virtue, in the practical sense of being better adapted to deal with the particular exigencies from which it draws its distinctive qualities Thus the ultimate of common bravery, qua individual virtue, may be due in a sense to its very imperfection qua Virtue In concluding this analysis, we may say that a consideration of the virtue of courage, in the context of the whole of the first six books of the *Nicomachean Ethics*, suggests the view that the more courage is a virtue, the less it is, in an important sense, courage This is confirmed by the way in which Aristotle refers to the higher kind of courage near the end of his account of that virtue in Book III When he speaks of the character of the man possessed of such virtue he identifies him as more nearly "possessed of virtue in its entirety," not identifying him primarily as "more brave," but rather "more virtuous." But, while he speaks of such a person as being unqualifiedly "more virtuous," he speaks of him in only a qualified way as being "more brave " Thus, of the man who is unqualifiedly "more virtuous" "but he is nonetheless brave," a negative way of asserting his equality (not superiority) to the ordinarily brave man, "and perhaps all the more so," a qualified way of affirming his superiority in bravery. Not to press the point too far, however, we must admit that, despite all qualifications, Aristotle clearly implies that the more virtuous man is ultimately braver, "because he chooses noble deeds of war at that cost." However, although this is ultimately true, it remains a fact that this increase in bravery is ambiguous, while the increase in virtue is unambiguous, and this paradox would be unintelligible if it were simply true that the virtues do not exist in separation from each other. It becomes intelligible if we grant that common bravery has an ultimate that is in some sense separate from that of Virtue.

### E. HEROIC VIRTUE

We will present one final example, from Aristotle's account of courage in Book III, to support our thesis concerning the necessary ambiguity of the "ultimate" of the virtue described there, and to show that Thomas fails to take note of this ambiguity. The passage to be examined is the beginning of the second of the three sections on courage [75] "What is terrible is not the same for all men, but we say there are things terrible to everyone—at least to every sensible man, but the terrible things that are not beyond human strength differ in magnitude and degree, and so too do the things that inspire confidence. Now the brave man is as dauntless as man may be Therefore, while he will fear even the things that are not beyond human strength, he will face them as he ought and as the rule directs, for honour's sake, for this is the end of virtue." [76] The problem involved in

this passage may be indicated as follows. Aristotle sets up two
classes of terrible things those that are not beyond human
strength (*secundum hominem*), and those that are beyond
human strength (*supra hominem*, literally "above man"). All
men, Aristotle says, will fear the things that are beyond human
strength, madmen excepted, but the brave man will also fear
many of the things that are not beyond human strength However, he will fear these as he ought, and act in accordance with
the dictates of reason in spite of his fear But a critical question
remains how will the brave man act in the face of the terrible
things that are beyond human strength? Aristotle, it must be
noted, not only does not distinctly answer this question, he does
not even distinctly raise it, it is only implied in the distinction
between the terrible things beyond human strength and those
that are not The nearest approach to a positive statement on the
subject is the remark that the brave man is "as dauntless as man
may be " Let us now see how Thomas interprets this apparently
deliberate indefiniteness [77]

We noted above[78] that Thomas failed to take account of the
connection between his own remark, that death might be desirable for some men, and Aristotle's remark that "what is terrible is not the same for all men " If he had noted that connection,
he would have had either to reject Aristotle's formulation of the
conception of courage (based on the terribleness of death), or
reject the view that men who consider death desirable, because
of their hopes for a better future life, are brave In commenting
on this passage, we are considering, Thomas says, that the vari-
ation in what men consider terrible is due to the difference in
the faculties (i.e., powers) of different individuals, so that, for
example, something may be terrible to a boy which would not
be terrible to a grown man [79] His meaning is, that to compare
the bravery of different persons we must equalize the factors of
age and experience e g , a boy might show greater courage than
a man in meeting a lesser danger, a pilot who is confident in a
storm at sea is not for that reason braver than the landsman with

no experience of such dangers to give him confidence,[80] in other words, what is terrible in individual instances is relative to the individual  Now this interpretation, although true, is not exhaustive  Its premise would seem to be that death is equally terrible to all men, and, on this basis, to go on to say that different dangers threaten different men with death. But it is difficult to believe that, a few passages after Aristotle has said that death is the most terrible of things, he should say that what is terrible is not the same for all men, without intending to suggest some reflection on the terribleness of death itself

Now, according to Aristotle, the brave man faces death in the greatest and noblest dangers. If this is true then death itself is not something terrible beyond human strength  More than that, we would have to say that death in the violent and painful forms that occur on the battlefield would not be considered by Aristotle as beyond human strength. Therefore it would follow that the terrible things beyond human strength are more terrible than death  But what does Thomas say about this class of "super-terrible" things? They are, he says, such things as earthquakes and floods, which human power is unable to resist [81] There would seem to be some warrant for this interpretation, as Aristotle a little further on gives the same examples when speaking of the kind of thing that only madmen would not fear [82] Yet the worst such natural disasters can offer is death, which, in itself, cannot be a "super-terrible" thing.

That Thomas has failed to grasp the extraordinary character of the "super-terrors" may be seen from the following consideration  Aristotle had originally said that death was the most terrible of all things  But even in the context of this assertion it was plain that death was not the most terrible thing simply. Death is an evil because it is a deprivation of life, which is a good [83] But the brave action is action for the sake of a good  Hence the goodness of the brave action must outweigh the evil of death.[84] Accordingly the baseness in failure to act bravely, in circumstances requiring courage, would be a greater evil for the brave man than death. Thus death is the most terrible thing only if we except the things that it is right to fear, but Aristotle takes it for granted that base and ignoble actions are more terrible to the brave man than death [85] This may seem too obvious to be worthy of mention. But it is necessary to labor the point because Thomas, in his examples of the "super-terrible" things mentions only earthquakes and floods, things super-terrible only within the dimension that premises death as the greatest evil. Yet it follows from what has been said that the real "super-terrors" are to be found in an entirely different dimension. The significance of this omission from Thomas' interpretation will become clear when we see how he answers the question, How does the brave man act in the face of the super-terrible things? According to Thomas the brave man will certainly fear such things (as only a madman would not) but, *in case of utility or necessity*, he will bear such things as he ought, according to the judgment of right reason, which is proper to man He will not, Thomas continues, because of fear of such things, depart from the judgment of reason, but he will suffer the terrible things of this kind, *however great*, for the sake of the good which is the end of virtue [86] Thus Thomas, commenting on the apparently non-committal statement that the brave man is as dauntless as man may be, a statement that hardly seems to specify *how* proof against terror man, as such, can be, ascribes to Aristotle an absolute and unqualified meaning. Here it would seem that Thomas is simply wrong, for the statement that the brave man is as proof against fear "as man may be" is a qualified one Moreover, the assertion that there are things "above man," beyond his capacity, could not apply at all to man's moral nature if Thomas were correct. We would certainly be justified in saying that Thomas' interpretation contradicts the impression (which may not be the last word on the matter) that Aristotle considers that there are limits to what the brave man, qua brave man, can endure.

In what follows, we shall show that there is a serious basis for Thomas' interpretation, but it is necessary first to dispose of a verbal difficulty arising from the difference between the English text of the Ross Oxford translation, and Thomas' more literally exact Latin translation. The English translation quoted above reads "Therefore, while he will fear even the things *that are not beyond human strength*, he will face them as he ought " The text of the *Versio Antiqua* reads "Timebit quidem igitur *et talia*, ut oportet autem." The Latin, which does not go beyond the original, says only that the brave man will fear "such things." The italicized passage in the English is therefore interpretation, rather than translation proper. This is important, because Thomas' commentary assumes that *"talia,"* "such things," refers to the terrible things that are *"supra hominem,"* "above man," i e., beyond human strength If Thomas were correct in his reading of the antecedent of *"talia,"* then his interpretation would, in fact, be merely a re-statement of what Aristotle says However, the most anyone could venture to say for Thomas here is that he is no more justified in assuming that "such things" refers unequivocally to the terrible things that are *"supra hominem"* than the English translator is in assuming they are *"secundum hominem,"* i e., not beyond human strength Now, we believe that the context distinctly favors the interpretation of the English translator, inasmuch as the last previous mention of terrible things referred to those *not* beyond human strength. It would, perhaps, be more correct, as well as more cautious, to say that Aristotle was here also deliberately non-committal This would be consistent, for if Aristotle says that the brave man is as brave as man may be, it would be natural for him to be equally indefinite in referring to the fears in the face of which he would be dauntless Certainly there are no grounds for Thomas' unequivocal interpretation of the passage in a sense directly opposite to that of the English translator.

But, although Thomas may be mistaken in the sense in which he takes the text here, we must note how consistent this sense is with the general line of his interpretation. Thomas failed, as has been shown, to discriminate any real class of "super-terrors," distinct from the class of terrible things that premises death as the greatest evil. From Thomas' point of view, the "super-terrible" things are such only in the sense that the brave man has no hope of resisting them successfully. They would deprive him of confidence, in the ordinary sense. They would not, however, deprive him of the capacity to suffer bravely, following the dictates of reason to the last. Hence, while they might deprive him of ordinary confidence, they would not deprive him of the power of confidence in his own virtue. The failure to discriminate the class of "super-terrors" is consistent with the premise that the reasonableness of the perfectly brave man can never be vanquished by terror. But let us also, in this connection, remember the Aristotelian warning "that with a true view all the data harmonize, but with a false one the facts soon clash."[87] If we appeal to the facts that are the basis of Aristotle's doctrine, what is the evidence on this problem? Do we or do we not find, on the basis of actual experience, that there is a class of terrible things beyond the capacity of the bravest man to endure? The answer would seem to support Thomas' premise. The pages of history are crowded with examples of men (and women) who have suffered the most extreme tortures for the sake of the good, as conceived by their rational faculties. If this is the case Thomas' interpretation might be said to represent correct Aristotelian doctrine, the apparent deviation from the text notwithstanding. But the evidence already adduced to show the difference between the ultimate of ordinary courage and the courage that is part of complete virtue must make us cautious of accepting such a deviation. In our view, the discrimination of "ultimates" makes possible a reading of the text that does violence neither to the facts nor the text. Indeed, as we hope to show, only such a reading is fully consistent with the facts. Thomas' interpretation, to the extent that it departs from the text, also departs from the facts.

To prove these contentions it is necessary to go further into the question of what Aristotle actually understands by the class

of terrible things "above man." Additional evidence is supplied
by another set of passages in Book III. These occur in the first
chapter, concerned with the nature of the voluntary and the
involuntary.[88] Having stated that the involuntary consists in
action done under compulsion or owing to ignorance, Aristotle
asks whether actions done from fear are voluntary or involuntary. He gives two examples: first, that of a tyrant ordering one
to do something base, having one's parents and children in his
power, "and if one did the action they were to be saved, but
otherwise put to death", and secondly, that of a man throwing
his goods overboard in a storm to lighten the ship. Both of these
actions fall into the class of "mixed" actions, in that they have
in them something of the voluntary and the involuntary: in the
abstract no one would wish to do them, but at the moment of
action they may be worthy of choice. In the case of the kind
of actions represented by the lightening of the ship, Aristotle
says decisively that this is voluntary (even though technically
"mixed"), because every sensible man would sacrifice his wealth
to save his life. But concerning the case of the tyrant and one's
children and parents, Aristotle says "it may be debated whether
such actions are voluntary or involuntary." And, since virtue
and vice can be predicated only of voluntary actions, it is de-
batable whether courage can be operative in the presence of
such fears. But the more decisive passages occur a little further
on in the same chapter. "On some actions praise is not bestowed,
but pardon is, when one does what he ought not under pressure
which overstrains human nature and which no one could withstand."[89] Now it is clear that the actions contemplated in this
passage are, in some sense, voluntary, otherwise Aristotle could
not speak of the man having done "what he ought not." But
if the actions were done under pressure "which *no one* could
withstand," then, from the moral standpoint, they would seem
to be involuntary, indeed, the distinction would appear to lose
its moral significance. The following are Thomas' comments on
this passage: some actions, done out of fear, do not merit praise,

but only pardon, so that someone is not much to be blamed, because he does certain things which he ought not to do, as when he does things not very serious, but yet not decent for one in his station, because of his fear of other evils, the enduring of which exceeds human nature, and which no one could bear, and especially for the sake of this cause, for example if he should be threatened with being burned to death, except if he should tell a jocular lie [90] Thus, where Aristotle says "praise indeed is not bestowed, but pardon is," Thomas adds *"non multum vitu-peretur,"* the pardoned person is "not much to be blamed", and when Aristotle says that he does what he ought not under pressure which "no one could withstand," Thomas adds, *"praecipue propter hanc causam,"* "especially for this cause," and continues with the case of the man threatened with death by fire unless he tell a *"jocosum mendacium,"* a "jocular lie " Thus, Thomas understands "pressure which no one could withstand" to refer only to cases where the greatness of the suffering is out of all proportion to the baseness of the action needed to escape the suffering. And even in such cases, Thomas unwillingly accepts what Aristotle literally says, that such actions are to be pardoned, by adding that they "should not be much blamed," implying that they nevertheless do deserve some blame Now Aristotle would certainly agree that the case Thomas allows is one for indulgence, but it is impossible that this could be an example of the extreme cases he had in mind Tyrants with hostages are not notorious for commanding people to tell jocular lies The pressure that they bring to bear is much more absolute than any mere disproportion between the evil to be suffered ·and the good to be gained

However, after saying that there is a pressure which over-strains human nature, and which no one could withstand, Aristotle goes on to say "But some acts, perhaps, we cannot be forced to do, but ought rather to face death after the most fearful sufferings "[91] This, it might be alleged, is evidence that Aristotle agrees with Thomas in believing that there are no terrors which can subvert the reason of a truly brave man. For if there are some things that the brave man cannot be forced to do because of their baseness, it would then follow that the base things he can be forced to do are not the ultimate in baseness If this is the case, then it is in fact a disproportion of the evil to be suffered to the good to be gained which underlies Aristotle's permissive principle in the passage in which he speaks of pressures overstraining human nature Thomas' interpretation would on this ground be correct, and although the example of the jocular lie might be somewhat exaggerated, the principle it illustrates would not be wrong However, this justification is based on one very doubtful premise namely, that the apparently contradictory elements in Aristotle's statements are not deliberate or intentional, and that they must be brought into harmonious consistency with each other.[92] For it must be noted that the two statements do, superficially at least, contradict each other. According to the first, there is pressure which overstrains human nature and which *no one* could withstand According to the second there are some actions we cannot be forced to do. But, in the face of pressure which no one could withstand, there are *no* actions which one could not be forced to do. Or, conversely, if there are actions which the brave man cannot be forced to do, there is no pressure which is absolutely beyond endurance What Thomas does is to choose the second of these two contradictories, believing that is what Aristotle really means, and he then interprets the former on the basis of the latter, assuming that if Aristotle said something different he could not have meant what he said

But in Thomas' paraphrase of the passage which he adopts as correct there is a significant omission Aristotle said, "But some acts, *perhaps*, we cannot be forced to do." Thomas omits the "perhaps," the "*adverbium dubitandi* " But this omitted adverb makes a great difference in the meaning of the apparent contradiction If we follow Thomas' own interpretive principle,[93] that Aristotle frequently uses "perhaps" in this work because of the uncertainty of the subject-matter, then we might be led to the assumption that the conflicting formulations are deliberate, and designed to reflect intrinsic difficulties Certainly the two statements do not embody the flatly contradictory propositions we suggested above, if one of them is qualified. They appear flatly contradictory only on the basis of Thomas' paraphrase, in which Aristotle's qualification is dropped. It was necessary for Thomas to drop the qualification before he could consistently disregard the antithetical character of Aristotle's formulation.

Let us now re-examine the elements of contradiction and antithesis in these two statements The first contains antithetical elements within itself. As noted above, action done under pressure which no one could withstand would seem to be, strictly speaking, involuntary In principle it would be the same as an "action" in which someone else moved one's limbs by main force. If this were what Aristotle meant then he would be inconsistent in speaking of such action as something one "ought not" to do Somehow, it remains true that the action under consideration is of such a nature that the agent does contribute something. But if he does contribute *something*, then why does Aristotle not say that this action is done under pressure which no one, *perhaps*, could withstand? It is striking, on reflection, that Aristotle does not qualify the statement "which no one could withstand"—the pardoning statement—while he does qualify the blaming statement ("some acts, perhaps, we cannot be forced to do," etc , going on to the condemnation of Alcmaeon) The emphasis is just the opposite of Thomas', Aristotle seems to go farther in pardoning than in blaming the base actions done under extreme terror.[94] Actually, however, this emphasis is more apparent than real, because the apparently unequivocal statement "which no one could withstand" *is* in fact already qualified in being classified as voluntary, as it is said to be an action that "ought not" to have been done The "perhaps" is implied in the antithesis, and it would have been redundant to have actually used it In addition, it would have weakened the force of the "perhaps" in the next sentence.

Aristotle's problem, in these passages, would seem to be to

find an adequate expression of the paradoxical fact, attested to by common opinion (that is, by the way in which praise and blame are usually bestowed) that there are base actions which, under certain circumstances, cannot really be blamed, and, conversely, that there are actions which, although the circumstances hardly permit them to be considered voluntary in the ordinary sense, do not, nevertheless, free the agent from the imputation of moral responsibility  The principle governing Aristotle's formulation would seem to be that, as long as it is possible to recognize an action as base, one has an obligation not to do it  The fact that there is a point at which this obligation ceases to bind does not imply an avenue of escape from the obligations of morality, because it is impossible to specify in advance what, in any given instance, that point will be. It is only after the fact, that a wise judge, knowing all the circumstances, could say whether the person in question had evaded his duty or had endured to the point at which it was humanly impossible to endure more  Although only the wise man can really judge well of any particular case, all men divine the principle the wise man applies to the individual case, viz , that we ought not to do base actions, and are to be blamed for doing them, but, just as in the case of physical stress, there is a point at which we cannot exercise our normal control over our limbs, so there is a point at which we lose control of our moral faculties [95] The case would be like men cast into the sea by a shipwreck, trying to stay afloat until help comes  Each will strive to stay afloat, but if help does not come, all will in time be overcome by exhaustion and perish, although some much sooner than others  So in moral matters, Aristotle seems to say, we are obliged to resist wrongdoing to the limits of our strength  But that there *is* a limit cannot be gainsaid, any more than it can be doubted that there is a limit to the time that the strongest swimmer can stay afloat  But this is no more an excuse for moral weakness than physical weakness is an "excuse" for drowning. In the case of the men struggling to survive in the water, the

assumption is (for all normal individuals) that there is no possible equivalent for the sake of which they would give up the
struggle to survive Similarly with the truly brave man, there
would be no equivalent for the sake of which he would give up
the cause of righteousness But just as, qua physical organism,
there is a point at which he is impotent to resist the forces that
assail him, qua moral organism there is a point at which he can
no longer resist terror

But, it might be objected, is not this example of the drowning
men the same as Thomas' example of the earthquakes and floods
that the brave man is powerless to resist? The cases, we submit,
are different, because in our example physical stress is only a
metaphor for moral stress. For a non-metaphorical example, we
return to Aristotle's that of a tyrant with a man's family as
hostages, commanding him to do something base Now Aristotle
clearly indicates that it is impossible to say, in the abstract,
whether a man ought or ought not to be pardoned for doing the
basest deeds to save his family One would have to know all the
relevant facts of the particular case in order to make an intelligent judgment For even if the deed clearly outweighed in baseness any personal suffering, if it was beyond all doubt something
that "ought not" to have been done, e g , betraying one's country and handing over one's fellow citizens to death or slavery,
it does not follow necessarily that the person involved could
have avoided doing it, *even if he was brave* Aristotle's saving
"perhaps" indicates, we believe, that in his view no simply true
general statement can be made on this question. Thomas, to repeat, says unequivocally, of the unequivocally brave man, that
he will obey the dictates of reason in the face of any terror,
however great But what of the apparently evident fact that
brave men (and women) have defied the worst tyrants can do
and, out of sheer courage, not insensitivity, obeyed the dictates
of reason to the last?

Let us take up this difficulty again from the example of physical endurance In general, physical fitness varies with two fac-

tors, natural physique and nurture on the one hand, and regimen
of diet and exercise on the other. Now, that a man breaks down
under a relatively slight stress, in a moment of danger, may be
involuntary. Fighting for his life he would of course wish for
the strength of Hercules. But he may nonetheless be fully responsible for his weak condition. Aristotle is perfectly clear
on this point [96] The case of physical and moral states is similar,
but Aristotle admits that the "ultimates" of both physical and
moral strength for different men vary, not only with the kinds
of lives they pursue voluntarily, but according to their natural
endowments, and to accidents beyond their control. We do not
blame a man blind from birth, but we do blame one blind from
drunkenness We do not blame "those who are ugly by nature,
we blame those who are so owing to want of exercise and
care."[97] It is clear that only those are to be blamed for lack of
virtue (physical or moral) who have not been prevented by
nature or chance from attaining virtue But the more difficult
question remains. Among those who are, apparently, well-en-
dowed by nature, and otherwise not hindered from attaining
virtue, there are also great differences in capacity This is evidently so in the case of physical strength. Of athletes born with
good physiques, and applying themselves with equal determination to the same regimen, some will nonetheless become much
stronger than others. Those who are relatively weaker cannot
be blamed for their weakness, as having through negligence
omitted anything that accounts for their relative lack of
strength The case is similar with moral capacity  of those who
are virtuous, some will be more virtuous than others. But is this
not paradoxical? If, following Thomas' reasoning, we say that
virtue is a power, and the definition of a power is of the ultimate, then the definition of virtue (and of each particular virtue) must be of the ultimate But if this is true then there cannot
be, strictly speaking, degrees of virtue. If the definition of a
virtue is the definition of an ultimate, then the ultimate is the
virtue. Virtue is a perfection, but in the strict sense there cannot

be degrees of perfection, only degrees of imperfection, for every
comparative implies some imperfection And if virtue is praiseworthy, only perfect virtue is, strictly speaking, praiseworthy,
for the partial virtue that is praiseworthy is not praiseworthy
qua partial, but qua virtue, i e, resembling the whole which is
virtue The praise of imperfect virtue would be derivative, i e.,
we would praise the imperfectly brave man because he approached the standard of the perfectly brave man. But on this
assumption knowledge of the latter would have to be prior to
and independent of our knowledge of the former [98] This must
be so, if the one serves as the basis of the other [99] But if we know
what the ultimate of virtue is, we have an obligation to be virtuous according to the dictate of that ultimate. Hence it follows
from Thomas' argument that any lack of virtue is blameworthy
The cases of physical strength and moral strength would seem
not to be altogether the same, because there is no absolute quantity which the strongest possible man could lift (or at least it
seems impossible to say what it would be), nor an absolute speed
which the swiftest runner could attain But there may be some
actions which we are absolutely prohibited from voluntarily
doing, or from refraining from doing. If so, blame would attach
to the commission or omission of these actions But if this were
the case, then there would be no room, in strict casuistry, for
pardon It is, we believe, evidence of the correctness of this re-
statement of Thomas' basic argument, that Thomas' interpretation, as was shown above, in effect cancels the pardon which
Aristotle explicitly grants to wrong actions done under extreme
duress. Thomas' interpretation leaves no real place for pardon,
only for pity, which is a kind of grief for a worthy man constrained to suffer an indignity, where reason dictates that suffering the indignity is the lesser of evils

But is it the case, as we concluded above, in harmony with
the argument there presented, that the cases of physical and
moral strength differ, in that the one admits of no absolutes,
whereas the other does? Aristotle seems to treat them as exactly

analogous. "Of the vices of the body, then, those in our own power are blamed, those not in our power are not And if this be so, in the other cases also the vices that are blamed must be in our own power "[100] Can one, that is, say with any more definiteness what it means to be absolutely brave, than one can say what it means to be absolutely strong? The answer, Aristotle seems certainly to imply, is no But, it may be replied, the notion of an absolute here does not demand mathematical precision [101] The man "who deviates little from goodness is not blamed, whether he does so in the direction of the more or the less, but only the man who deviates more widely "[102] The precise point of virtue cannot be ascertained, one can only know that it is somewhere between reasonably well-defined limits But this does not make the conception of *the* intermediate point as defining the virtue irrelevant, nor does it invalidate the precise conception of the ultimate as defining the virtue as a power The important difference between Thomas and Aristotle does not lie in the fact that Thomas demands more precision in his conception of the "ultimate." The most significant difference, as was suggested at the outset of this analysis,[103] is that the conception of the ultimate does not at all apply to the virtue of courage, because of the fact that in the context it is actually recognized, i e , known, only by reason of the fact that it is praised. The analogy of physical and moral virtue is exact All men who approximate a certain measure of physical strength are recognized as strong, i e., in contrast to those who are weak Similarly, there is a generally recognized standard, with reference to which men are called brave Let us again take note of what that standard is.

Aristotle has said, to return now to our point of departure, that the brave man is as proof against fear as man may be By his qualification he leaves open the question whether human virtue, as such, is a shield for the brave man against those terrors which are said to be "above man." As Aristotle later speaks explicitly of heroic virtue, as distinct from mere human virtue, it follows that it is at least problematical whether the brave man, qua brave man and not hero, can bear any terrors whatever. Aristotle's ambiguity at this point can, therefore, hardly be construed as accidental This ambiguity is demanded by the context Aristotle could not say that the brave man is not proof against fear, nor could he, in terms of ordinary praise and blame, describe the dimension of heroic virtue Thomas, of course, can take no note of the ambiguity, because the entire plan of his analysis allows no room for the possibility that a whole dimension of courage is not fully accounted for in the present context The standard for Aristotle, in the present context, is that which is relative to praise and blame, or, more exactly, it *is* praise and blame. Virtue is known to Aristotle first of all as a praiseworthy quality. Hence it is perceived among the things that are praised. Because of the honor, i e , praise, bestowed on those who die, or face death, in battle, courage has been perceived to be the virtue which enables a man to meet a noble death in battle. But by following the "facts" so closely, we arrive at the following paradox. If degrees of courage are measured on a scale in which death in battle is the highest point (as it must be if the definition of courage is based strictly on the "facts" of praise and blame), then the fear of death in battle must be considered the greatest fear. But then it can be no derogation of a man's courage that he is not able to sustain a greater fear. Thus a man would not be called truly brave who could not sustain the greatest fears that were "*secundum hominem*," within human strength, but on the other hand he could not be dispraised as being deficient in courage for not being able to bear terrors that are "*supra hominem*," above man, the latter being roughly equivalent to whatever is more terrible than death in battle. We arrive at the conclusion then, that although a man who can bear super-terrible things might, in a sense, be more courageous, a man who could not bear them would not, for that reason alone, be any the less brave, i e , no one would blame him for it. To state this even more explicitly one man may have more courage than another without the other being in any way deficient in courage Yet this paradox is also confirmed by observation, i e, observation of the way in which praise and blame are actually bestowed For even the honors of the battlefield distinguish between the courage required by legal justice (which Aristotle calls complete virtue), and that which is "above and beyond the call of duty." In other words, the dimension of common opinion itself recognizes its own inadequacy for the role of anything like an "ultimate" criterion. It recognizes that what is most truly noble is "beyond praise." Yet, what is noble is recognized as praiseworthy. This, however, contradicts Thomas' reasoning, according to which the recognition of the imperfect presupposes knowledge of the perfect. The only solution of this difficulty lies in the proposition that the noble things, for most people, lie only in the dimension of opinion, not knowledge Of course, this proposition, as it implies a depreciation of morality, is not made explicit by Aristotle in this context. The ambiguities preserve the moral phenomena by concealing the truth about morality that would be destructive of morality. Yet it cannot be said that Aristotle conceals anything What we have tried to show is that the ambiguities are inherent in the subject matter, and it is the part of exactness to preserve them in the manner in which they are found. But, when we are led by Aristotle from the more superficial (although crucially important) levels of the moral phenomena to deeper levels, we are then forced to reflect on the inadequacy of the moral phenomena qua moral phenomena Thomas, in his own moral doctrine, presupposes knowledge of the virtues through a natural habit of understanding loosely called conscience, or, more exactly, synderesis [104] The natural knowledge of the virtues is required as a condition of the promulgation of the natural moral law Praise and blame, in Thomas' system, are basically a reflection of that natural knowledge From Aristotle's point of view, however, it would seem that men learn of virtue and vice from the fact that one is praised and the other blamed. From Thomas' analysis of courage we must conclude that he unjustifiably imputes to Aristotle his own view.

There is then a dimension of virtue which is beyond praise—and hence also beyond blame Deficiencies in heroic virtue are not blameworthy as are deficiencies in ordinary virtue Heroes are quasi-divinities, for it is a well-nigh universal opinion that "men become gods by excess of virtue."[105] But the idea of an excess of virtue is, strictly speaking, illogical, certainly it is illogical from the point of view of Thomas' "ultimate " It is, of course, equally illogical from Aristotle's point of view, because the very expression is self-contradictory [106] But this confirms our contention that, according to Aristotle, the element of morality is opinion, not knowledge. The praise of heroic virtue is like the praise of God It bears no proportion to the worth of the object, as in the praise of human things. We do not measure the worth of God by our praises, as we do when discriminating between acts of greater or less courage Gods and heroes receive as their due the praise that is beyond praise And that very fact—that there is a universal opinion attesting the existence of a dimension of virtue above the apprehension of man as man—is the empirical basis of Aristotle's procedure The empirical facts of praise and blame attest the proposition that morality is restricted to the dimension of opinion, and hence that the "ultimates" of morality, if such an expression be at all permissible, lie beyond the scope of morality proper.

## CHAPTER VI

# MAGNANIMITY AND THE LIMITS
# OF MORALITY

### A. MAGNANIMITY AND THE RELATION OF PRAISE TO OPINION
### ABOUT THE GODS

AT THE conclusion of the analysis of courage our contention that the concept of the "ultimate" was inapplicable
to the definition of courage was confirmed by pointing out that
courage was defined by Aristotle with reference to the facts of
praise and blame, and that the facts concerning praise indicated
a sphere of virtue beyond praise Or, more exactly, it was seen
that the highest kind of praise was a praise beyond praise, i.e,
the praise of an object not commensurable with praise as such
Of such a kind is the praise of the gods, or of divine things. But
the magnanimous man, Aristotle says, is above all concerned
with honor, which is the greatest of the external goods, and
"that which we render to the gods, and which people of position most aim at."[1] If then magnanimity is especially concerned with honor, and the highest kind is that which we render to the gods, and it is the highest kind that the magnanimous
man aims at, then it is for something divine that the magnanimous man strives But the element of praise is opinion We have
seen one sign of this in the incommensurability of the highest
kind of praise with its object. Now every act of praise is the
expression of an opinion, hence praise of the gods involves an
expression of opinion concerning the gods In order to understand magnanimity, therefore, it would appear necessary to
understand the relation of praise to opinion about the gods.

Let us consider first a passage in Book I, where this topic is
discussed The question is asked, "whether happiness is among
the things that are praised or the things that are prized."[2] What

is here called "prized" is literally rendered by "honored," as it is in Thomas' Latin translation. The problem raised by the distinction between what is praised and what is honored is due to the following reflection. Happiness, it is universally admitted, is the final end and aim of all our actions Now the goodness and badness of actions is first perceived as the praiseworthy or blameworthy quality of those actions Yet if happiness is *the* end, then the goodness or badness of actions must ultimately be referrable to happiness That is, what is good or bad in actions, is good or bad because it contributes to or detracts from happiness But if what is praiseworthy is praiseworthy because it is a means to happiness, then happiness, which of necessity is not and cannot be a means to anything, is not praiseworthy It is something better than what is praiseworthy, as the end is better than the things that are for the sake of the end Praise, therefore, according to Aristotle, is properly an opinion that something contributes to an end that is itself better than the thing praised Praiseworthy things are, therefore, not desirable solely for their own sakes. Things desirable solely for their own sakes are honored, and those who possess such things are not for that reason praised but, rather, called blessed and happy

Aristotle's remarks about the gods in this context are worthy of particular note. After making clear the foregoing, namely, that what is praised is praised relatively to something better than what is praised, he continues "This is clear also from the praises of the gods, for it seems absurd that the gods should be referred to our standard, but this is done because praise involves a reference, as we said, to something else."[3] Aristotle says that the gods are praised—which, indeed, was the practice of pagan religion, and is the practice of the biblical religions, substituting only God for gods[4]—but he says that this praise is absurd. In the preceding paragraph we said that praise, according to Aristotle, was essentially related to what is imperfect, while happiness and the gods are perfect. But to praise what is perfect is, from Aristotle's point of view, to fail to understand the meaning of perfection And the element of opinion in the praise of the gods would then be shown by this inner contradiction in the very fact of praise of the gods. Moreover, as the foregoing quotation shows, praise involves a reference, and to praise the gods means that the gods are referred to non-gods. This means in fact, that the gods are referred to *us* But to measure the greater by the less is absurd. Hence to praise the gods seems altogether absurd.

Yet is the praise of the gods simply absurd? Let us consult the "facts," the phenomena under consideration. Praise of the gods is inseparable from prayers to the gods Prayers to the gods are requests of the gods. And requests of the gods imply that the gods are capable of bestowing benefits or inflicting injuries Praise of the gods is, therefore, inseparable from some kind of belief in particular divine providence. And this, we may say, would to Aristotle be the basic absurdity in the opinion implicit in the praise of the gods To impute a providential character to God or the gods is to him equivalent to imputing moral virtue to the divine nature And Aristotle maintains in Book X[5] that the imputation of moral virtue to the gods is entirely absurd Yet Aristotle's argument showing that the imputation of moral virtue to the gods is absurd is based on the premise that the gods are perfect, blessed, and happy. But this is also an ingredient of the opinion implied in the praising of the gods Opinion concerning the gods is, then, from his point of view, inconsistent, it is partly true and partly false But it is significant that the "purification" of opinion concerning the gods is left by Aristotle until Book X. On the basis of our previous analysis we can see why that is necessary. To treat the several moral virtues on their own levels it was necessary to present them in a way familiar from the common experience of mankind The accounts of the virtues are, of course, clearer than what most people know about the virtues from their experiences, yet the accounts are intended to clarify what everyone does experience But these accounts lead to difficulties,

difficulties which cannot be solved without going beyond morality in this primary sense The common understanding of morality itself recognizes its own inadequacy, in a way, by recognizing the existence of a dimension of morality above common morality This we indicated by the common apprehension of heroic virtue Heroic virtue, being "above man," is therefore something "divine " But, as human virtue is, for the mass of mankind, primarily moral virtue, and as heroic virtue is primarily understood as super-human virtue, divine virtue is primarily understood as super-human moral virtue

This is not to deny that, within the moral horizon viewed by Aristotle, there may be acts of reverence, respect, or homage which are not praises or requests Nevertheless, we maintain that praise, prayer, and request, as distinct from honor, are, from his point of view, inseparable Prayers, strictly speaking, *are* requests The connection between praise and prayers would be as follows we praise the virtues, and, in praising the gods, impute virtue to them But this must be moral virtue, and hence human virtue. For only human virtue is a means to an end, and hence only human virtue is praiseworthy If the gods are praiseworthy, then they must be capable of human virtue But then they must be capable of achieving a human good Now a human good is primarily what is good for human beings From this point of view, the gods are either human beings (even if "super-human"), or capable of doing good to human beings This, to repeat, is confirmed by the fact that the gods *are* objects of prayer, and prayer is always directed toward what is good for human beings.[6]

Praise, therefore, expresses the opinion that the object of praise is capable of achieving a human good. Prayer, as distinct from praise, is a request for a human good Now the gods, in granting our requests, must act, and in acting, act for the sake of an end. The end aimed at cannot have been achieved before the action (otherwise the action would not take place, or if it did take place it would be irrational). But every end is a good,

and thus if the gods act there must have been a good achievable by action which was not achieved by the gods *before* each
such action  Hence if the gods fulfil prayers they cannot be
perfect beings  To pray to the gods argues of necessity their
imperfection, as it argues their capacity for practical, i e ,
morally virtuous action  But it is reasonable that if we pray
to the gods we should praise them  Of course, in Book X[7] Aristotle argues that the imputation of moral virtue to the gods is
absurd, and elsewhere[8] that God is an end and never a means
to an end  But we may say that, within the dimension of morality, which is the dimension of opinion, not of knowledge, as
happiness is identified with moral perfection, the happiness of
God is identified with super-human practical or moral virtue [9]

Now, to strive for something it is necessary to have a motive,
as an end  To strive for that moral perfection "divined" by
common opinion requires a motive transcending that supplied
by the ordinary criteria of praise and blame  If man as man is
only capable of a certain degree of moral virtue, but a higher
degree is evidently possible, then the higher degree is due to
something divine in man  Man goes beyond his mere humanity
when he strives to attain super-human, i e , divine, excellence
But if a man knows that the gods have no moral virtue, if he
knows that morality is merely a human affair, then what motive
does he have for a moral perfection which, when looked at
from the point of view of human things, appears as something
divine?  To insist that heroic virtue is not something divine
would be destructive of the horizon within which heroic virtue
appears  It would be destructive of the moral phenomena, because the moral phenomena become less intelligible, if not unintelligible, in the premature glare of a philosophic critique
showing the impossibility of the common opinions about the
gods  Magnanimity is that virtue which perfects all the moral
virtues, it is "a sort of crown of the virtues, for it makes them
greater",[10] and the motive for magnanimity is precisely the desire to achieve a divine good  Note that Aristotle says "crown

of *the* virtues," not *moral* virtues, as we say. The omission of the distinction is of course necessary to preserve this horizon. It is, however, clear from the whole *Ethics* that magnanimity is not the perfection of *every* virtue, e g , philosophic wisdom. But from this point of view we see the reasonable element in the otherwise absurd opinion that the gods are benefactors It may be true that gods, in the philosophic sense, cannot be benefactors, but the magnanimous man is presented by Aristotle as being a great benefactor. And in striving for divine honor the magnanimous man strives above all to be a benefactor [11] There are two references to divinity in the chapter on magnanimity the one mentioned above, that the greatest of external goods is honor, which we render to the gods; and another, relating how Thetis approached Zeus when she had a favor to ask [12] It is not unimportant that the mention of Zeus occurs in the context of the discussion of the magnanimous man's extreme concern to be a benefactor.

But to understand the meaning of the magnanimous man's concern with divine things, we must remind ourselves of what Aristotle says on the subject in Book X "Therefore the activity of God, which surpasses all others in blessedness, must be contemplative, and of human activities, therefore, that which is most akin to this must be most of the nature of happiness "[13] The divine good *is* contemplation But is the magnanimous man, in striving for a divine good, striving for philosophic wisdom? The answer is a manifest no There is no suggestion of any philosophic attributes in the description of the magnanimous man The description of the magnanimous man is, precisely, the description of the highest *non-philosophic* human type [14] The magnanimous man is an example of the *highest* type, even from his own point of view, "in so far as something divine is present in him," and he too obeys the injunction Aristotle addresses to potential philosophers not to "follow those who advise us, being men, to think of human things, and, being mortal, of mortal things, but... make ourselves immortal."[15]

The magnanimous man is, however, non-philosophic in his attitude toward the divine something in him. This is necessarily so,
for the magnanimous man, qua magnanimous, is a man of practical virtue. But the practical virtues aim at an end which is not
a perfect end. "Now the activity of the practical virtues is ex-
hibited in political or military affairs, but the actions concerned
with these seem to be unleisurely [i.e., not pursued purely for
their own sake]. Warlike actions are completely so (for no one
chooses to be at war, or provokes war, for the sake of being
at war; any one would seem absolutely murderous if he were
to make enemies of his friends in order to bring about battle
and slaughter), but the action of the statesman is also unleisurely, and—apart from the political action itself—aims at des-
potic power and honors, or at all events happiness, for him and
his fellow citizens—a happiness different from political action,
and evidently sought as being different."[16] In other words, the
end aimed at by the greatest actions of the practical virtues is
an end beyond the practical virtues themselves. This is not in
contradiction to the dictum that "good action itself is its end,"[17]
but it means that good action in the sense of practical or moral
action is not the highest end or good. The consummation de-
voutly wished by the great statesman is not one which he himself, qua statesman, enjoys. Yet, although Aristotle says in
Book X that the end aimed at by political action is evidently
sought as being different from the good contained in the political action itself, it does not follow that the statesman understands this the way Aristotle understands it. There is, of course,
no necessity that prevents the great statesman from understanding the superiority of the contemplative to the practical life.
But if he does so he will no longer be a mere statesman, indeed,
he will be a statesman only by necessity, in so far as he is constrained by circumstances to turn from philosophy to politics.[18]
But he would never wish to spend his time in anything but the
pursuit of wisdom. Yet the very fact that Aristotle paints for us
a full length portrait of the magnanimous man, in pursuance of

his uniform aim of presenting the various moral phenomena in
their own terms, i.e., as they actually appear to the agents characterized by them, indicates that the magnanimous man is *sui
generis* motivated by the desire for the good contained in
super-human *practical* action. "And even apart from argument
it is with honor that proud [i e., magnanimous] men appear to
be concerned, for it is honor that they chiefly claim, but in
accordance with their deserts."[19] Even if, as Aristotle says a
little further on, the magnanimous man contemns honor itself,
it is nonetheless true that the virtue which he thinks is inade-
quately measured by the honor rendered to him is practical or
moral virtue. For it is characteristic of him "not to aim at things
commonly held in honor, or the things in which others excel,
[but] to be sluggish and to hold back, except where great
honor or a great work is at stake, and to be a man of few deeds,
but of great and notable ones "[20] The magnanimous man, however much he contemns honor, is nonetheless supremely concerned with the kind of excellence reflected in the non-philosophic opinion which identifies heroic virtue and divine virtue
And this opinion ultimately refers divine things to a human
standard, because it only "divines," i.e, does not know, the
truth concerning the nature of divine things.

## B. FRIENDSHIP AND HONOR

We will try to substantiate the foregoing reflections and de-
velop the problem of Thomas' critique of magnanimity by the
following further considerations. At the beginning of the account of magnanimity Aristotle says that it "seems even from
its name to be concerned with great things "[21] The magnanimous, i e, great-souled man, would seem to represent human
perfection. Human virtue is virtue of the soul (i e, of the rational and appetitive parts of the soul), and the greatest soul
must be that which has actual virtue in the highest degree That
the magnanimous man is such a man would seem to be borne
out by the statement that magnanimity "seems to be a sort of

crown of the virtues, for it makes them greater, and is not found without them "[22] Magnanimity implies the presence of all the virtues,[23] but it is not merely a sum of them all, rather it is their sum plus an "X" which brings them all to a pitch of perfection they would not have severally, or as a mere collectivity. But, although the magnanimous man is great "in every virtue,"[24] he is nevertheless above all concerned with one thing. "If, then, he deserves and claims great things, and above all the greatest things, he will be concerned with one thing in particular. Desert is relative to external goods, and the greatest of these, we should say, is that which we render to the gods, and which people of position most aim at, and which is the prize appointed for the noblest deeds, and this is honor, that is surely the greatest of external goods."[25] We may note, parenthetically, another distinction in the "levels" of virtue each virtue, taken together with magnanimity, is greater than it would be by itself. Hence it follows that each virtue, as a principle of virtuous action, is insufficient for attaining the level reached by the same virtue when operating as part of magnanimity. But each virtue supplies the motive, i e., the end, which is the cause of the virtuous action, for "the end of every activity is conformity to the corresponding state of character."[26] But the motive that magnanimity adds to that of virtue apart from magnanimity appears to be honor, or something connected with honor. That there is something problematic in the magnanimous man's concern with honor we have already seen, for we have seen that he contemns honor at the same time that he is so concerned with it. Yet he seems to be so much concerned with it because "that is surely the greatest of external goods" Moreover, as noted above, honor seems especially to be connected with the divine good. But in Book IX, in a very different context, when Aristotle raises the question as to whether the happy man will need friends, he says that "it seems strange, when one assigns all good things to the happy man, not to assign friends, who are thought the greatest of external goods."[27] There is then apparently a contradiction between what Aristotle says is the greatest of external goods in Book IV and Book IX. And we have seen that honor is either the good, or the measure of good, which raised the moral virtues to a new "ultimate." But the possibility that friendship is a good, or the measure of a good, that transcends the sphere of honor, raises the question as to what exactly is the status of the good connected with magnanimity in the hierarchy of goods achievable by action. To answer this question we must discuss the relationship of honor and friendship.

If we compare the two statements it would appear at first that the former is the more emphatic of the two  "that [honor] is surely the greatest of external goods", as compared with "friends. . are thought the greatest of external goods." But a moment's reflection teaches us that the actual emphasis must be the opposite  how *could* honor in any ultimate sense be a greater good than friendship? We may see this confirmed by the attitude of the magnanimous man himself. For to him even honor is a little thing,[28] yet it is said of him that "He must be unable to make his life revolve around another, *unless it be a friend*"[29] The contempt which the magnanimous man feels even for honor is clearly absent from his feeling for a friend. The principle involved is clear  he contemns honor because he knows that "there can be no honor that is worthy of perfect virtue"[30] But the friend of the magnanimous man in the strict sense must himself be an example of perfect virtue. And hence the magnanimous man must hold such a friend, as well as himself, in higher esteem than any honor  As we learn in Book IX, all friendship, and all virtue, are ultimately based on self-love,[31] and a friend is a kind of other self, so that, in effect, we are better able to love ourselves when we have a friend like ourselves to love at the same time, and we *do* love a friend for the same reason that we love ourselves[32] But the perfection of friendship, like happiness, must be relative to self-sufficiency. And friendship, like happiness, must be activity. But the most self-sufficient kind of activity is philosophic activity,[33] and hence friendship must above all consist, as Aristotle says, in "living together and sharing in discussion and thought," which means primarily in sharing a philosophic life. Of course, it is true that "sharing in discussion and thought" does not necessarily imply philosophy Any friends who share any activities, e g , hunting, drinking, dicing, athletic exercises, will discuss and think about these activities together [34] But in all cases other than philosophy the discussion and thought are derivative from activities which are not themselves identical with discussion and thought. Only in a philosophic friendship are the discussion and thought which characterize friendship not derivative from other activities, thus only in a philosophic friendship is the activity of friendship self-contained in the activity of discussion and thought It follows then necessarily that only in philosophic activity can the activity of friendship be perfect activity, and thus that only a philosophic friendship can be a perfect friendship

If, then, we raise the question as to why the magnanimous man is primarily concerned with honor and not with friendship, the answer would seem to be connected with the fact that the magnanimous man, not being a philosopher, cannot be a party to a perfect friendship. The magnanimous man represents perfection in the sphere of the practical virtues, and hence is perfect in relation to honor. He is, however, imperfect in relation to friendship, and for that reason *honor is said to be*, with respect to him, the greatest of external goods. Other considerations will lead us to the same conclusion. It was stated in the preceding paragraph that only in philosophic friendship is the essential activity of friendship not derivative from other activities. In this connection we may try to imagine a friendship between two magnanimous men. Each will strive to be the benefactor of the other, yet each is ashamed to receive benefits, and is displeased at the recollection of benefits received [35] There is, we may say, something awkward in the very notion of such a friendship Of course, it will no doubt be the case in fact that the truly magnanimous man will be aware that "it may be nobler to become the cause of his friend's acting than to act himself," and accordingly "he may even give up actions to his friend "[36] Yet it is somewhat doubtful whether the magnanimous man, qua man of practical virtue, is quite so delicate in his moral perceptiveness. The distinction just noted is made by Aristotle near the end of Book IX, in the context of that part of the analysis of friendship where it is gradually made clear that the essence of friendship lies in philosophic activity The case of the magnanimous man is suggestive of that paragon, Henry V, as characterized by Shakespeare Before the battle of Agincourt, when the English face a greatly superior enemy, the King's cousin Westmoreland wishes for "But one ten thousand of those men in England that do no work today!" Henry replies [37]

> If we are marked to die, we are enow
> To do our country loss, and if to live,
> The fewer men, the greater share of honor.
> God's will! I pray thee, wish not one man more.
> By Jove, I am not covetous for gold,
> Nor care I who doth feed upon my cost,
> It yearns me not if men my garments wear,
> Such outward things dwell not in my desires
> But if it be a sin to covet honor,
> I am the most offending soul alive.
> No, faith, my coz, wish not a man from England
> God's peace! I would not lose so great an honor
> As one man more, methinks, would share from me
> For the best hope I have

It may be that Aristotle's magnanimous man is not quite so covetous of honor as Henry seems to be, or that Henry's emphasis on honor may be in part stimulated by the fact that there was no chance of reinforcements from England, and hence the necessity of rousing his commanders' valor to the highest pitch. Yet it is true that honor is something that tends to be diminished as it is shared. As Hobbes says, "glory is like honor, if all men have it, no man hath it."[38] If, then, honor is of such nature that sharing tends to its diminution, there is something about honor inconsistent with friendship For it is of the nature of friendship that friends have things in common,[39] and the goodness of the things they share must be enhanced, rather than diminished, by the fact that they are common. But there is only one good of which this is intrinsically and unqualifiedly true. And that is truth itself. Truth is the one good that is in no way affected by being shared, which cannot, indeed, be made private property by anyone, and accordingly must be shared by all who possess it And there is no ground for competition in such friendships, for other goods, e g , wealth and honor, are divided when they are shared, but the truth is not a divisible good. When the truth is shared one does not give up any part of it. Rather is the contrary true in sharing what one has learned with a friend one communicates in speech But speaking and thinking are correlative, and the activity of thinking is increased in the friendly communication of knowledge Hence one can better contemplate such truth as one may possess by means of friendly intercourse, so that in philosophic friendship the act of sharing increases both the proper and the common store of the good aimed at.

The virtue of magnanimous men, we may say, becomes active primarily as a result of great crises, of situations of great need of their fellow-citizens They are, as we have seen, great benefactors. But their benefactions have to do primarily with what is useful in the salvation of their country, above all in war. Their actions are intelligible, therefore, primarily as actions directed toward that good of which honor is thought to be the proper prize or reward. Friends, however great a role they may play in the actual lives of such men—and it may be very great—cannot be considered central for their activities the way honor is. We can imagine magnanimous men in a noble comradeship of arms, and perhaps other comparable great endeavors, but it

is difficult to imagine their friendship as an active relationship
except with reference to such external stimuli. Their friendship
and their greatness both would seem to depend upon great
crises in human affairs—unfortunate crises, which they themselves, as virtuous men, would never wish for.[40] What would
William of Orange or Marlborough have been without Louis
XIV, Pitt without Napoleon, Washington without George III,
Lincoln without the slave interest, Churchill without Hitler?
This indeed is the paradox of moral virtue, but it is a paradox
which cannot be emphasized on the level of moral action itself,
because the supreme efforts and sacrifices demanded by morality require that the end contained in moral action itself
appear as a supreme good. As has been shown above[41] Aristotle
makes it very clear in Book X that this is not the supreme good.
Yet, in portraying the man of supreme practical virtue he is at
pains to preserve the horizon within which moral action does
appear as something supremely good. To preserve this horizon
Aristotle must present the magnanimous man as concerned
above all with honor, because honor enforces the virtuous
man's consciousness of his virtue, and hence makes his virtue
more pleasant to him and accordingly a more fitting motive
for those great deeds which are the consummation of his virtue.
Indeed, if we examine the matter more closely, we will see that
honor, even for the magnanimous man, is in a way reducible to
friendship, but in such a way that the emphasis remains on
honor  In Book I Aristotle speaks of those who identify happiness with honor, which is, he says, "roughly speaking, the end
of political life." "But it seems too superficial to be what we
are looking for, since it is thought to depend on those who bestow honor rather than on him who receives it, but the good
we divine to be proper to a man and not easily taken from him.
Further, men seem to pursue honor in order that they may be
assured of their goodness, at least it is by men of practical wisdom that they seek to be honored, and among those who know
them, and on the ground of their virtue, clearly, then, accord-

ing to them, at any rate, virtue is better."[42] Now the magnanimous man, as the man chiefly concerned with honor, is clearly the political man par excellence And as such, he needs friends, because he cannot enjoy honor unless there are men of practical wisdom to assure him of his own virtue They too then are "other selves," in the sense that their goodness is a necessary condition of the magnanimous man's consciousness of his own goodness And, as the magnanimous men love themselves for their own virtue, they must love their friends as a condition of loving themselves Yet the fact remains that the virtuous activities, because of which they love both themselves and their friends, are primarily intelligible as *honorable* activities, rather than *friendly* activities For, as we have seen, the practical virtues find their supreme expression in the political sphere, whose good is the honorable good, with respect to which friends are valued either as instruments in the performance of the activities, or as conditions of our consciousness of the virtuousness of the activities The friends are not intrinsic to the activities, as they are in the sphere of the theoretical virtues.

We must now see how Thomas treats this question of the priority of friendship and honor A decision on the question turns, ultimately, on what status is accorded the good achievable by magnanimity among the goods achievable by man Broadly speaking, Aristotle's answer to this question admits of no doubt the good achievable by practical wisdom is secondary to that achievable by theoretical or philosophic wisdom And Thomas cannot and does not seek to make any qualification of this broad conclusion But within the framework of this broad conclusion Thomas does make certain qualifications, qualifications which, it is believed, have the effect, if their implications are fully traced, of contradicting this manifest broad conclusion.

Let us first compare Thomas' comments on the two contradictory statements regarding the greatest of external goods. Concerning that in Book IV, where honor is said "surely" to be the greatest, Thomas says that honor is the "*optimum*" of all external goods. But when Aristotle, in Book IX, says that friends "are thought the greatest of external goods," Thomas says that a friend is "*quoddam maximum*," a *certain* maximum among external goods  Thus Thomas, in paraphrasing Aristotle in the commentary, qualifies the latter statement, but not the former  This, taken in conjunction with other evidence indicates, we believe, a preference for the statement in Book IV  We may note, incidentally, that in the former case Thomas paraphrases "greatest," which is "*maximum*" in the Latin text of the *Ethics*, by "*optimum*"  Now "*maximum*" has the same ambiguity in Latin that "greatest" has in English  it may emphasize quantity or quality [43]  Aristotle suggests in the section on magnanimity itself that quality and quantity have a certain connection, particularly in the moral sphere  "for pride [i e , magnanimity] implies greatness [magnitude], as beauty implies a good-sized body, and little people may be neat and well-proportioned but cannot be beautiful "[44]  Yet in Book X Aristotle, speaking of the philosophic life, says that we should live "in accordance with the best thing in us, for even if it be small in bulk, much more does it in power and worth surpass everything "[45]  Thus there would seem to be a kind of quantitative factor connected with the excellence of the moral life which plays no role in the excellence of the life of reason  Yet Thomas speaks of honor as "optimum," but friendship as "maximum," although the Latin text of the *Ethics* is "maximum" in both cases  Moreover the former is spoken of by Thomas unqualifiedly as the "*optimum*" of *all* external goods, whereas the latter is spoken of merely as a *certain* "*maximum*" of external goods. Thus Thomas seems to imply that magnanimity, in its concern with honor, is more connected with the perfection of reason than it would be if its primary concern were with friendship  But this implication, if actually intended, would be directly contrary to what has been said above as to Aristotle's conception as to the relation of friendship and honor.

In order to appreciate the bearing of this apparent implication in Thomas' commentary, we must return to our analysis of friendship, and carry it a few steps further. We have seen that only a philosophic friendship can be a perfect friendship, because only in such a friendship can the activity of the friendship be as self-contained as possible, and the common good of the friendship, truth, be perfectly consistent with that self-love which Aristotle says is the proper basis of all human motivation.[46] The connection between truth and friendship is perhaps best expressed in the famous passage referring to Plato or the Platonists in Book I. Aristotle regrets having to attack the doctrine of "ideas," "Yet it would perhaps be thought to be better, indeed to be our duty, for the sake of maintaining the truth even to destroy what touches us closely, especially as we are philosophers, for while both are dear, piety requires us to honor truth above our friends."[47] The etymological connections are somewhat obscured in the translation [48] friendship is "*philia*," and philosophy ("*philo-sophia*") means love of, or friendship for, wisdom (whose object is truth). Thus philosophers are friends of each other, but qua philosophers they are lovers of truth first, and of each other only secondarily, as fellow-lovers of truth. Aristotle says that "both are dear (*philoin*)," but we must prefer truth to our friends,[49] the reason clearly being that we could not *be* friends to our friends, unless we preferred the truth to them. But, we must again recall, philosophic friendship is the most perfect friendship, and the good aimed at in common by such friends is the greatest of all goods. Now the aim of fellow-philosophers, both individually and collectively, is the possession of truth. And this truth is everywhere and at all times the same. For "what is healthy or good is different for men and for fish, but what is white or straight is always the same", while on the contrary "if the state of mind concerned with a man's own interests [i.e., practical wisdom] is to be called philosophic wisdom, there will be many philosophic wisdoms."[50] The absolute identity of the good aimed at by all philosophers is beyond dispute. But, to the extent that this good is gained, i.e., to the extent that the philosophers have actual understanding, to the extent that they know, as distinct from only inquiring,[51] they will partake of the same activity. Indeed, in knowing, as distinct from inquiring, they will partake of a perfect activity (*energeia*), the activity of "immobility," in which more pleasure is found than in movement, i e., the imperfect movement (*genesis*) of coming into being.[52] But this activity must be identical for all, as the objects of truth are identical for all, and thus the consciousness of all individual philosophers, to the extent that they possess truth, will be identical. For the truth which philosophers are concerned with is what is of necessity, what is universal, and beyond all particularity.[53] Hence the consciousness of all individual philosophers, when active in accordance with the perfection of wisdom, and to the extent that they are thus active, involves a withdrawal from all particularity, all individuality. The perfection of wisdom, as it is a consciousness of what is universal and necessary, involves the destruction of all consciousness of what is particular and ephemeral, including the consciousness of one's individual identity In this sense philosophy, for Aristotle as well as Plato, meant "learning to die."[54] We see then that friendship is the external good most closely connected with the highest internal good, the activity of wisdom We see also that the perfection of self-love, which is assisted by a philosophic friendship, aims toward a consummation in which self-consciousness itself is transcended This transcending of self-consciousness would seem to be included in (although perhaps it may not exhaust) what Aristotle means when he advises us to "make ourselves immortal"[55] Friendship, we would conclude, is first among the external goods for the same reason that the activity of wisdom is first among the internal goods. And Thomas' equivocation on this point, if it be such, amounts to an equivocation concerning the status of philosophy. And, we suggest, he does equivocate on this point because of the heterodox notion of immortality to which it leads

That Thomas equivocates on this point we may suggest, from a merely external point of view, from the fact that there is no emphasis, comparable to Aristotle's, in his own doctrine, on friendship proper  For example, in Book III of the *Summa contra Gentiles,* when he asks an apparently exhaustive list of questions as to what happiness is, including the question whether happiness consists in honor (chap 28), he never asks whether happiness consists in friendship  Also, in the *Summa Theologica,* there is no question on friendship proper. In the *Secunda Secundae,* Question 114 is "De Amicitia seu Affabilitate," concerning friendship or affability, meaning thereby the social virtue of friendliness, which Aristotle discusses in Book IV, as part of the general discussion of urbanity,[56] and not the comprehensive topic of Books VIII and IX  In the *Secunda Secundae,* the treatise on justice, Questions 57 to 122, occupies more than a third of the whole  In the *Nicomachean Ethics,* on the other hand, friendship, which is not properly treated in a single question of the *Summa Theologica,* is the subject of two full books, whereas justice is the subject of only one  It is true that Thomas identifies friendship, in the *Summa Theologica,* with charity.[57] But charity is the greatest of the theological virtues, and, as there are no theological virtues in Aristotle's doctrine, it cannot be properly identified with Aristotle's conception of friendship in the *Ethics* [58]

### C  THE SUPERIORITY OF THE MAGNANIMOUS MAN

The nature of Thomas' reservation in favor of honor as opposed to friendship may become clearer from other comments he makes on magnanimity. The magnanimous man is presented by Aristotle, according to our analysis, as being preeminently the man of practical virtue, inasmuch as he is the type most concerned with honor  And Aristotle has said in Book I that "consideration of the prominent types of life shows that people of superior refinement and of active disposition identify happiness with honor, for that is, roughly speaking, the end of the political life "[59] Of course, Aristotle makes it clear that the type concerned with honor is really concerned with virtue, but it remains true that the type concerned with honor because of virtue is nonetheless the one which finds greatest scope for virtue in the political life But, as we have shown above, this type must be concerned rather with "outward" things than "inward" things, because the very nature of practical or moral virtue, which is always directed toward something other than itself, is such that it can be actualized in the highest degree only as a relation with others.[60] Yet the whole emphasis of Thomas' interpretation of magnanimity is on its "inwardness " For example, when Aristotle says that the magnanimous man would never fly from danger, or wrong another, "for to what end should he do disgraceful acts, he to whom nothing is great?"[61] Thomas says that the magnanimous man does not place so great a value on any *external thing* (*rem exteriorem*), that for the sake of it he should wish to do anything base [62] And again, when Aristotle says that "at honors that are great and conferred by good men he will be moderately pleased, thinking that he is coming by his own or even less than his own, for there can be no honor that is worthy of perfect virtue, yet he will at any rate accept it since they have nothing greater to bestow on him,"[63] Thomas says that the magnanimous man considers that no honor *outwardly* shown *by man* is a worthy premium of virtue [64] And again, in the same paragraph, Thomas notes that the magnanimous man accepts his honors equably, considering that *men* do not have anything greater to bestow on him We may ask, at this point, why Thomas calls any honor outward or external, if honor is defined simply as an external good. Moreover, we may ask what contrast Thomas has in mind when he speaks of honor shown by *man*, inasmuch as Aristotle makes no distinction at this point Aristotle distinguishes the honor that is paid by good men from that of low or vulgar men, but Thomas drops this distinction, and hence implies a different one  Again, when Aristotle speaks of magnanimous men as being thought "disdainful" (*despectores*, literally "lookers down") because they place a slight value even on honor, and hence contemn still more the other things that most men value (and, accordingly, the men who value them), Thomas comments that they are judged to be "*despectores*" for this reason, that they contemn *exterior* goods, and value the interior goods of virtue alone [65] And again, on the theme of the magnanimous man's contemptuousness, when Aristotle says, "Nor is he given to admiration, for *nothing* to him is great", Thomas insists on the qualification that nothing of the things that occur outwardly are great to the magnanimous man, because his whole life is concerned with the interior goods, which are truly great [66] And still once more, when Aristotle speaks of the deportment of the magnanimous man, that it is unlikely for one "who thinks *nothing* great to be excited,"[67] Thomas again insists, "nothing of what is external "[68]

Let us now analyze more closely Thomas' critique of the magnanimous man's haughty, despising, contemning nature. In all of the above passages, it may be noted, Thomas has conveyed the impression that this haughtiness, this sense of his absolute superiority to all others, is more appearance than reality. Thomas would have us believe that it is the magnanimous man's knowledge of the inferiority of all external goods that makes him depreciate all estimations of worth founded on the appreciation of external goods  Yet we have seen that the conception of magnanimity is founded on the opinion that divine excellence is a kind of super-human excellence, and, accordingly, that a kind of assimilation to God or the gods is possible by means of great deeds, which are actions of super-human practical or moral virtue  Thomas seems to ascribe a kind of meditativeness to the magnanimous man, whereas any actual reflectiveness in such a non-philosopher, and hence non-contemplative, would only be a reflection on his own great deeds, and the

ı

great virtue which produced them Men who achieve such
great deeds are honored in life and after death with the same
kind of honor that we pay to the gods, and in this sense achieve
at least a semi-divine status, and the pleasure of the magnanimous man, as it does not come from the contemplation of necessary truth, must come from the contemplation of himself But
Thomas does not suggest that this is what he means by "interior
good " To repeat our former argument, the good achievable by
practical action is an imperfect good. A supreme example of
practical virtue is the action by which one's country is saved
in war, yet such virtue must be valued because of the value of
peace As warlike actions are of no use in peace, there must be
other actions, peaceful actions, which are more valuable than
any warlike actions, because of which warlike actions may
themselves sometimes be valued Yet the man who is called
upon to make the supreme sacrifice in war, if he is to have
a really sufficient motive for sacrificing his life virtuously (i e,
if he is to have true virtue as distinct from political or citizen virtue),[69] must be motivated by the opinion that the good
achieved in his virtuous action is the highest good achievable by action Now when Aristotle speaks of the great deeds
of the magnanimous man he particularly emphasizes his greatness in the face of danger, which can only mean his greatness in
war For example "And greatness in every virtue would seem
to be characteristic of a proud man And it would be most un-
becoming for a proud man to fly from danger."[70] Thus, after
speaking of his greatness in every virtue, Aristotle immediately
emphasizes his courage, which we saw was defined primarily in
reference to war and battle And again, "He does not run into
trifling dangers, nor is he fond of danger, because he honors
few things, but he will face great dangers, and when he is in
danger is unsparing of his life, knowing that there are conditions on which life is not worth having "[71] We should think it
a reasonable inference from these passages that the magnanimous man, as presented in Book IV, is of the opinion that the

greatest good is achievable by the supreme actions of practical virtue, and that great deeds in battle are examples of such actions But if this is true, then the distinction between the magnanimous man and the many whom he despises cannot be founded on the distinction between knowledge and opinion concerning the highest good In this respect the magnanimous man, qua magnanimous man, is on a level with the others When Thomas says that the magnanimous man would never do anything disgraceful because he does not value any *external* thing sufficiently to wish to do anything base, he implies that the magnanimous man has another good, different from that to be achieved in the virtuous action itself. But what this is, Thomas does not say And when Thomas adds the qualification *external* to Aristotle's statement that nothing is great to the magnanimous man, he seems thereby to depreciate the magnanimous man's own motive, namely consciousness of superiority, and realization of that superiority in great deeds. Similarly, when Aristotle says that the magnanimous man speaks and acts openly, "because he is contemptuous,"[72] Thomas hastens to add that it is not to be understood that he despises others in the sense of depriving them of due reverence, but that he does not value them beyond what he ought.[73] Yet, we must ask, what kind of reverence can a man to whom nothing is great pay to others who are his inferiors? For if "the end of every activity is conformity to the corresponding state of character,"[74] and if magnanimity is a state of character in which *nothing* is great to its possessor (i e., greater than itself), then the notion of *anything* greater of necessity changes the motivation, and hence the state of character and action produced by it. We do not deny that Thomas is correct in implying that Aristotle believed that there was something greater than the virtue of the magnanimous man, but we believe that he is incorrect in implying that the magnanimous man, qua magnanimous man, thinks so Aristotle, in accordance with his uniform aim of presenting the various moral phenomena on their own levels (as well as the

various levels of the moral phenomena), is in Book IV presenting the magnanimous man in his own terms.

Let us turn again to the passage discussed in chapter 1, concerning the alleged ingratitude of magnanimous men, as they are said
"to remember any service they have done, but not those they
have received (for he who receives a service is inferior to him
who has done it, but the proud man wishes to be superior), and
to hear of the former with pleasure, of the latter with displeas-
ure."[75] Thomas, it will be recalled, says that this characteristic
is not of the magnanimous man's choosing, but is a consequence
of his disposition, whereby he thinks more frequently of what is
more pleasant to him—i e , doing benefits—and hence seems to
forget the benefits he has received, because he thinks less of what
is unpleasant to him—namely, receiving benefits, which place
him in an inferior position It is, says Thomas, against the magnanimous man's will that he be placed in the position of an inferior, which is what happens when he is a recipient of a benefit.
But, Thomas adds, by choice the magnanimous man does not forget benefits received [76] Now Thomas is certainly correct in saying that the magnanimous man does not intend to be ungrateful.
Yet it remains true that there is an appearance of ingratitude
about him. Now Aristotle must have been as well aware of that
as Thomas, but Aristotle does not attempt to excuse this trait,
in fact he emphasizes it, illustrating it by a reference to Zeus,
which would imply that this jealous regard for superiority had
something particularly divine about it. There is nothing in
Thomas' interpretation to explain Aristotle's silence on the very
point which Thomas labors. Moreover, if the magnanimous
man himself is perfect in every virtue, as Aristotle says, and
hence, if he is perfect in gratitude, which is a virtue, then how
is it that he is not able to prevent himself from giving the impression of ingratitude by being forgetful of benefits received?
Or, more specifically, why is it that the pleasure he receives in
doing good deeds causes him to forget the good things done to
him? Can good action be the cause of even an appearance of

evil? Is not this loss of memory, which Thomas says he does not choose, and hence must be against his will, a weakness, and hence a sort of vice? If it be said that the magnanimous man does not really forget, then the implication is that he feigns forgetfulness But this Thomas denies, when he says that the magnanimous man does not choose to forget Of course, to feign forgetfulness of benefits received would indeed be vicious, particularly from Thomas' point of view, because that would deprive the benefactors of their "due reverence," which Thomas insists the magnanimous man does not do [77] But if the magnanimous man does not feign forgetfulness, then he *does* forget, and this, to repeat, is itself a weakness or deficiency Thomas, it must be admitted, has not "saved" the magnanimous man as a prototype of perfect virtue.

But from Aristotle's point of view, it is clear, the magnanimous man does not need to be saved in the aforesaid sense The traits which Aristotle ascribes to the magnanimous man are those which he evidently believes, on the basis of observation, actually do characterize the highest human type, as viewed within the dimension of morality To measure this type by a higher standard is to transcend this dimension But if we transcend this dimension we no longer see things as they appear within the dimension The magnanimous man's world is in one respect at least like the world of the child, as explained above.[78] He knows that morality is something good, and hence that those who excel all others in the actions of the moral virtues are the best To explain to him that morality is good because it is a means to an end that is better than morality, would be destructive of the motive that makes him concentrate all his energies in supreme actions of moral virtue, in which he thinks that he will attain a supreme good Similarly, as the opportunities for great actions are comparatively rare (he is "a man of few deeds"),[79] his greatest preoccupation in between his moments of action must be the contemplation of his own greatness.[80] His concern with his own greatness has something overweening

about it for, aiming at divine honors, he is divinely jealous of
his superiority It is most significant, we believe, that in the
context of the discussion of magnanimity in Book IV, Aristotle
mentions the chief of the Olympian gods, and emphasizes his
quality as a moral agent, although in Book X he says that the
gods cannot have moral qualities This we take to be strong evidence that Aristotle intends to portray magnanimity, in the earlier book, within the moral horizon alone. This does not mean
that Aristotle denies that the magnanimous man may not at the
same time be something more than magnanimous But we could
not understand the state of character, magnanimity, as corresponding to the man characterized by it, if we tried to understand it as part of a state of character higher than itself. It may
be true that the philosopher is also magnanimous, but if it is
true then it is so only in the sense that his capacity for great
actions is the same, certainly his motive is no longer the same
But, even though his motive is no longer the same, it will remain
the case that those who do not understand his motive, which
means all non-philosophers, will perforce *interpret* his motive
as being that of the non-philosophic magnanimous man In
other words, whether or not the magnanimous man is more
than a man of practical or moral virtue, qua magnanimous he
will appear the same, to all who remain within the practical
or moral horizon Now, in effect, this means, to most men But,
certainly in Book IV, Aristotle is reconstructing the moral
horizon of most men, the horizon within which men are moved
to act by the appearances of the things that seem good to them
Thomas, in repeatedly qualifying Aristotle's description of the
magnanimous man, in order to "save" his character in accordance with what Thomas evidently considers a higher standard
of perfection, mistakes Aristotle's intention in these passages
Aristotle's aim is not to save the reputation of the magnanimous
man, but to save the phenomenon of magnanimity. Evidently,
the magnanimous man is not himself aware of any need to
be saved.

## CHAPTER VII

# THE AMBIGUITY OF "MAN" AND THE LIMITS OF HUMAN HAPPINESS

### A A REVIEW THE LEVELS OF MORALITY

WE HAVE shown at some length the inapplicability of Thomas' principle of the "ultimate" to Aristotle's presentation of the various moral virtues. It was this same rigidity in the conception of the virtues which motivated the repeated emphasis, in the comments on magnanimity, on a quality which Aristotle does not evidently impute to the magnanimous man in his merely moral character But we must seek to go further behind the principle of the "ultimate" itself. Magnanimity, we saw, perfected the other moral virtues. But magnanimity itself is evidently carried to a higher perfection by legal justice, the comprehensive form of justice, in which "every virtue is comprehended," and which is "the actual exercise of complete virtue."[1] Yet at the beginning of Book VIII we are told that justice itself is carried to a higher degree by friendship And the perfection of friendship, we saw, was partnership in philosophic activity Aristotle, we may say, leads us by almost insensible degrees beyond the moral dimension, even before he explicitly proposes the philosophic life as the happy life in Book X. We may thus distinguish at least six levels within the moral dimension itself The first broad division was between virtue and heroic virtue (we omit continence, which is not called a form of virtue, although it is a good state) Second, the distinction in Book VI between natural virtue and strict virtue, the latter implying the presence of practical wisdom But, as we saw above,[2] natural virtue is also distinguishable from ordinary virtue, which is based on habituation, but does not imply the presence of practical wisdom. In the chapter on magnanimity, how-

ever, we saw that ordinary virtue is carried to a higher degree
as part of magnanimity, and now that magnanimity is carried to
a higher degree by legal justice The perfection of justice by
friendship carries us again into the region of heroic virtue, and
we will not try to make any further distinctions within this
realm. The principle of the "ultimate" cuts off this very subtle
and suggestive development, which goes on within the entire
*Ethics* But the transition from justice to friendship, and from
friendship to philosophy, emphasizes what was, of course, implicit from the beginning namely, the ultimate dependence of
morality upon a trans-moral good, a dependence not only for
its justification, but, ultimately, for its very being

### B THE INDEPENDENCE OF THE MORAL DIMENSION

We emphasize "ultimately," because it is Aristotle's method
to treat the whole of morality, and even the various levels of
morality, as having a kind of independent existence, which
must be grasped primarily (but not ultimately) from the point
of view of those who actually live on these various levels
Thomas, as we shall try to show in the next chapter, treats
morality as having actually an independent existence, and as
being intrinsically rational, rather than rational only with a
view to the rationality of its ultimate justification [3] As we have
interpreted Aristotle, all morality, as such, is motivated only by
an opinion as to what is good, and in this sense cannot be intrinsically rational Indeed, we might say that the perfection of
morality, for non-philosophers, is better attained with the aid
of an illusion than with the truth about morality, namely, that
it is not the highest good On the lowest level of morality, that
of courage, this is obvious men going into battle must somehow believe that the supreme sacrifice is for the sake of the supreme good, that is, they must believe this if they are to be
truly brave, and not motivated either by mere sense of shame
or desire for the external good of honor The political community itself cannot survive—and the moral life of the citizen

qua citizen would be impossible—if it were believed that the "last full measure of devotion" was directed to a transient and evanescent good Yet "sub specie aeternitatis" every political community is transient, and everything that has come into being must pass away The moral life means essentially an attachment to mortal things, yet the fact that true happiness can be found only in an attachment to immortal things is reflected on the moral level by the opinion—the necessary but untrue opinion—that an immortal good is attained in the highest consummation of moral virtue.

Yet, we must add, this untrue opinion is only in a sense untrue, and to fail to understand the sense in which it has truth would be to fail to understand the motivation behind Aristotle's scrupulous regard for the moral phenomena on their own level, which also means in their own right We may illustrate Aristotle's decent regard for the opinions necessary for the proper functioning of the moral life from his own personal will, as reported by Diogenes Laertius Apart from a beneficent and paternal care for the future well-being of all members of his household, slaves as well as family, he also attends piously to the memories of all those for whose "happiness after death" he may have been thought in any way responsible, and to all other duties of piety "My executors shall see to it when the images which Gryllion has been commissioned to execute have been finished, that they be set up, namely that of Nicanor, that of Proxenus, which it was my intention to have executed, and that of Nicanor's mother, also they shall set up the bust which has been executed of Arimnestus, to be a memorial of him, seeing that he died childless, and shall dedicate my mother's statue to Demeter at Nemea or wherever they think best. And wherever they bury me, there the bones of Pythias shall be laid, in accordance with her own instructions And to commemorate Nicanor's safe return, as I vowed on his behalf, they shall set up in Stagira stone statues of life size to Zeus and Athena the Saviours "[4] Some modern writers have taken this as evidence that

Aristotle was not really free from pagan superstition This, of course, is altogether nonsense, especially as Aristotle himself says, at the end of Book IV, that things that are disgraceful ought never to be done, regardless of whether they are disgraceful in truth, or only according to common opinion [5] The corollary of this would be that one ought not to omit doing actions that are considered decent and good, even if they are so only by opinion and not truth. The only evident exception, would be if common opinion enjoined as good, actions which were in truth evil or indecent But behind this regard for common opinion is the principle that certain things are indeed decent and honorable and noble, and that to act indecently or dishonorably or ignobly is in itself, and *in truth* a vice, a deficiency, and an imperfection And the man who is imperfect in this respect lacks something as a human being, and hence cannot be happy For although morality may rest on opinion, in one sense it is nonetheless objectively true that the moral good is a human good, and proper to human nature as such For example, to feel a regard for the dead to whom we have been bound by friendship or duty, is an essential element of our humanity To act on these feelings in performing obsequies, and carrying out their wishes as if their well-being still depended on us, is what every decent human being must do, so long as he functions as a member of a human community. Aristotle expresses this perfectly in the chapter in Book I on how the fortunes of descendants and friends affect a man's happiness "The good or bad fortunes of friends, then, seem to have some effects on the dead, but effects of such a kind and degree as neither to make the happy unhappy nor to produce any other change of the kind "[6] In other words, even though we may *know* that the dead are beyond fortune and misfortune, a decent man cannot fail to honor the memory of the worthy departed. The contrary, Aristotle says, "seems a very unfriendly doctrine," and "one opposed to the opinions men hold," which, Thomas rightly observes, cannot be completely false [7] In other words, to the extent that we

live on the moral and political level we must act in reference
to certain opinions, in order to live as well, and hence as happily, as it is possible to live on that level But this is the level on
which most men live all their lives, and even philosophers live
most (albeit not the most important part) of their lives. That
this level is not the highest level does not detract from its
proper dignity.

C THOMAS' RESERVATIONS IN FAVOR OF PERSONAL IMMORTALITY

But Thomas' insistent reservation in favor of the magnanimous man's "inner" life does not imply the same reservation
that Aristotle may be said to have in favor of the contemplative
life. It implies rather a reservation in favor of a conception of
personal immortality, for which there is no apparent basis in
the *Nicomachean Ethics*. Yet Thomas interprets the moral phenomena described by Aristotle on the basis of such a conception, and virtually imputes the doctrine to Aristotle himself. He
certainly denies vigorously that Aristotle held any notions that
would be incompatible with the Christian doctrine of personal
immortality. We may take as our starting point the passage in
Book I quoted in the preceding paragraph When Aristotle
speaks of the dead not being affected in their happiness or un-
happiness, Thomas says, it is to be understood that he refers to
the dead "not as they are in themselves," but "according as they
live in the memories of men " Thomas thus admits that Aristotle
does not speak of the dead as if they were still living, in another
existence, by saying that he does not refer to them "as they are
in themselves " The emphasis of the passage, according to
Thomas, is the fragility of that felicity which depends on human opinion [8] But, says Thomas, whether the souls of men do
in some way live after death, and whether they know what
happens here, does not pertain to the matter at hand, as the
Philosopher *here* deals only with the felicity of the present
life And, Thomas continues, questions of this kind, which require long discussion, are *here* passed over, because in this sci-

ence, which has to do with actions, they would be superfluous. But, Thomas concludes, "alibi haec plenius disservimus," *elsewhere* we have discussed these subjects more fully.[9] Thus Thomas repeatedly stresses that Aristotle *here* limits himself to what has to do with this life, implying that *he* (Aristotle) discusses what has to do with the other life elsewhere But in the decisive statement just quoted Thomas uses the *first* person, which would seem to refer to himself, Thomas, and not Aristotle. But to speak thus in a commentary is, to say the least, ambiguous [10] Apart from this point, we must note the incorrectness of the assumption governing the entire series of comments, namely, that what happens to the soul in another life is irrelevant from the point of view of action in this life. We have discussed this in a former chapter,[11] in which it was clear from Thomas' own remarks that the opinion that the soul might suffer great good (or, by implication, great evil) in another existence, could have the greatest influence on human actions in this life For Aristotle to pass over a discussion of life after death, *because* it is irrelevant from the point of view of ethics, as Thomas says he does, is intelligible *only* on the assumption that he did not believe in personal immortality But further, in view of Aristotle's procedure of discussing all relevant opinions, even though they are in the main discarded, we must say that the notion of personal immortality is one to which he did not even give serious consideration [12]

At what pains Thomas is to counteract this manifest impression that Aristotle does not consider personal immortality seriously we must now see. In Book III Aristotle remarks that "there may be a wish even for impossibles, e g immortality "[13] Thomas, in his comments, promptly adds "according to the state of this corruptible life."[14] And, in the discussion of courage, when Aristotle says that death is thought to be "the end,"[15] Thomas adds "of the present life "[16] When, in Book I, Aristotle says that it is quite absurd to speak of a dead man as happy, "especially for us who say that happiness is an activity,"[17] Thomas again insists that Aristotle does not *here* speak of the felicity of a future life, but only of the present life, whether it can be attributed to a man while he is living or only when he is dead.[18] Still again, when in Book III Aristotle speaks of death being particularly painful for the virtuous man, who is "knowingly losing the greatest goods,"[19] Thomas repeats his insistence that Aristotle does not speak of what pertains to the state of the other life *in the present work*.[20] This repeated insistence that Aristotle does not speak "here" and "in the present work," with its evident inference that Aristotle does, would, or could speak of it elsewhere, is accompanied in another passage by a curious complication In an early passage of Book I, where Aristotle is discussing in a general way the criterion of self-sufficiency as applicable to happiness, Thomas again remarks that in this book the Philosopher is speaking only of the happiness which is possible in this life, but he then adds that the felicity of the other life "exceeds all investigation of reason "[21] Thus, on the one hand Thomas insists tirelessly[22] that Aristotle omits discussing the life after death because it would take him beyond the confines of ethics proper, but then says that such an inquiry exceeds the power of reason. Now if it exceeds the power of reason, how could Aristotle have written on the subject *anywhere?* The principles of such discourse must be presumably derived from revelation, if they are not accessible to reason Thomas seems almost to forget that Aristotle did not have this dispensation We noted above the passage in which Thomas, after saying that Aristotle does not treat of the life after death *here*, says *we* have dealt more fully with this topic elsewhere Thomas, we would conclude, not only identifies himself in the commentary with Aristotle, qua philosopher, but Aristotle with himself qua theologian.

### D THE AMBIGUITY OF "MAN"

But we must see a more serious aspect of Thomas' reservation to Aristotle In Book I Aristotle concludes his discussion of the question as to whether it is possible to call a man happy when he is still alive, and hence possibly destined to the misfortunes of Priam, by saying that he is to be called happy "who is active in accordance with complete virtue and is sufficiently equipped with external goods, not for some chance period but throughout a complete life" And, Aristotle concludes, "we shall call happy those among living men in whom these conditions are, and are to be fulfilled—but *happy men*."[23] Thomas comments as follows. we call such happy *as* men, who in this life of changeability cannot have perfect beatitude And, because there is no natural desire that is vain, it can rightly be thought that there is reserved to man a perfect beatitude after this life [24] Now we see that Thomas finds Aristotle's limitations of happiness, implied in the word "man" to be an indication that man has another life after this life, that is, that the defective nature of happiness in this life provides prima facie evidence of the existence of another life The implied reasoning is as follows there is a natural desire for perfect happiness, yet perfect happiness is impossible in this life, but no natural desire can be vain, hence perfect happiness must be possible in another life [25]

We must now turn briefly to the texts which are most pertinent for understanding this ambiguity in "man" In answering this question, we are again answering the question as to the status of the good connected with moral virtue It was noted above that the good achievable by magnanimity, considered as the perfection of practical or moral virtue, was only secondary among the goods achievable by human beings Yet, from another point of view it could have been regarded as first among the goods achievable by man as man, because in Book X Aristotle says that the higher good will not be achieved by him "in so far as he is man, but in so far as something divine is present in him "[26] There are, no doubt, a number of ambiguities in "man", and some, but not all, are of the simple variety, in which the two meanings are far apart e g., soul and body, reason and desire.[27] We may state the difficulty as follows. Virtuous activity is activity in accordance with reason. But rational activity may mean activity in obedience to reason, or the activity of reason itself.[28] And again, the activity of reason itself may mean the activity of reason in issuing commands, to be obeyed by the part of the soul that merely acts in accordance with reason, or it may mean the activity of reason that issues no commands, and has nothing to do with anything outside itself.[29] A difficulty arises from the fact that the one element in man called reason has the dual function, first, of issuing commands for practical action (the activities in accordance with which comprise the moral virtues), and second, of actualizing the objects of pure thought, i e, of contemplation. Reason, as such, is divine, but the divine reason issues no commands.[30] There is, as we have repeatedly stressed, no particular providence in Aristotle's natural theology, hence there is no "assimilation" to God possible through the perfection of reason in the sphere of practical action Yet when Aristotle speaks of "man as man" he does not simply oppose man as moral being to man as divine being. For the divine thing in man *is* "man himself, since it is the authoritative and better part of him."[31] Hence the expression man as man may mean man qua moral being, or man qua divine being, or, again, it may refer to man qua divine being, but with reference to the limitations on the actualization of his divinity because of the fact that the divine element in him is limited by his composite nature as soul-in-body.[32] In other words, as man is a composite being, "man as man" may refer to his composite nature, but man in another sense *is* reason, which is divine, and not composite. The composite nature of man may be proper to him in the one sense, but in the latter sense, the sense in which reason is intrinsically non-composite, the composite nature of man is extrinsic to reason, and hence to man.[33]

### E THE PERFECTION OF HUMAN HAPPINESS

We have drawn out this paradox to make as emphatic as possible the identification in the foregoing passage, of "man him-

self," with what Aristotle calls, without qualification, "divine."
Now Thomas repels any suggestion that Aristotle actually
identifies the element in man which is divine, with what is
simply divine. For, obviously, what is simply and absolutely
divine is God  The divinity of man must be, from Thomas'
point of view, qualified and contingent  We must see how
he maintains this view in the face of Aristotle's text. First it is
necessary to quote the passage in which Aristotle concludes
that happiness is identical with contemplation  "If happiness is
activity in accordance with virtue, it is reasonable that it should
be in accordance with the highest virtue, and this will be that
of the best thing in us. Whether it be reason or something else
that is this element which is thought to be our natural ruler
and guide and to take thought of things noble and divine,
whether it be itself also divine or only the most divine element
in us, the activity of this in accordance with its proper virtue
will be perfect happiness."[34] Let us note the following concerning the foregoing passage. Aristotle does not specifically say at
this point whether reason is or is not the best thing in us, but he
leaves no doubt on that question elsewhere, nor does Thomas
have any doubt about that. It is a separate question however
whether the best thing in us (which is, of course, reason) is
divine, i e., participates directly in the divine nature, or whether
it is only the most divine thing in us, i e , approaches more
nearly the divine nature than any other part of us  In other
words, is the most divine thing in us simply divine, or is it only
like what is divine?  The answer seems perfectly plain and unambiguous, as far as this passage is concerned, and we believe
in the Ethics as a whole as well. Aristotle does not decide the
question. He says that in either case the activity of this element,
in accordance with its proper virtue, will be perfect happiness.
The decision on this problem is apparently considered by Aristotle to be a metaphysical question, belonging outside the
sphere of ethics proper. The reason it belongs outside the
sphere of ethics is that, whatever the status of the best thing in

us, 1 e , whether it is actually divine, or only most like what is divine, its activity will be perfect happiness Aristotle does not say that, if the best thing in us is only quasi-divine, its perfection is relative to quasi-divinity, but imperfect relatively to the higher perfection of simple divinity. He says that its activity *is* perfect happiness [85] There is no hint even that Aristotle regarded the virtuous activity of what was best in us here and now as inadequate for meeting the requirements of what he understood happiness, in the best sense, to be But let us suppose that Aristotle did believe (although he does not clearly say so in the *Ethics*) that the best thing in us attains only to a likeness of the divine nature, implying that our faculty of knowing is of necessity limited to an imperfect kind of knowledge, as different from God's knowledge as the blind men's account of the elephant is from that of a person with vision Would it follow that he believed that the other kind of knowledge is accessible to man in another existence? It is impossible to infer from the present passage that Aristotle regarded this inferior kind of knowledge as being inferior from the point of view of happiness The only question from Aristotle's point of view would be whether the universe, and reality, is so constituted that man's nature permits him to know the truth the way God knows it, or in an inferior manner Whichever turns out to be the case, *that* knowledge is man's happiness. To say that the inferior manner of knowing leaves man with an unsatisfied desire for the more perfect kind of knowledge is not, from Aristotle's standpoint, an effective argument to the contrary. It is true that Aristotle maintains that no natural desire is vain But it does not follow that a desire for what is beyond man's nature would be admitted by him to be a natural desire A man may desire many things that are beyond his natural capacities, as Aristotle says in Book III,[36] mentioning immortality in particular He may desire to fly like a bird, or run like a deer. And anyone who became obsessed by any such desire would as surely be frustrated as someone who became possessed of a desire to see God in his essence, *if* such a desire exceeded the natural capacity of man. To wish for what is beyond our capacity is, from the point of view of natural reason, as represented by Aristotle, to wish for what is impossible, to wish that reality be different from what it is. But, as knowledge is an actualization of what is real, a wish for reality to be different from what it is, in order that we may know it, is a wish that can lead only to insanity For reality, in the strict sense, is what is of necessity, what cannot be otherwise. The nature of man, as a determinate species (apart from all individual men as such) exists of necessity. To wish the nature of man to be different is to wish an essential ingredient of reality to be different But this would not be essentially different from wishing that man was so constituted that he could fly like a bird, or run like a deer To cultivate such desires, in both cases (as in the cases of other desires, which grow by being indulged, either in imagination or fact) would lead to being enslaved to the desires, and, where the desires are incapable of fulfilment in reality, to frustrations and hallucinations.

Now let us state Thomas' comments on the question as to whether the best thing in us is divine, or only most divine The signs of the excellence of the intellect, Thomas says, are shown by a comparison with higher beings, namely, divine things This comparison, he says, is two-fold first, according to habitude, as only the intellect has knowledge of things essentially good, which are divine things, second, the human intellect is compared with divine things, according to "connaturalitatem," as it shares a common nature with them, which is different according to the differences of the sciences [37] Here Thomas distinguishes the habit, or virtue, from the activity in accordance with the virtue. Intellect as a habit is divine in the sense of being proportioned to a divine object, but the activity of the mind is even more "of a nature" with the divine objects toward which it is directed But, as we shall see from the next comments, Thomas does not mean that this "connaturalness" of reason and its divine objects is in any sense an identity

Thomas then grasps the horns of the dilemma, and first attacks the Averroists *certain* persons, he says, have said that the human intellect is eternal and separate. [If it were eternal, all intellect would be one, and the same intelligence would have to serve all individual men, who come into existence and perish, therefore there would be no such thing as an individual mind, only individuals having mind ] And according to them intellect would be divine in the sense that we call things separate and eternal divine. Others, however [meaning himself, inter alios], say that the intellect is part of the soul [meaning that there is a part of each individual soul, which is intellect or mind], *as does Aristotle* And according to this latter view intellect is not something simply divine, but it is the most divine of all the things that are *in us*, because of the greater agreement it has with the separate substances, inasmuch as its operation takes place without any corporeal organ [38] Thus Thomas gives an unequivocal answer, in the name of Aristotle, to a question which Aristotle deliberately does not answer in the *Ethics* [39]

In the light of this "decision" by Thomas we may return to the passage in which Aristotle speaks of man living the contemplative life, not in so far as he is man, but in so far as something divine is in him Thomas, commenting, says that man in contemplating does not live as man, i e , as composed of diverse elements, but according as something divine is in him, namely, as he participates in a *similitude* of the divine intellect And again, when Aristotle says that the life of the mind *is* divine in comparison with human life, Thomas says that it is *in a way* divine [40] Then comes the one great passage of the *Ethics* in which Aristotle apears to speak favorably of the idea of immortality "But we must not follow those who advise us, being men, to think of human things, and, being mortal, of mortal things, but must, so far as we can, make ourselves immortal, and strain every nerve to live in accordance with the best thing in us "[41] Thomas comments  the Philosopher says that this is false [that we should aim at human wisdom etc.] because man ought to *intend* immortality as far as he is able, and in his whole life, as far as possible, make himself live according to his intellect, which is the best of those things that are in man, *which is indeed immortal and divine* [42] In other words, where Aristotle says we should *make* ourselves immortal [Thomas' Latin text has *"facere,"* which bears the same sense as "make" in English], Thomas substitutes *"intendere,"* which means aim at, direct one's self toward, or act with a view to. But aiming toward something is not the same thing as achieving it, and "make" carries the sense of achievement. The reason Thomas substitutes *"intendere"* for *"facere"* is clear from the sequel the intellect is said by him to *be* immortal and divine. In other words, it is immortal independently of any efforts we make We cannot *make* ourselves immortal if we already *are* immortal But, we must ask Thomas, if we already are immortal what sense is there in Aristotle's saying that we should *make* ourselves immortal? [43]

Let us return now to Thomas' attack on the Averroists There are two other places in the commentary in which he also singles them out, although not by name, for criticism The first occurs in the comments on the passage in Book I where Aristotle asks "whether happiness is to be acquired by learning or by habituation or some other training, or comes in virtue of some divine providence or again by chance", and continues "if there is any gift of the gods to men, it is reasonable that happiness should be god-given." [44] Now from the passage on the gods in Book X [45] we know that the activity of the divine nature is contemplative and nothing else, according to Aristotle Yet in his paraphrase Thomas says, "if happiness is not sent *immediately* by God, but comes as a result of virtue, etc ," thus suggesting the possibility that happiness *is* sent *mediately*, and hence providentially. What Aristotle actually says is that *if* there were divine providence, it would be reasonable to assume that happiness would be god-given. He does not attack the popular notions of the gods, but shows the element of truth in them, and, by implication, the element of untruth, in saying that "even if it is not god-sent but comes as a result of virtue and some process of learning or training    [it is] among the most god-like [literally, most divine] things " As we shall see, the question of the immortality of the soul is closely connected with that of divine providence, as well as that of the eternity of the visible universe. Thomas' insistence that Aristotle does not deny providence, even when he does not affirm it, is a sign of his keen awareness of these connections But we have shown that Aristotle explicitly denies providence in the most crucial passages, and Thomas' persistent suggestion that he does not deny it, in peripheral passages, is of no force.

But if happiness comes as a result of learning or training, "It will also on this view be very generally shared, for all who are not maimed as regards their potentiality for virtue may win it by a certain kind of study and care "[46] Thomas comments as follows  "This view [that happiness is a result of virtue, which nearly all may share] is agreeable with respect to happiness inasmuch as the end of any nature is common to all those who share that nature  For nature does not fail from what it intends, except in a few cases  And thus if happiness is the end of human nature, it is fitting that it be common to all or most of those having human nature  And this is made possible if it is due to a human cause " And then, after some further paraphrasing, the following  "from the aforesaid it is clear, that the felicity concerning which the Philosopher is speaking, does not consist in that "*continuitate ad intelligentiam separatam*" [i e , being joined or united to the separate intellect], through which man knows all things, as *some* have stated, for this does not come about in many, rather in none in this life."[47]

Before discussing these comments of Thomas, we will set forth his last important reference to the view of Averroes in the commentary on the *Ethics*  This occurs in Book X, in the final discussion of happiness, in which Aristotle proves that the wise are most dear to the gods  The context is similar to that

of the passage in Book I discussed above. "For *if*," Aristotle
begins, "the gods have any care for human affairs, as they are
*thought* to have, it would be reasonable . etc "[48] And Thomas,
paraphrasing "If it be supposed that God has a care and providence for human things, *as is the truth of the matter*, etc "[49]
And when Aristotle, in continuing, says "it is reasonable that
*they* should delight in that which was best and most akin to
them [i e , reason]," Thomas says "it is reasonable that he [i e.,
God] be pleased concerning men by that which is best *in them*,
and what is 'cognatissimum' [this is an exact translation of
what is called "akin" in the English, and means, literally, born
together, or of the same blood or nature], that is, 'simillimum,'
most like God "[50] In other words, where Aristotle says that the
reason of the gods and man is "cognate," Thomas interprets
"similar," again shifting the emphasis away from the identification of God and man It must be stressed, however, that we
do not argue that this identification *can* be made without qualification, because the *Ethics* is not conclusive on this point,
rather it seems deliberately inconclusive, as has been shown
above In another passage of Book X Aristotle says "while the
whole life of the gods is blessed, and that of men in so far as
some *likeness* of such activity belongs to them ," thereby
lending some support for Thomas' interpretation But, again,
in the passage immediately preceding the one just quoted, Aristotle says "and of human activities, therefore, that which is
most akin [again, "cognatissima"] to this [the activity of God]
must be most of the nature of happiness "[51] It might be argued
that Aristotle simply used the terms "cognate" and "similar"
indiscriminately, and this may, in a sense be said It is true in so
far as he has not decided the issue as to whether human thought,
in its perfection, is similar to or identical with divine thought
But it is hardly imaginable, after Aristotle has stated the issue
so clearly, that he would fail to be aware of the importance of
lending color to one view or the other in an indiscriminate use
of qualifying terms On the whole, "cognate" predominates

over "similar." Thomas, however, does not suggest that the two terms are interchangeable, rather he implies that the former is always reducible to the latter. This is made doubly emphatic in the foregoing comment by the words "in them" which have been italicized Thomas stressing that God cares most for what is best *in man*, and obscuring the fact that at one point Aristotle had said that what is best in man *is* divine This is again emphasized in the next paragraph of the commentary, when, after Aristotle has said that "they [i e , the gods] should reward those who love and honor this [i.e., reason] most," he comments "The wise man loves and honors intellect, which is most loved by God *among human things* "[52] Thomas never relaxes his effort to prevent the identification of human and divine reason.

Aristotle concludes this passage on the relation of the wise man to the gods as follows "He, therefore, is the dearest to the gods And he who is that will presumably be also the happiest, so that in this way too the philosopher[53] will more than any other be happy." Thomas, in his comments, says that he is most happy who is most loved by God, who is the fount of all good things, and it follows that as happiness is spoken of with reference to what is loved by God, the wise man is most happy. From which it is clear, Thomas concludes, that Aristotle places human happiness in an operation of wisdom [*sapientia*], as described in Book VI, and not in the "continuatione ad intelligentiam agentem," i e , being joined or united to the agent intellect, as *some* [Averroists] have imagined And finally "it must be noted that in this life *he* [i e , Aristotle] does not posit perfect happiness, but only such as befits human and mortal life, whence as he said in the first book, happy *as men*, etc."[54]

Now we may note the following First, Thomas pronounces, in Aristotle's name, in the last passage quoted, the dictum that perfect happiness is not to be had in this life. But we have already shown that Aristotle does say, that the virtuous activity of the best thing in us "will be perfect happiness "[55] Second, that Thomas quotes an apparent qualification by Aristotle, but that this qualification is drawn from a passage in Book I, but applied by Thomas to the happiness described in Book X. But what is the context of the passage in Book I? The theme is whether a man can be called happy before he is dead, and beyond the caprice of fortune's wheel But it is plain that Aristotle is speaking there primarily of the moral life, because he has not at this point even considered the contemplative life When in Book I he takes up the various types of life which might be identified with happiness, he says that he will consider the contemplative life at a later place, and in fact does not consider it explicitly until the middle of Book X [56] That he refers to the moral life in the passage Thomas takes in evidence is partly shown by the fact that he takes the misfortunes of Priam as a supreme example of the kind of turn of fortune's wheel which prevents one from calling a man happy until he is dead Priam, of course, is an example of a non-philosophic man.[57] But if we examine Aristotle's solution to the problem of how we can tell whether a man is happy before he is dead we will see a distinction that Thomas does not make A happy man, Aristotle says, is one "who is active in accordance with complete virtue and is sufficiently equipped with external goods, not for some chance period but throughout a complete life " But, he continues, must we not add "and who is destined to live thus and die as befits his life?" But, it must be asked, who *is* destined thus to live and thus to die? The answer is, *no one* It has been sufficiently shown that there is no doctrine of particular divine providence in the *Ethics,* but there is a doctrine of chance, or real contingency in the events of the sublunar world, in the second book of the *Physics* It would follow that no one is *destined* to happiness, although some may by good fortune actually live and die happily But Aristotle says in the same passage "the future is obscure to us, while happiness, we claim, is an end and something in every way final " If this were true it would follow that we cannot call anyone happy who is subject to fortune. Now it would be reasonable to suppose that Aristotle uses the expression "destined" in this context, in the same way in which he speaks, in the chapter that follows, of the good or bad fortunes of friends having "some" effects on the dead. It is the same dimension of opinion that considers the supreme acts of the practical virtues as achieving immortality. We saw that the idea of the supreme acts of moral virtue being rewarded with immortality is partly true and partly false. it is false that the acts of *moral* virtue are so rewarded, but it is not simply untrue to say that the acts of virtue are so rewarded. That immortality *is* the reward of the highest virtue of the highest part of the soul is indicated by Aristotle in Book X. This fact is reflected in an incorrect, but not completely false opinion, on the moral level. Of course, the immortality that is somehow possible is not personal. But in the same sense as immortality is possible, a perfect happiness beyond the reach of fortune is possible. For the activity of speculative wisdom, according to Aristotle, is relative to the objects of knowledge "that are highest by nature," and these are "of necessity", and they are eternal, ungenerated and imperishable.[58] Now, it is not necessary to insist upon Averroes' interpretation, that the mind of the wise man is simply identical with the objects of speculative knowledge and hence with God, when it is active, to see that the contemplative life is far freer from fortune's wheel than the moral life. All practical or moral actions are directed toward man and his works, friends, children, country. Even works of art, or philosophic treatises, these we *know*, even if they survive millennia, must some day pass away. But the wise man's attachment is to something that cannot pass away. And, as the objects of his supreme attachment are beyond the reach of fortune, so is he, in this most important sense, beyond its reach. Thomas does not make any distinction between the relation to fortune of the happiness of the moral life and that of the contemplative life. And therefore his comment in Book X, referring to the qualification of the moral life in Book I, and applying it to the contemplative life, is entirely indiscriminate.[59] Such a failure of judgment, however, was implicit from the beginning of our analysis, when it was shown that Thomas did not observe, or account for, the process of development within the whole *Ethics*

### F THOMAS AGAINST AVERROES

Let us now consider more specifically Thomas' attack on the Averroists' doctrine concerning the separate intellect, in so far as that attack takes place within the commentary on the *Ethics*, and in so far as that implies a distinct judgment on Thomas' part as to the meaning of the *Ethics* We must emphasize, in regard to this most sensitive and controversial issue, that we are not here concerned with the truth of Averroes' teaching concerning the soul, or of Thomas' We are only concerned in establishing Thomas' interpretation of the *Ethics* and in assaying the validity of that interpretation As stated in chapter II,[60] a reliable interpreter is one who does not arrogate to himself superior knowledge in the act of interpreting, indeed, a serious interpretation is always one which seeks light from the author being interpreted Our primary concern is with Aristotle, and our concern with Thomas is due to his great prestige as an interpreter of Aristotle, and to the fact that he apparently agrees with the principle stated above, and presumably approaches the text of the *Nichomachean Ethics* with the purpose of establishing exactly what Aristotle meant Of course, Thomas possessed principles which he considered superior to those of Aristotle, namely, those he believed were revealed by God in the Old and New Testaments, and handed down by the church But, according to Thomas, natural reason has a proper function within a sphere of its own, and it is very important to know that teaching on its own terms, and from its own point of view Thus political science makes use of military science, and the latter is subordinate to the former But it does not follow that the statesman knows what the best strategy and tactics are The general, qua general, knows better than the statesman what is

the best military way of achieving a given military objective
The statesman, besides setting the goals for the general, may
rightly overrule the general, because of non-military considerations which are deservedly of greater weight But that does
not mean that the statesman is a more competent judge of military matters [61] One example of this distinction in the commentary occurs in Thomas' remarks on Aristotle's statement regarding magnificence—that it is concerned with expenditures
for the gods[62]—when he says that "Here the Philosopher is
speaking according to the custom of the gentiles, which, the
truth having been made manifest, has been abrogated Whence
if anyone *now* should spend anything for the cult of a daemon,
he would not be magnificent, but sacrilegious "[63] Here Thomas
certainly implies that in the absence of revelation the actions
described by Aristotle *are* virtuous, according to the teaching
of natural reason The teaching of natural reason is now over-
ruled in this particular by divine revelation. But Thomas is not
prevented, in this case, from pointing out what the teaching of
natural reason is, according to Aristotle, independently of its
later alleged abrogation Thus Thomas does not here prevent us
from seeing what is *still* the teaching of natural reason, on the
basis of Aristotle, for those who, like Aristotle, have not been
illumined by the light of revealed truth

To return to the separate intellect, Thomas' attack was two-
fold first, in the earlier passage (paragraph 170 of the commentary), he said that the Averroist doctrine of the separate intellect was inconsistent with Aristotle's statement that happiness
will be very generally shared For, said Thomas, the continuity
with the separate intellect is that through which a man knows
all things. But this happens to few, rather none, in this life Yet,
this objection of Thomas to the Averroists falls to the ground
for the evident reason that it fails to take into account the distinction between the happiness of the moral life and that of the
contemplative life We have seen how Thomas indiscriminately
applies the qualification Aristotle places upon happiness, in con-

nection with fortune, to both kinds of life In the same way he disregards the fact that it is only the happiness which is "in a secondary degree" happy,[64] which, according to Aristotle, is very generally shared  It is this secondary kind of happiness which Aristotle, in Book X, emphatically says befits our "human estate," and which is contrasted with the divine status of the contemplative life  The happiness which is in this sense human is generally shared, and it is also in this sense that our happiness, being human, is particularly at the mercy of fortune's wheel.

The second prong of Thomas' attack on the Averroists was that the activity of the separate intellect, by which it knows all things, was not possible in this life. This objection, however, depends upon the identification of the separate intellect with the individual immortal soul  In the later passage (paragraph 2135) Thomas explains his position by saying that Aristotle places human happiness in an operation of wisdom, and not in "continuity with the agent intellect, as some imagine."[65] What the issue is here we may easily apprehend from Thomas' remark in the very next paragraph (2136), namely, his oft-repeated theme that perfect felicity *according to Aristotle* is not possible in this life  If the activity of the intellect is possible in the manner interpreted by the Averroists, then, to the extent that it happens, the happiness Thomas says is reserved for another life is possible in this one. From this point of view personal immortality becomes both impossible and superfluous.

Let us see what Thomas' grounds are, as stated in the commentary, for contradicting the view that there is an activity of the intellect, possible in this life, which *is* the highest form of happiness. In paragraph 2084, Thomas distinguished two postulates of the position he attacks  that according to it the human intellect is *eternal* and *separate*. Thomas admits that what is eternal and separate (from all matter) is in a way divine  But, says Thomas, the intellect is *part* of the human soul, according to Aristotle. And from this point of view it is not *simply* divine, but only the most divine thing in us, because it is like the separate substances, in that its operation takes place without any bodily organ Thus Thomas, interpreting Aristotle, implies that the intellect is immaterial, but not eternal Let us take this together with Thomas' statement in paragraph 2107, that the intellect *is* immortal. We thus see that Thomas interprets Aristotle's position as implying that the intellect is immortal, but not eternal But if the intellect is not eternal it must, from Aristotle's point of view, have come into being, it must have been generated And if it was generated it *must* perish In Book VI Aristotle says that "things that are of necessity in the unqualified sense are *all* eternal, and things that are eternal are ungenerated and imperishable "[66] It is hardly necessary to collect passages in which Aristotle equates the immortal with the eternal.

In Book III of *On the Soul*, however, he speaks of intellect thus "Actual knowledge is identical with its object in the individual, potential knowledge is in time prior to actual knowledge, but in the universe as a whole it is not prior even in time Mind [i e , intellect] is not at one time knowing and at another not. When mind is set free from its present conditions it appears as just what it is and nothing more this alone is immortal and eternal (we do not, however, remember its former activity because, while mind in this sense is impassible, mind as passive is destructible), and without it nothing thinks "[67] Here Aristotle distinctly identifies the mind that is in us, even if only potentially, with a mind which is apart from us as individuals, and which is eternal He distinctly refers to its former activity —meaning evidently before our birth as individuals—but says that the part we remember with is mortal That is reasonable, for a mind that is eternal and always active does not need a memory Now grave difficulties exist as to whether or how far Aristotle thought that the activity of mind in mortal men ever attained to the condition of seeing itself "as just what it is and nothing more " But there is no reasonable doubt that Aristotle regarded the activity of this eternal mind—to the extent that we are able to make it active in us—as the best thing in ourselves, and that our making ourselves immortal depends on this and this alone. Nor does Thomas' attempt to distinguish between the operation of wisdom and that of the separate intellect constitute a real objection. Consider the following from the treatise just quoted "Once the mind has become each set of its possible objects, as a man of science has ..." Here the operation of wisdom is identified with that of the separate intellect, an operation whereby the mind, through the action of the agent upon the passive intellect, "becomes," i.e, becomes *identical* with its objects [68]

There seems little doubt that Thomas virtually imputes to Aristotle his own view that human souls are brought into being by creation, which is the only way in which he could consistently speak of them as not eternal yet immortal What Thomas says is, however, absolutely inconsistent with manifest Aristotelian doctrine. The view he is attacking, however, is not, in the particular cited, inconsistent with what we can assert with confidence to be true of Aristotle

Thus Thomas agrees with Averroes that the intellect is immortal and divine, but is inconsistent (as an interpreter of Aristotle) in saying that it is not eternal. If it is eternal, however, there can be only one intellect for all men, inasmuch as individual men, and hence individual souls, are always coming into being. Then if all men share intellect, what they share is not something merely common to them, but identical for all. Thomas labors to prevent this conclusion, but it is inevitable if intellect is eternal But if this is true, personal immortality is impossible on an Aristotelian basis, and is inconsistent with such basis.

As to Thomas' contention, that Aristotle says that intellect is only part of the soul, we refer to our remarks concerning the ambiguity of "man" As we saw, Aristotle distinguishes our "composite nature," in accordance with which we live a distinctly "human" life (the moral life), from the divine thing in us which is not composite and which, although small in bulk,

surpasses everything else in worth.[69] This latter thing, reason
(i e, the activity of the intellect), "more than anything else is
man "[70] Thus there are here two distinct meanings of "man".
qua composite, and qua non-composite and divine. Intellect is
clearly a part of the soul according to the former meaning of
man. But, according to the latter meaning, its status as a mere
part cannot be maintained unequivocally. We conclude then
that Thomas' charges against the Averroists in the commentary
correspond with distortions in his interpretation of the doctrine of the *Ethics*, and of Aristotle's philosophy in general

# CHAPTER VIII

## NATURAL RIGHT AND
## NATURAL LAW

### A. STATEMENT OF THE PROBLEM

WE PROPOSE now to discuss Thomas' comments on the subject of natural right in the fifth book of the *Ethics.* Before doing so, however, some preliminary observations on his discussion of this subject elsewhere than the commentary on the *Ethics* may not be inappropriate We noted in our introductory chapter[1] that the doctrine of natural law is the basis of what might today be called Catholic social science Moreover, it was noted that Thomas is the classic exponent of that doctrine, and Aristotle his chief authority for the teachings of natural reason. Natural law, according to Thomas, is the rational creature's participation in the eternal law, i.e , that participation possible to natural reason It is contrasted with eternal law, by which God rules the entire universe, and divine law, which is revealed by God directly and not through reason alone (although the same things may, incidentally, be contained in both divine and natural law, e g , the second table of the Decalogue). The existence of natural law is presumably attested by Scripture in the words of St Paul "When the Gentiles, who have not the law, do by nature those things that are of the law, these, having not the law, are a law unto themselves."[2] Aristotle is the supreme example of a Gentile who had not the law, yet who, aided only by his own powerful intellect, sought to understand nature's intentions with regard both to man and the universe as a whole That Aristotle may have been wrong about the universe as a whole is quite understandable, from Thomas' point of view, inasmuch as Thomas believed that the universe as a whole was not intended to be understood by

167

man in this life, nor in the next without the assistance of divine grace But Thomas did believe that man had a natural end,[3] imperfect compared with his supra-natural end, but attainable by the perfection of man's merely natural faculties, and congruent with, although not a sufficient preparation for, his other-worldly end Presumably Aristotle is a sufficient guide to that merely natural end, and presumably the Thomistic doctrine of natural law, qua natural, cannot be based on principles which were not equally available to Aristotle Moreover, unless he corrects Aristotle, it is only reasonable to assume that Thomas understands his own natural law doctrine to be identical, in principle, with the moral doctrine of Aristotle Yet Thomas nowhere, to our knowledge, criticizes Aristotle as a teacher of what may be known by unassisted natural reason regarding human actions [4] All his explicit "corrections" are based on apparent contradictions in Aristotle's text, which he resolves in terms of Aristotle's own principles [5]

Yet a curious fact strikes one in examining the plan of the *Summa Theologica* It is that the subjects of law and justice occur in different major subdivisions of the work Law is treated in the First Part of the Second Part, and justice in the Second Part of the Second Part. Moreover the term "jus" (the object of justice, usually translated "right" in English, but sometimes "law") seems hardly to occur in the treatise on law, whereas the converse is true in the treatise on justice, where "jus" is common but "lex" is uncommon. Nor is there anywhere a discussion of the precise relation between "jus naturale" and "lex naturalis "[6] Now this is not unimportant because there is nowhere in Aristotle's *Ethics* or *Politics* any mention of natural *law*. There is only a single doubtful mention of natural law in the *Rhetoric* [7] But in the context of a discussion of the means of forensic persuasion one can draw no serious conclusions from it alone The reason why there is no mention of natural law in Aristotle may be gathered from Thomas' own definition of law "Law is nothing else than a certain ordinance of reason for the common good, by him who has the care of the community, and promulgated "[8] There are four criteria for a law that it be reasonable, for the common good, made by one responsible for the community, and promulgated. But of these four criteria only two could possibly be said by Aristotle to emanate from nature· reasonableness and goodness, which are really correlative terms. The other criteria depend upon a *legislator*, which, in the case of a natural law, would mean a divine legislator An ordinance is imposed, says Thomas, "on others," which would imply providence Without particular divine providence there can be no doctrine of natural law in the Thomistic sense But such a natural law doctrine implies divine revelation because the fact (as distinct from the possibility) of divine providence, is evidently not naturally known to all men But to be binding the natural law must be known in its legal character, that is, it must be known *to be promulgated*.[9] Yet, for one who was perhaps the wisest of the pagans to deny this crucial premise of the natural law—as Aristotle does in denying particular divine providence—would certainly seem to suggest that the legal character of the natural law is most immanifest to unassisted natural reason.

But, it may be objected, while the strictly legal character of the natural moral order may not have been visible to Aristotle, natural right comes to virtually the same thing Man's natural end, it may be said, is reached partly through moral perfection This perfection means happiness, so far as that is possible for most men, and is a contribution toward happiness even for philosophers. To fail to be virtuous is to fail to be happy, and thus it may be said that violations of the demands of the virtues lead automatically to punishment. As virtue is its own reward, vice is its own punishment For the order of natural morality to be called natural right rather than natural law makes no great difference it has a quasi-legal character all the same This argument would roughly parallel that of Plato's *Republic:* that justice is the health of the soul, and as such is intrinsically good and choiceworthy for its own sake. Moreover, the implication is that every fully rational man would choose justice, as he would choose health.[10] There is, however, this difference. a person who does not pay heed to the demands of nature in the sphere of bodily health usually learns rather quickly from experience what those demands are, at least in an approximate way. But how does one learn what the rules for the health of the soul are? If it be said that experience teaches us "honesty is the best policy," and "crime does not pay," one need only refer to the ring of Gyges in Glaucon's great speech in the second book of the *Republic,* to point up the irrelevance of this answer. The crucial point is this. we do not need any experience, in the sense in which the rules of prudence are derived from experience, to know that bodily health is good, and similarly with "intelligence, sight, certain pleasures, and honors."[11] We know intuitively that they are desirable, even apart from any result that may come from them. But, the question is, is moral virtue of this character? "All men," Aristotle says at the beginning of the *Metaphysics,* "by nature desire to know" and all men desire by nature to be healthy, for the same reason that they desire to live. But do all men by nature desire to be morally good?

Now if all men by nature desired moral excellence, in the same way that they desired knowledge and health, it would follow that they had the same intuitive knowledge of moral virtue and its goodness that they have of health and theoretical knowledge. We do not imply that Aristotle would say that there is natural knowledge of health like that of the physician, or of truth like that of the philosopher. The natural knowledge of health is that by which we know we are possessed of the desirable capacity to act as a healthy man acts (i e, we know when we are well and when we are ill)[12] And the natural love of knowing, as Aristotle says, is "shown by the delight we take in our senses ... and above all others the sense of sight . . [which] most of all senses makes us know and brings to light many differences between things."[13] The love of knowledge, and even the instinctive recognition of the character of all knowledge, that it consists in making distinctions, is shown in the behavior of little children. The question then is, is there anything in the nature of man (and particularly the child) which leads him to know the goodness and desirability of certain kinds of moral conduct, analogous to the way in which he is led to recognize the intrinsic goodness of theoretical knowledge, which is naturally appreciated as a result of the wholly natural operation of our senses and our power of making distinctions?

### B THE THOMISTIC DOCTRINE OF A NATURAL HABIT OF THE MORAL PRINCIPLES

Let us first see how Thomas answers this question in the *Summa Theologica* The first article on natural law[14] asks, whether the natural law is a habit. The answer is, natural law is not a habit in the strict sense, the sense in which it means that *by which* we know or do something But there is a secondary sense, the sense in which we say the doing, or knowing of something is a habit. In this sense, says Thomas, the natural law is a habit "Accordingly, since the precepts of the natural law are sometimes considered by reason actually, while sometimes they are in the reason only habitually, in this way the natural law may be called a habit So, too, in speculative matters, the indemonstrable principles are not the habit itself whereby we hold these principles, they are rather the principles of which we possess the habit " But, we must now ask, what is the character of the habit whereby the precepts of the natural law are held? Everything would appear to depend upon this. All the moral virtues are habits, according to Aristotle, "but *none* of the moral virtues arises in us by nature."[15] However, the precepts of the natural law are not themselves habits, but rather directions as to what we should do in order to acquire the virtues Aristotle says "we become just by doing just acts, temperate by doing temperate acts, brave by doing brave acts."[16] Presumably the precepts of the natural law tell us, Do brave acts! Do temperate acts! Do just acts! at the same time informing us, in a general way, as to what brave, temperate, and just actions are. The question, then, is whether there is a natural habit by which we are commanded to do the acts of the virtues, and by which we have a sufficient knowledge of these actions to be able to carry out the commands This would evidently *have* to be the case if the natural law is promulgated, and, of course, if it were not promulgated it would not have its strictly legal character

Thomas, of course, says that there is such a natural habit. In the passage quoted from article one of the question on natural law, it may be seen that he compares the habit whereby the precepts of the natural law are held to that whereby the principles of speculative reason are held. This intellectual virtue, called "intuitive reason" in our English translation, but also translated intellect, mind, or intelligence, is the only natural virtue. It is the habit of mind by which we grasp the first principles from which all demonstration starts, it supplies the premises gathered by induction from sense perception, and the principles of reasoning itself, e g, the law of contradiction The habit of knowing the things that we do know by intuitive reason we have from nature, we cannot be taught these things any more than we can be taught the law of contradiction, or to see or hear. Again, the question is, whether we know the precepts of the natural law by a habit as natural to us as that by which we know the data of sense perception, or that a whole is greater than any of its parts Thomas answers this question in the affirmative.

The second objection of article one is as follows· "Further, Basil says [a church father, not a philosopher] that the conscience or synderesis is the law of our nature, which can only apply to our mind. But synderesis is a habit, as was shown in the First Part Therefore the natural law is a habit." And the

reply "Synderesis is said to be the law of our intellect because it is a habit containing the precepts of the natural law,
which are the first principles of human actions." Note then,
that Thomas places synderesis on the same level as the intuitive
reason, as a habit which bears the same relation to human
actions as intuition does to human thought [17] We must now
turn to the First Part,[18] to the thematic discussion of synderesis,
to see if Thomas actually says that it is in us by nature The
question in the context there is, whether synderesis is a special
power of the soul distinct from other powers. The answer is
that synderesis is not a power, but a habit Thomas appears to
associate Aristotle with his decision on this point, by quoting
the Philosopher to the effect that "rational powers are related
to opposites. But synderesis does not regard opposites, but inclines to good only." Thus with Aristotle's help Thomas settles
the question that synderesis is a habit but not a power. He
never asks the question whether there is such a habit, or how
we know that there is such. The only authority distinctly cited
for the existence of synderesis is Basil. However, in the first
objection of the present article he mentions Jerome, as making
a division of the soul that included synderesis as a power. One
thing, however, is perfectly clear, namely that there is no mention of synderesis (or of any possible equivalent) by Aristotle.

Thomas' argument, in the body of the article just referred to,
is as follows "Now it is clear that, as the speculative reason
reasons about speculative matters, so the practical reason reasons about practical matters. Therefore we *must* be *naturally*
endowed with not only speculative principles, but also practical
principles Now the first speculative principles bestowed on us
by nature do not belong to a special power, but to a special
habit, which is called the 'understanding of the principles,' as
the Philosopher explains Hence, the first practical principles,
bestowed on us by nature, do not belong to a special power,
but to a special *natural* habit, which *we* call synderesis " Thus
Thomas borrows the idea of a natural habit of the principles

relative to the end, which Aristotle sets forth with regard to speculative knowledge, and says that the same thing *must* be true in the sphere of moral action. Why it must be true Thomas nowhere says. Nor does he offer any evidence *that* it is true.

### C. THOMAS' IDENTIFICATION OF NATURAL RIGHT AND NATURAL LAW

We will now see that Thomas imputes his own opinion to Aristotle in regard to this key feature of his natural law doctrine. It will be our final task to show that this imputation is incompatible with the teaching of the *Nicomachean Ethics* as a whole, as that teaching has been developed in the course of our interpretation. It will be necessary to quote extensively both text and commentary on the crucial passages concerning natural right.[19] Aristotle begins "Of political justice [i.e., the politically just, *jus*, the object of justice, distinct from the habit, *justitia*] part is natural, part legal." Thomas, in his comment, says the citizens do justly what nature imprints on the human mind, and what is laid down by law [20] But Aristotle has not said anything about nature imprinting or bestowing anything If it be granted that the principles of justice are implanted in us by habituation in the actions of the virtue, yet this implanting, according to Aristotle, is the result of moral education, and not any action of nature. But the subject of this chapter is not the virtue of justice, not that whereby any principles could be said to be imprinted, but the *justum politicum*, the politically just. Then Aristotle continues, "natural, that which has everywhere the same force and does not exist by people's thinking this or that." And Thomas " 'Justum naturale' is what has everywhere the same power and virtue *for leading towards the good and turning away from the evil.*"[21] Again, Thomas imputes an active agency to natural right, where Aristotle speaks only of its intrinsic rightness What Aristotle appears to us to mean, is that what is right by nature does not depend upon any human opinion for its *being right*

It is entirely a different matter to discuss the agency *by which* it is acted upon. Thomas continues. "this indeed happens [that natural right has everywhere the same force] because nature, which is a cause of just things, is the same among all But the just which is due to having been laid down by some city or prince, has power among them [i e., the citizens] to the extent of the jurisdiction of that city or that prince." But, Thomas continues, Aristotle explains this in another way when he says "that the 'justum naturale' does not consist in seeming or not seeming, that is, it does not arise from any human opinion, but from nature " And then comes the following crucial passage of the commentary "For just as in speculative matters there are certain things naturally known, as indemonstrable principles, and others closely following upon them (*propinqua*), and certain things that the industry of men finds out, and what follow upon them, *thus also* in matters of action there are certain principles *naturally known, as if* (*quasi*) indemonstrable principles and [others] linked to them, as, evil is to be avoided, no one is to be unjustly harmed, one should not steal, and the like Others are thought out by the industry of men, which are here called legally just "[22] Thus Thomas apparently takes Aristotle's statement, to the effect that what is naturally right or just does not depend on opinion, as an outright endorsement of his own doctrine that there is a natural habit of the understanding, by which *we know* what is, in principle, right and wrong according to nature

A problem is caused by Thomas' use of the expression "quasi" in the foregoing passage. It is not clear whether Thomas means that the principles of practical operations are "quasi-indemonstrable," in that they are capable of some demonstration, or that the concept of demonstration is only "quasi" applicable to practical principles, which are primarily precepts or commands, and not truths. The latter would appear to be the case In the passages in the *Summa Theologica* in which he draws the analogy of the habit of the practical principles and that of the *intel-*

*lectus,* Thomas speaks usually of "the principles" or "the principles naturally known." Here he speaks of the *indemonstrability* of the speculative principles and, as it seems to us, sensible of the defect in the analogy, calls the habit of the practical principles "quasi" indemonstrable Thomas appears in this context to regard the natural law as a kind of geometrical system.[28] In a system of geometry there are axioms and definitions, postulates required to operate with them, theorems deduced from the axioms, definitions and postulates, and corollaries inferrable from the theorems, and so apparently with the precepts of natural law. In the body of the article on synderesis in the *Summa Theologica* Thomas avoided using "indemonstrable" as applied to first principles. It is easy to see why An axiom or definition of speculative reason is not altogether like a precept of practical reason. A precept is a command. "Do this!" is a different kind of statement from, "This is white," or even "This is just." A person may recognize a given action as right or just, because it is demonstrably "equal," but persist in believing that, because justice is "another's good," he ought not to do it voluntarily and for the sake of being just. What makes a precept a precept is that we recognize it as having been commanded, or as being in some sense authoritative A command is an act of the will. But how do we know when a thing has been ordained? In the case of human law it is clear we are apprised by the agencies of the law as to what the law-making authority has willed But natural law is not human law to be apprised of an ordinance of a supra-human will it would seem necessary that we be informed by a supra-human agency Now how could this take place except through divine revelation? We can intuitively know an act of will only by a direct communication from the willing agent. We cannot even *know* what is morally right on the basis of a revelation handed down by others, we can only believe on that basis Even supposing that moral virtue is a means for happiness (although, as Thomas admits, on the basis of natural reason this is true only in a contingent sense),[24] and that we all necessarily want to be happy Does it follow that we know what moral virtue is? It would first have to be true that we all know what happiness is but the many identify happiness with sensual pleasure,[25] and even the arguments of the wise have no power to stimulate the masses to virtue "For these do not by nature obey the sense of shame, but only fear, and do not abstain from bad acts because of their baseness but through fear of punishment . and have not even *a conception* of what is noble and truly pleasant."[26] We must conclude, therefore, first, that it is a logical fallacy to call an act of the will an "indemonstrable" proposition, because what is willed is not of necessity, as what can be willed can be not-willed, and to know a thing which could have been otherwise depends upon experience of the event Thomas, we believe, was aware of this, and for that reason called the principles of the practical reason "quasi-indemonstrable." Secondly however, we must again insist that such evidence is never treated by Aristotle as being even within the realm of the possible, because it depends upon an act of particular providence, and in any case has nothing to do with "natural" doctrine. Thirdly, the notion that what is naturally right is so because it leads to happiness, toward which all men are naturally disposed, and that hence it is naturally known, is explicitly denied by Aristotle as regards the mass of mankind Whether or not the wise may be said to have a natural habit of the principles of practical action, distinct from the habit of intuitive reason, we shall shortly discuss

We have seen therefore that Thomas identifies Aristotle's doctrine of natural right with his own doctrine of natural law, but he ignores the tremendous difference implied in the distinction between "*lex*" and "*jus*," as well in the commentary as in the great *Summa* In the next passage of the *Ethics* Aristotle explains that what is legally just is what "is originally indifferent, but when it has been laid down is not indifferent." He gives four examples the price of a prisoner's ransom, regulations governing sacrifices to the gods, laws passed for individual cases, "e g., that sacrifices shall be made in honor of Brasidas,", and the provisions of decrees. Thomas, after carefully explaining the differentia of the legally just, then proceeds to tell how the legally or positively just "arises from the natural." That the one does "arise" from the other he testifies on the authority of Cicero's *Rhetoric*. The relevance of this authority is not explained. There are two ways, Thomas says, in which something can arise from natural right first, as a conclusion from premises [as the conclusions "arise" from the axioms and postulates in geometry], and these conclusions are part of natural right because they follow necessarily from the premises, but as natural right is always and everywhere the same this does not fit legal and positive right, and thus as it is an evident principle that no one is to be unjustly harmed, it follows that one should not steal, which indeed pertains to natural right. The second way in which something arises from natural right, says Thomas, is "per modum determinationis," by way of determination, and it is in this way that all positively or legally just things arise thus, it is naturally just that theft should be punished, but that it should be punished by this or that penalty, this is a matter for positive law.[27] But, Thomas continues in the next paragraph, one must attend to the circumstance that the legally just, according to the second mode, may arise from the natural in two ways one way with a mixture, and another without any admixture of human error, and this, Thomas says, is demonstrated by Aristotle's example For, says Thomas, it is naturally just that a citizen, who is captured through no fault of his own, should be rescued, and, consequently, that he should be redeemed but the determination of the price to be paid pertains to legal right which proceeds from the foregoing natural right without any error Moreover, it is naturally right that honor should be shown to a benefactor, *but* (says Thomas) that divine honor should be shown to man, and that sacrifice should be made for such, this is due to human error.[28] It would seem superfluous, in the light of the preceding chapter, to discuss the impossibility of an attack, upon Aristotelian grounds, in the name of morality, on the customs of pagan religion. The very idea of magnanimity we saw depended on the paying of divine honors to super-human virtue. And we saw above, on Thomas' own admission, that magnificence, one of the "great" virtues, involved great expenditures on sacrifices to "daemons" and heroes More important, however, is Thomas' insistence that natural right forms the framework for the legal code of all communities everywhere His assertion, to repeat, is this there are certain principles of natural right, which are naturally known by nearly all men everywhere [excepting only mental deficients, and those brutalized by extraordinarily corrupt customs], these give rise to an extensive code of right or just things, which are deduced from the principles, and are made legally just by enactment of the ruling authorities in political communities. These deductions from the principles of natural right are, however, still natural right, because they are as universally applicable as the principles from which they are deduced It is only the application of these universally, and hence naturally right precepts, to particular or local situations, that gives rise to purely legal right From this we would have to conclude, however, that the content of natural right *is* everywhere the same, and so, that the naturally just framework of every just legal code everywhere in the world would have to be the same. This, it must be noted, is a very rigid conception. An objection to it would appear to be contained in the famous passage which follows on the mutability of natural right.

In the most enigmatic passage of the *Nicomachean Ethics* Aristotle says "with us there is something that is just even by nature, yet all of it is changeable, but still some is by nature, some not by nature. It is evident which sort of thing, among things capable of being otherwise, is by nature and which is not but is legal and conventional, assuming that both are equally changeable. And in all other things the same distinction will apply, by nature the right hand is stronger, yet it is possible that all men should come to be ambidextrous." Thomas' accounting for the mutability of natural right follows one very simple principle natural right is true for the most part, but is not true in a few cases, for the same reason that nature generally succeeds in its intentions for the most part, but fails in a few cases. Thomas first gives the example of the man who has had a sword deposited with him, "and nothing seems more just than that a deposit should be returned", yet a sword should not be returned to a man who demands it in a rage, nor should money be returned to a traitor to his country, who would use it to buy arms.[29] That deposits be returned is naturally just in most cases, but the rule is altered in the few.[30] The reason why this is so, according to Thomas, is as follows "It is to be noted that the natures (*rationes*) of changeable things are unchangeable, thus anything natural to us as pertaining to the very nature of man, in no way may be changed. But what follows (*consequuntur*) our nature, as dispositions, actions, motions, are changed in a few cases And similarly these things which pertain to the nature of justice itself in no way can be changed, for example that one should not steal, which is to do what is unjust. But those things which follow are changed in the minor part."

That this explanation is quite inadequate we may now see According to the English translation, Aristotle says that the naturally and the legally just are equally changeable. Thomas' text says they are "*ambo mobilia similiter,*" i.e , both similarly changeable, or both changeable in like manner. The force of this we would construe in the same way as the English text. The point is that Aristotle makes no distinction between the changeability of natural and legal right. Thomas, however, emphasizes that natural right changes only "*in paucioribus*" and "*in minori parte*" The example of the change in the relative dexterity of the right and left hands is remarkable for its a-moral connotation. Thomas' examples are not of this character His examples and his explanation presuppose a failure of nature which causes a departure from the rule. Aristotle's example could be interpreted as suggesting a possible perfection of nature: although most men are naturally right-handed (or left-handed), it might be thought *better* to be ambidextrous. That men should be ambidextrous is a natural possibility, a possibility that may be realized under favorable circumstances.

Some light on what this possibility may be may perhaps be gleaned from the following. "Similarly, the things which are just not by nature but by human enactment are not everywhere the same, since constitutions are not the same, though there is but one which is everywhere by nature best" Here the mutability of *legally* just things is attributed to the variety of constitutions or regimes and not simply to the application of general rules to particular cases. But has not Aristotle also said in the first chapter of Book V that all legally just things are "in a sense" just?[31] Now, if they are only "in a sense" just, they are not simply just But, although the legally just is here contrasted with the simply just, the simply just is *in a sense* present in the legally just In other words, the legally just qua legal, is neither simply just nor simply unjust. But legal justice commands all the acts of all the virtues from the point of view of the common good, as conceived by any given political order or regime. But some political orders are better than others. Therefore, the general character of morality will vary from regime to regime. Now if the general character of morality varies, then the precepts of a universal code cannot determine what is naturally just for all men everywhere. Thomas' rigid scheme is inconsistent with Aristotle's principle that what is just is roughly equated with what is legally just, if what is legally just depends upon the nature of the regime and *not* upon a code of natural right. But what if it be supposed that the constitution or regime is a very poor one? We refer, first, to Aristotle's statement at the end of Book IV, concerning shame [32] the good man will defer to the standard of common opinion, even if it be wide of the truth. And, as to changing the constitution, we may quote a passage from the *Politics*, concerning revolutions: "And of all men those who excel in virtue would most justifiably stir **up** faction, *though they are the least given to doing so* "[33] Aristotle does not, of course, say that good men never revolt, but it is apparent that they would never do so except in extreme cases The good man, therefore, defers to the law of imperfect communities, and hence to its moral code, and what the good man does *is* morally right. In other words, not to obey the law and customs of one's community is usually unjust, and hence contrary to *natural right*. As natural right enjoins obedience to any legal justice which may reasonably be said to aim at the common good, it would seem to follow that for the most part, the mutability of natural right follows, *pari passu*, the mutability of constitutions

### D THE INCOMPATIBILITY OF THOMISTIC AND CATHOLIC NATURAL LAW AND ARISTOTELIAN NATURAL RIGHT

Natural right is said by Aristotle to be *part* of political right. It is not simply correct to say that natural right is the norm for legal right, because the relation is not simply that of superior to inferior, but of parts of a whole  The common good is the end of the political community  Some communities have very imperfect notions of what constitutes the common good, yet the preservation of that imperfect order may yield more of what is truly good than any attempted change  It may be that the given imperfect order is the best possible under the circumstances. It would then be naturally right to preserve that imperfect order, and even the man who had the naturally best for his standard would act accordingly.

Aristotle says that there is but one political order that is by nature best, and the best is best everywhere and always. But it does not follow that the best order of society is realizable everywhere and at all times  It is the standard for all moral and political judgment everywhere and at all times, but not in the way that Thomistic natural right or law is. The latter is everywhere immediately applicable, as a standard of right and

wrong, for the guidance of all legislators, as a test for all positive law, and even as a measure for all private morality. The
function of the best polity is perhaps best described in the opening paragraphs of the fourth book of the *Politics* Just as the
good gymnastic trainer knows what is the best regimen for the
person with the best natural endowment and equipment, so he
must also know what modified regimen is best for the person of
average physique, as well as what is best suited for various other
special circumstances. He must know what is absolutely best
first, of course, in order to know what the best adaptation is
under the various limitations imposed by circumstances on the
various handicapped bodies that he wants to help But just as
the diet and exercise that is best for the perfectly endowed
body might be crippling for many less well endowed, so a
political prescription that was not adapted to the individual
circumstances of times, places, and persons would be inappropriate What is best in itself is always and everywhere the same,
but what is right or just in any particular case depends upon
the particular circumstances If a deviation from the best polity
be regarded as a failure of nature, it is nonetheless true that
some deviation is what is right and just in nearly all cases for
Aristotle does not expect the best polity to be actual in many
places and at many times The natural equipment required for
perfection in the individual is extremely rare, "a result of some
divine causes. present in those who are truly fortunate "[34]
How much rarer still the conjunction that permits of such fruition for a whole society' What is naturally best is distinct from
what is naturally right The former is the standard to which
the wise legislator and statesman looks, in order to know the
true *direction* of all sound policy What is just, however, is
what is fitting here and now But to attempt to apply what is
best to all polities would be as doctrinaire and impractical as to
write medical prescriptions from a textbook without considering the bodily condition of the individual patient

The lack of connection of Aristotle's doctrine of natural

right, with the Catholic Natural Law, as expressed by Thomas, can be readily inferred from some of the precepts which supply the content of the latter and which are most widely known today In the best polity described in books seven and eight of the *Politics* it is explicitly stated that it is the function of the legislator, to "direct his attention above all to the education of the youth, for the neglect of education does harm to the constitution The citizen should be moulded to suit the form of government under which he lives "[35] As, according to Aristotle, the political community is the most perfect kind of human community, the art of "politike" is supreme over "oekonomike," and the statesman to the head of the household The family is prior to the state in order of generation, but not in order of perfection It is with a view to the perfection of the latter that the life of the former must be regulated, and the notion that the head of the family has an independent natural right to educate his children, because the family is "prior" to the state, is entirely alien to Aristotle's thought.[36] Similarly with birth control Aristotle explicitly says that population limits shall be decided by law, and abortion procured, if necessary, to keep within the limits set.[37] It is reasonable to assume that, if he sanctions abortion, he would not object to easier methods of keeping population within limits, by preventing unnecessary conceptions. In the passage just referred to Aristotle also requires exposure of deformed children which, under the heading of euthanasia, would be absolutely forbidden by the Catholic Natural Law. These instances, however, do not mean that the practices Aristotle considered fitting for the best polity would be universally applicable, certainly birth control would be forbidden where population was a radical necessity, and education under parental guidance might be considered preferable to that of an inefficient public school system. There is no rule or precept of natural right, according to Aristotle, which may not change with circumstances.

E THE ULTIMATE DEPENDENCE OF MORALITY ON THE
THEORETICAL PRINCIPLES

That there is no evidence that Aristotle held to the notion
that there was a habit of the principles of practical reason comparable to intuitive reason, we have seen. We shall briefly present evidence that such could not have been his view, and that
from his point of view the only possible natural habit of understanding is that of the speculative principles We quoted
above the passage in which Aristotle said that the mass of mankind do not have even a notion of what is by nature noble.[38]
We may also note the passage in the *Politics*[39] in which Aristotle
clearly says that the virtue of the subject, as distinct from that
of the ruler, is only true opinion. "The subject," says Aristotle,
"corresponds to the maker of flutes and the ruler to the flute-
player who uses them " The man who possesses the virtue of a
ruler is the one whom Aristotle calls a good man, but he must
possess the virtue of practical wisdom However, only a few
people can be expected to be wise, although many can be virtuous (i e., as subjects). Yet if all had a habit whereby they *knew*,
in principle, what was good and bad, the many too could become good This is what Thomas implies is the case, but it is
explicitly denied when Aristotle says that the most that the
many can hope for is true opinion. Prudence, or practical wisdom, is for Thomas exclusively concerned with discerning the
right means to the right ends This is what Aristotle also says is
its function, but Aristotle understands the function of practical
wisdom in a wider sense. A practically wise man is one who understands what happiness is, and why the virtues are good. He
alone *knows* that they are good, because he alone knows the
end for the sake of which they are good [40] But does the wise
man have a natural habit of these moral principles? Here we
must distinguish the "phronimos" from the "sophos," the practically wise from the simply or philosophically wise man If the
"phronimos" believes that the life of moral virtue is simply the

happy life, then he too is living within the dimension of opinion, because, according to Aristotle, this is not simply true. If,
however, he understands that the happiness of the moral life is
happiness only in a secondary sense, then the happiness at
which he will aim primarily will be that of wisdom proper, in
other words he will, in principle, be a "sophos," and not merely
a "phronimos." But the only natural principles leading to wisdom proper are those of intuitive reason, and it is only in the
light of wisdom proper that one can *know*, as distinct from
opining, the truth about morality, as well as of the supra-
moral sphere of human existence.

This ultimate dependence of all knowledge, moral as well as
theoretical, upon the theoretical principles alone has been
adumbrated in the previous chapter by the progression of moral
"ultimates" from natural and common virtue to friendship [41]
And we saw that the perfection of friendship depended upon
philosophic activity. In the famous demonstration of the necessity of friends, at the end of Book IX, the crucial minor premise
of the first syllogism, is that human life is defined by reference
to the power of perception or thought. The idea is the same as
that in the opening lines of the *Metaphysics*, quoted above.[42]
The necessity of friendship is then strictly derived from the
goodness of the activity which arises from the natural habit of
the speculative principles But friendship is the perfection of
justice, which itself is the perfection of all the moral virtues.
Hence the perfection of all the moral virtues is ultimately
derived from the principles of the speculative reason.

## F. CONCLUSION

In chapter II[48] we said that Thomas rarely, if ever, attempts
to explain any statements of Aristotle except in terms of other
of his statements, and that nothing extraneous to the *Ethics* is
permitted to serve as the basis for interpretation of the *Ethics*
We must, perforce, now qualify this by saying that, although
Thomas never appeals to any non-Aristotelian principles to

interpret Aristotle's words, he nonetheless imputes non-Aristotelian principles to Aristotle, although treating them as if they were Aristotelian. We conclude then that Thomas' assumption as to the harmony of natural and revealed doctrine, at least in so far as Aristotle is to be considered a representative of the former, is entirely unwarranted. Thomas' "success" in creating the appearance of such harmony, is due, we believe, entirely to his imputation to Aristotle of such non-Aristotelian principles as the following·

1. Belief in divine particular providence.
2. Belief that perfect happiness is impossible in this life.
3. Belief in the necessity of personal immortality to complete the happiness intended, evidently, by nature.
4. Belief in personal immortality
5. Belief in the special creation of individual souls.
6. Belief in a divinely implanted "natural" habit of the moral principles

These principles are all at least virtually imputed to Aristotle in the course of the Commentary, as we believe has been shown  In view of Thomas' standing as a "harmonizer" of philosophy and revealed theology, and his apparently sincere conviction concerning the independence of the two within their proper spheres, we may well suppose that he made the fewest possible slips or errors in borrowing from the one to interpret the other  Yet all the principles listed above are principles of revealed theology  It is hardly necessary to emphasize their importance in Thomas' system of revealed theology [44]

We also conclude, then, that the objections to Aristotle's moral and political philosophy, upon which we laid such emphasis in chapters II and III,[45] have no weight whatever. The facts of observation, which Aristotle explicitly made the supreme criterion of his doctrine, do not bear witness against him.

Thomas, certainly, does not make the apparent differences between pagan and Christian ethics seem other than real differences, except by making the principles of Christian ethics, as he understood them, serve actually, if not avowedly or consciously, as the basis of his interpretation of Aristotle's *Ethics*.

# POSTSCRIPT

THE intention of this study was not to enter into a critical discussion of the enormous secondary literature on the relation of Thomism to Aristotelianism. That would require another study, at least as long as the present one In view of the fact that our conclusions have been based on an original analysis of sources not heretofore, to our knowledge, the subject of any similar inquiry, this would seem permissible. We would like, however, to notice a book published after the present study was completed, and which supports at least the premises of our thesis regarding the relation of Thomism to Aristotelianism in the sphere of moral philosophy. In *A History of Philosophy*, Vol II, *Mediaeval Philosophy. Augustine to Scotus*, Fr. Frederick Copleston, S J., makes a number of remarks indicating the opinion that Thomas has misinterpreted Aristotle in some of the decisive points emphasized in the present study. The reader is urged to consult the whole of the excellent account of Thomas' philosophy by Fr Copleston, and in particular the discussion of the "latent tensions" in the Thomistic synthesis (a discussion which runs throughout the account and is not confined to the section bearing that heading) There is room here to quote only a few typical passages.

Concerning the end of human life, Copleston says flatly, that "What Aristotle calls happiness, St Thomas calls imperfect happiness or temporal happiness or happiness as attainable in this life."[1] According to Copleston, there is no question but that, according to Aristotle, man's end is to be acquired in this life "as far as the ethics of Aristotle is concerned there is no hint of any vision of God in the next life."[2] Concerning the controversy with the Averroists, Copleston remarks that "St Thomas interprets the notoriously obscure passage in Aristotle's *De Anima* as teaching the individual character of the active intellect in individual men. It is impossible to say with certainty that the Thomistic interpretation of Aristotle is wrong, though I incline to this opinion."[3] Our opinion on this point, as will have been seen, is less reserved, because we regard as decisive Aristotle's assertion that mind is eternal, and his repeated assertion that it is identical (in actuality) with eternal objects.[4]

Concerning the notion of a natural desire for eternal life[5] Copleston has this to say "In the *De Veritate* (27, 2) St. Thomas says that man, according to his nature, has a natural appetite for *aliqua contemplatio divinorum*, such as it is possible for a man to obtain by the power of nature, and that the inclination of his desire toward the supernatural and gratuitous end (the vision of God) is the work of grace. In this place, then, St. Thomas does not admit a 'natural desire' in the strict sense for the vision of God, and it seems to me only reasonable to suppose that when in the *Summa Theologica* and the *Summa contra Gentiles* he speaks of a natural desire for the vision of God, he is not speaking strictly as a *philosopher*, but as a theologian and philosopher combined, that is, presupposing the supernatural order and interpreting the data of experience in the light of that presupposition."[6] This valuable reference to *De Veritate* establishes two propositions contended for in the present study that in the two *Summae* Thomas speaks not as philosopher simply, but, on the other hand, that it is still possible, according to Thomas himself, to speak as philosopher simply. It should hardly be necessary to emphasize that, however, in the commentary, Thomas does not speak as a purely philosophic interpreter.

But what is a "combined" philosopher and theologian? Clearly, one who subordinates philosophic to theological principles, and interprets the data of philosophy from the viewpoint of theology. But can the data of philosophy, thus interpreted, be still described as philosophic? The issue is well expressed by Copleston "I do not think that St. Thomas is considering the hypothetical state of nature at all when he speaks of the *desi-*

*derium naturale* [i.e , in the sense presupposing grace], and if this is so, it obviously means that his moral theory is not and cannot be a purely philosophical theory. His moral theory is partly theogical and partly philosophical  he utilizes the Aristotelian ethic but fits it into a Christian setting  After all, Aristotle was himself considering man in the concrete, as far as he knew what man in the concrete actually is, and St. Thomas, who knew much better than Aristotle what man actually is, was fully justified in utilizing the thought of Aristotle."[7] Copleston, himself speaking as a divine, quite properly attributes to Thomas a superior knowledge of "what man in the concrete actually is." But it is equally clear that the measure of this superiority is not the measure of philosophic knowledge. The superior knowledge to which Copleston alludes is the knowledge of man's fall and redemption  But clearly, this is knowledge supplied by faith, which, on Thomas' own principles, is a special gift of God, whereas philosophic or scientific knowledge is knowledge which is intrinsically capable of communication to all men everywhere, because it is based on evidence which all men everywhere can see with their own eyes, without any special act of Providence.

Concerning the more specific question of ethics, Copleston writes as follows  "Finally, one can point out that St. Thomas's realization of God as Creator and supreme Lord led him, in company, of course, with other scholastics, to recognize *natural* [our italics] values which Aristotle did not envisage and could not envisage once given his view of God. To take one example, that of the virtue of religion (*religio*). Religion is the virtue by which men pay to God the worship and reverence which they owe Him as 'first Principle of the creation and government of things.' ... Aristotle [however] did not look upon God as Creator nor as exercising conscious government and providence, but regarded Him as the final Cause alone. The virtuous man of Aristotle is, in a sense, the most independent man, whereas the virtuous man of St Thomas is, in a sense, the most dependent man, that is, the man who realizes truly and freely expresses his relation of dependence on God [i e., a personal God who governs human affairs]."[8] First, in regard to the word *natural*, as used above, Copleston follows Thomas in this usage, but clearly, it represents a transference to the word of a new meaning, a meaning with which natural reason alone could not have endowed it. In regard to this very virtue of *religio*, Thomas himself says,[9] "even in those things which order us in relation to God, some are moral (precepts), which reason itself *'informed' by faith,* (*fide informata*) dictates as that God is to be loved and worshipped." It is difficult to avoid the conclusion that the entire notion of natural law, in the Thomistic sense, is— in fact if not in intention—a dictate of reason "informed by faith." For the specific differences between the Thomistic and Aristotelian conceptions of God are not the differences between two equally philosophic notions If unassisted natural reason could have arrived at the conception of a personal Deity, consciously governing the world, why should Thomas have thought that reason would stand in need of faith in order to recognize the obligations of divine worship? According to M Gilson,[10] Thomas "certainly identified" Aristotle's "fundamental principles . with those of natural reason itself." But assuredly nothing in Aristotle's philosophy is more fundamental than his conception of God. If Gilson is correct concerning Thomas' attitude toward Aristotelian principles, as we believe, then Thomas' arguments in support of his conception of God would be arguments of reason "informed by faith," and not of reason simply.

This essay is devoted to what the author considers the fundamental problem of present-day social science The urgency of the need for an adequate social science today stems from the nature of present-day political problems No one doubts that these problems are global in scope The contest that is joined today will certainly be decided, in part at least, by the nature of the convictions that reasonable men, and men of good will,

in all lands, can be brought to share. Obviously the view that
any opinion as to what is good is equally good, the characteristic tenet of present-day positivism and relativism, cannot supply a frame of reference within which differences can be reasonably composed [11] But our social science, if it is to be of any
use, must be addressed to Moslems and Jews as well as to Christians, to Buddhists and Hindus as well as to believers in the
Bible, it must, finally, be addressed "not only to those who enjoy the blessings and consolation of revealed religion, but also
to those who face the mysteries of human destiny alone."[12]

# NOTES

## CHAPTER I

1. See especially Leo Strauss, "The Social Science of Max Weber," *Measure*, spring, 1951, pp 204–30

2 E g , the choice between a sales tax and an income tax ultimately reflects the choice between democracy and oligarchy.

3. In effect, this means that pragmatists grant equal rights in full only to other pragmatists.

4 ("Loeb Classical Library"), p xxiv.

5 That is, he admits the truth, or correctness, of that part of the *Ethics* which has been bred into the Englishman's moral nature, without wondering what principle it is that enables him to discriminate the sound from the unsound

6. Cf. Plutarch, in his *Life of Alexander*, Dryden trans ("Modern Library" ed ), p. 801 "Aristotle ... speaks . of these doctrines as in fact both published and not published as indeed, to say the truth, his books on metaphysics are written in a style which makes them useless for ordinary teachings, and instructive only, in the way of memoranda, for those who have been already conversant in that sort of learning " It is not unlikely that, if this remark is true of Aristotle's *Metaphysics*, it applies in only a lesser degree to the *Nicomachean Ethics* Compare Plato *Seventh Epistle* 341B–342A, esp the following "But thus much I can certainly declare concerning all these writers, or prospective writers, who claim to know subjects which I seriously study, whether as hearers of mine or of other teachers, or from their own discoveries, it is impossible, in my judgment at least, that these men should understand anything about this subject There does not exist, nor will there ever exist, any treatise of mine dealing therewith But were I to undertake this task it would not, as I think, prove a good thing for men, save some few who are able to discover the truth for themselves with but little instruction" (Plato's *Epistles* ["Loeb Classical Library"], pp 531, 533). Although neither of these statements has the authority of completely authenticated texts, they express the conception of the "two teachings" which seems to have been basic for all pre-modern interpreters From this point of view, the conflicting interpretations of both Plato and Aristotle, which have characterized the whole tradition stemming from them, would be evi-

dence, not (necessarily) of lack of clarity on their part, but of the fact that their works were read and interpreted by both philosophers and nonphilosophers But Plato and Aristotle, who did not believe that every man could be a philosopher, provided for this contingency by seeing to it that no interpretation could claim to be authoritative, just because it would always be contradicted by another interpretation This would prevent nonphilosophers from replacing the test of truth with that of authority. For real philosophers there never could be any authority but the truth itself

7 Cf Prologue to Part I

8. This does not mean, of course, that any correction of Aristotle by Thomas is due to his holding certain doctrines by faith alone There is no reason why Thomas may not have criticized Aristotle in the same way that Aristotle criticized Plato The question is whether, to the extent that Thomas himself identifies Aristotle's teaching with natural reason itself, he represents it accurately or is forced into "accommodations "

9. I here follow the view of Professor Pegis (*Basic Writings of St Thomas Aquinas* [New York  Random House], Introduction, p xlix), that the commentaries, above all, represent "a long and minute effort to arrive at the real thought of the Philosopher "

10  II 2. 129. 3, repl obj. 5.

11 Paragraph 764  All references to the *Commentary on the Nicomachean Ethics*, by Thomas (hereinafter referred to as "Commentary") are to the edition edited by Pirotta, published by Marietti (Turin, Italy, 1934) and to the numbered paragraphs therein It is my general practice throughout to quote Thomas indirectly, to bring out his meaning as clearly as possible Even in quoting indirectly, however, I have tried to translate literally, without consideration for English style All italics, in direct or indirect quotation of Thomas or Aristotle, are my own References to Thomas' Latin text are to the *Versio antiqua* which accompanies the *Commentary* The first words of each passage of the text are repeated by Thomas in the body of the *Commentary*, which is evidence that this is the version Thomas actually used The *Versio antiqua* was traditionally ascribed to William of Moerbeke, but recent scholarship inclines to the view that it was done by Robert Grosseteste

## CHAPTER II

1 Aristotle *Nicomachean Ethics* (hereinafter cited as "*NE*") 1098$^a$29 ff  Unless otherwise specified, all references to the *Nicom-*

*achean Ethics* and translations from it are from the edition translated by W D Ross ("Student's Oxford Aristotle," Vol. V [Lon-
don Oxford University Press, 1942])

2. Cf above, chap 1, pp 1-4 Compare the following, from
Judge Goddard's charge to the jury in the Hiss perjury case (*New
York Times*, January 21, 1950) "Reasonable doubt does not mean a
possible doubt or a fanciful doubt It means a doubt which is reasonable in view of the evidence or lack of evidence.... It is not necessary for the Government to prove the guilt of the defendant beyond
all possible doubt. If that were the rule, very few people would ever
be convicted It is practically impossible for a person to be absolutely
sure and convinced of any controverted fact which, by its nature,
is not susceptible of mathematical certainty. In consequence the
law says that a doubt should be a reasonable doubt—not a possible
doubt . . . If, after a careful and full consideration of all the testimony, and the exhibits, you are convinced of the defendant's guilt,
and such conclusion is one in which you yourself would be willing
to rely upon [*sic*] and to act upon in the more important matters
of your own private life, then it may be said that you have no reasonable doubt." One must, of course, note that juries decide questions of fact, not questions of right. However, the question of moral
certainty would be the same The method of Aristotle's *Ethics*
suggests that there is an implicit consensus on general principles of
right upon which all reasonable men would act, in Judge Goddard's
sense.

3. We must underscore this point In what follows we do not
imply that Aristotle's teachings are identical with right reason and
that therefore every deviation of Thomas necessarily implies a
corruption of truth or a conflict of reason and revelation. Obviously, this study would not make sense if it were possible to assume
that every deviation from Aristotle was a corruption of the truth
it would imply that we knew what the truth was, and hence knew
that Aristotle was right But if we knew this, there would be no
reason to turn even to Aristotle for guidance It is only the *possibility* that Aristotle may have known the truth about things that
we find baffling that leads us to study him with all seriousness

4 *NE* 1104ᵃ10

5. Cf above, p. 6.

6 Cf. above, n. 2.

7. P. 6.

8. *Leviathan*, chap. xlvi, p. 374 (folio pagination).

9. Cf. Philipp Frank, *Foundation of Physics* (Chicago University of Chicago Press, 1946), p 2 "Aristotle's philosophy of physics is a petrifaction of a physical theory which covered the experiences of Greek and oriental artisans about physical phenomena." What Frank means, of course, is that Aristotle's doctrine of natural ends, or nature working for ends, is a "theoretical" expression of the artisan's tendency to ascribe to invisible beings the same agency in the production of natural things as the artisans have in producing artificial things Presumably, thus, Aristotle's *Physics* is just another expression of the conception embodied in Gen 2 7 This is only a short step from the Hobbesian view of Aristotle It might not be an altogether inappropriate comment on Frank's objection to Aristotle that, whereas Aristotle's physics covers the experience of artisans, modern physics does not.

10. *NE* 1098$^b$9.

11. *Ibid* 1145$^b$ ff.

12. ("Loeb Classical Library"), p 376, note b.

## CHAPTER III

1. *NE* 1107$^a$30

2. *Ibid.* vii 3, esp. 1147$^a$1–10 and 1147$^b$11–19

3. E g, *Commentary*, pars 1119–25.

4. Cf Plato's *Apology* 34E, 36B, and Matt. 27 12–14, Mark 15 3, Luke 23 9 It has been assumed here, gratuitously to be sure, that Socrates is a legitimate example of what Aristotle would consider the highest human type, but to any objection we reply, as we believe Aristotle would, "If Socrates cannot serve as an example, who can?" Actually, we know from Aristotle's elegy to Plato ("who alone or first of mortals clearly revealed, by his own life and by the methods of his words, how a man becomes good and happy at the same time," quoted by Jaeger, in his *Aristotle* [Oxford, 1934], p. 107) that he reserved the very highest praise for him, and there can be no question as to who the model of human perfection was for Plato.

5. Cf Shakespeare, *King Henry V*, Act IV, scene 1 "I am afeard there are few die well that die in battle, for how can they charitably dispose of any thing when blood is their argument."

6. *Social Contract*, Book IV, chap. viii ("Everyman's" ed , p 119)

7 The extreme formulation of the nature of justice is in Plato's *Republic* (414 ff ), where the citizens are taught that they are literally children of the soil of the fatherland (or motherland) that is,

that their native land and fellow-citizens have natural claims upon them which cannot be compared to any other natural claims. In other words, the citizen's nature shares no common bond with anyone outside the city, and morality is thereby limited to the city. That the idea of the community of all mankind through reason was not a later, Stoic discovery is shown by Hippias' speech in the *Protagoras* (337C-D) That Plato rejected this as an inadequate basis for a practical moral teaching does not necessarily imply an inadequate understanding of the doctrine itself

8 Socrates' "contract" with the laws of Athens, as sketched in the *Crito*, indicates the imperfect obligation to obedience due to the laws of an imperfect city. There is, and can be, no contractual obligation to obedience in the *Republic* The obligation to obey wisdom is perfect, without any contract. The obligation of the wise to obey the unwise is at best problematic

9 This does not mean that there would be no principles of natural justice between all men as men but that the perfection of justice was considered possible only in the political relationship and hence that all relations of justice were considered derivative from this For the Christian, all duties of man to man are considered ultimately to be derived from duties to God and hence not to rest on a political foundation There is no foundation for justice as such, in Aristotle, independent of civil society

10. *NE* 1134$^{b}$19

11. This is not contradicted by the distinction between the good man and the good citizen Cf below, pp. 181, 182, concerning how the good man will act in an inferior polity

12 *Summa theologica* i 2. 58 5

13 *Ibid.* 66. 3.

14. *Ibid.* 66 5.

15 *Ibid.* ii 2 45 3, where Thomas says that the wisdom (*sapientia*) that is a gift of God is both theoretical and practical, but not the wisdom that is a virtue in the Aristotelian sense Concerning the difficulty this raises for Thomas' natural law doctrine see below, chap viii, n 10, p 222.

16 *NE* 1141$^{b}$20

17 In what sense it would be obligatory upon them would seem to present a problem if they are obliged to be morally virtuous because they are incapable of true wisdom, then their obligation would arise out of an imperfection But the good qua good is some-

thing perfect What kind of good is it, then, that requires imperfection as a condition of its goodness? That this problem is fundamental may be seen from the fact that the gods, who are truly good, would not possess moral virtue (cf *NE* 1178$^b$7 ff.)

18 *Ibid* 1140$^b$6

19 Cf above, pp 8, 9

20 We do not wish to seem to have posed a false problem for Thomas in the foregoing. It is not implied that Thomas thought there was no difference between a pagan ethics based purely on natural reason and Christian ethics The theological virtues, having for their end an end different from the natural virtues, would differ as that end differs We do imply that Thomas assumed that the full realization of the virtues devoted to the one end would in no way necessitate an inhibition of the virtues devoted to the other end—an a priori assumption not warranted by natural reason alone. The view we impute to Thomas is implicit, we believe, in the following quotation from a distinguished present-day Catholic writer "As grace does not destroy nature, so the institution of the Church has not destroyed the spontaneously natural aspirations of man to a good political society, and this society is as autonomous as the social instinct that produces it. Again, as the harmony of nature and of grace presupposes their enduring distinction, so the harmony of the two powers is conditioned by the fidelity of each to its own nature and end" (Father John Courtney Murray, "Governmental Repression of Heresy," *Proceedings of the Catholic Theological Society of America*, p 34). Aristotle's *Ethics* we take to be what Thomas regarded as the most adequate expression of the ethics of that natural political order to which Father Murray refers But when, in the sequel to the foregoing, Father Murray writes that "grace completes nature, not by invading the order of nature but by elevating it," he also makes the assumption we have ascribed to Thomas, but which cannot be made on the basis of unassisted natural reason—the only basis permissible for social science. That is, nature elevated by grace is different from nature simply, just as reason "informed" by faith is different from reason simply In other words, the harmony which is, in fact, alleged to exist, is the harmony of elevated nature and grace. But an ethics of elevated nature is not the same thing as an ethics of nature It is the purpose of this inquiry to discover whether Thomas can show that the ethics of nature simply is not inconsistent with, or incompatible with, an ethics of grace or elevated nature.

## CHAPTER IV

1. *Commentary*, par. 1

2. W. D Ross, *Aristotle* (London Oxford University Press, 1926), p 236, quoted by Sabine, *A History of Political Theory* (New York Henry Holt & Co, 1937), p 89

3 *Phaedrus* 264C Cf *Poetics* 1150$^b$25–36, where Aristotle discourses on the necessity governing the sequence in a well-constructed plot It is not unreasonable to suppose that he would apply this criterion to every kind of serious writing.

4. See below, pp. 48 ff.

5. *NE* 1115$^a$5–1117$^b$20.

6 *Commentary*, par 583

7 See Table 1 (p 38) The two tables accompanying this chapter were prepared independently of those in the Marietti edition.

8 ("Loeb Classical Library"), p 192.

9. *Commentary*, par 1954

10. *NE* 1095$^a$1–10.

11. Cf Henry Adams, *Mont St. Michel and Chartres* (New York Houghton Mifflin Co, 1905), on the architectural character of Thomas' theological system, esp. pp. 345 ff.

12. I e, in the sense that, as one lays one brick on another, the building progresses toward completion, while a growing organism, although also progressing toward perfection, "develops," i.e., discloses new potentialities.

13 *NE* 1122$^a$35.

14. Thomas does, in his own way, recognize this, as he notes that courage and temperance are virtues of passions we share with the brutes, while the passions connected with wealth and honor are distinctively human (and hence "higher") Yet the fact that he recognizes this makes even more remarkable his failure to emphasize the whole "ascent." Of course, in his own doctrine magnanimity, e g, is presented as a part of courage (*Sum. theol* II. 2. 129 5), which would be simply incompatible with Aristotle's view as we conceive of it here.

15. I have, throughout, used the literal rendering "magnanimity," instead of the "pride" of the Ross translation.

16. *NE* 1119$^a$22.

17 *Ibid* 1119$^a$25.

18. *Commentary*, par 1292

19 *NE* 1145$^a$15

20. *Ibid* 1117$^b$1–20

21 *Ibid* 1104$^b$5–9

22 *Ibid* 1169$^a$17–26 Thomas notes that these two passages treat of the same theme, but he does not note the differences in treatment Compare *Commentary*, pars 591 and 1879, 1880

23 *Ibid* 1175$^b$15–20, compare with 1104$^b$5–9

24 A sufficient reason is, of course, found in the fact that continence is not a virtue, although it is a "good" state The specious forms of courage are, after all, forms of courage Continence is not a form of temperance

25 *NE* 1117$^b$16–19

26 This is not strictly true, as a moral action is defined by the end for the sake of which it takes place, and the end here is different In a sense, the truly brave action is more difficult because it involves more mental stress, i e , a higher degree of practical wisdom, but in the external sense they both, i e , the truly brave man and the citizen-soldier, act in identically the same way in the same situations The crucial point in the resemblance of the two is in their relation to pleasure and pain for both, the act of cowardice would outweigh in pain the act of courage This is not true of the other specious forms of courage

27 *NE* 1169$^a$18–25.

28 Cf *The Eight Chapters of Maimonides on Ethics*, trans and ed Joseph I Gorfinkle (New York Columbia University Press, 1919), chap vi, pp 75 ff Maimonides' solution of the difficulty is as follows the things called "evils" by the philosophers are the things that all people agree are evil—the things Thomas would include in Natural Law—and Maimonides agrees that the person who desires these things, e g , theft, robbery, fraud, even while abstaining from them, is inferior to the person who has no such desires But, he says, the things contained in the ceremonial law, e g , partaking of meat and milk together, a man should desire and he should refrain from them solely because the Law has forbidden him Compare also Kant, *Foundations of the Metaphysics of Morals*, trans L W Beck (Chicago University of Chicago Press, 1949), esp. pp 58 ff Kant represents the theological vein in its extreme form (without the theological motivation), in representing an action as having moral worth *only* when it is in opposition to, or at least totally unconnected with, our inclinations. Perhaps a still better representation of the theological vein is that of the modern Catholic spokesman, Msgr. Fulton J Sheen The following is from an ar-

ticle in the *New York Times*, February 27, 1950 "Referring to the Gospel record of Christ's temptation by the Devil, Msgr. Sheen warned his hearers against being discouraged by temptation 'There is no sin in being tempted, no matter how often it occurs,' he declared He added that persons who resisted temptation acquired merit and that temptation 'keeps us humble ' " The foregoing, it seems to us, is a perfect illustration of the opposition of Aristotelian and Christian ethics. Msgr. Sheen distinctly elevates continence over temperance Moreover, humility, the sense of our imperfection, is said to be a good thing Compare Aristotle's magnanimous man, to whom "nothing is great" ($1123^{b}33$) and his good man, who would never be ashamed of himself ($1128^{b}26$)

29 *NE* $1178^{b}15$.

30. Luke 15·7.

31 I.e., as the brave act may result in death, it cannot lead to any further end for the brave man. Of course, by saving the lives or freedom of others, the brave man may contribute to a further end. But life and freedom, while conditions of the good life, are minimal conditions, temperance is one of the most difficult conditions

32. *NE* $1177^{b}26$.

33. In Xenophon's discussion of Socrates' virtues, courage is not even mentioned. Cf *Memorabilia* 1 5, where temperance is spoken of as the foundation of virtue.

34 *NE* $1103^{b}15$-20

35. *Ibid* $1116^{a}26$

36. *Ibid* $1146^{a}34$-$^{b}2$

37. Cf above, p. 34, concerning the relation of appearance and reality in moral matters

## CHAPTER V

1. Above, p. 47

2 *NE* $1095^{a}16$, $1097^{b}21$.

3 *Ibid* $1095^{a}$ ff

4 Cf below, pp. 73, 74.

5. This has already been shown, to some extent, in the case of temperance and continence.

6. See Table 2, *a"*.

7 Above, pp 51, 52

8. *Commentary*, par. 536.

9. *Virtus determinatur secundum ultimum in potentia.*

10 E G , i 2. 55, 1, obj. 1, *ibid. 55. 3*, 56 1. O.t c , 64 1, obj. 1, 66. 1, obj 2.

11. 281ª6–20

12 *NE* 1094ᵇ19–23.

13 *Ibid* 1104ª1–5.

14. Above, pp 54, 55.

15 *NE* 1129ᵇ25–30.

16 *Ibid* 1155ª25.

17. *Ibid* 1115ᵇ6.

18 *Commentary*, par. 536.

19 *Ibid* , par 590

20. Compare Hobbes, *Leviathan,* on "fear of powers invisible," e g "This perpetuall feare, always accompanying mankind in the ignorance of causes, as it were in the Dark, must needs have for object something And therefore when there is nothing to be seen, there is nothing to accuse, either of their good, or evill fortune, but some Power, or Agent Invisible." And the following "The force of Words, being ... too weak to hold men to the performance of their Covenants, there are in mans nature, but two imaginable helps to strengthen it. . . . The passion to be reckoned upon, is Fear, whereof there be two very generall Objects one, The Power of Spirits Invisible, the other, the Power of those men they shall therein Offend" (pp. 53, 71, folio pagination), cf. Gibbon, *Decline and Fall of the Roman Empire,* chap 1 ("Modern Library" ed., I, 5) "To the strength and fierceness of barbarians, they added a contempt for life, which was derived from a warm persuasion of the immortality and transmigration of the soul "

21. *Commentary*, pars. 531 ff

22 See Table 1, passage 11, *NE* 1115ª32.

23 *Commentary*, par. 537

24. Cf. *Summa theologica* ii 2 123 5, repl obj. 1.

25 *Commentary*, par 538

26 *NE* 1115ª31.

27. *Commentary*, par 539

28 Cf *Prior Analytics* 70ª3

29 Cf. *NE* 1094ᵇ7–10 and *Commentary*, par 30

30 E g , the religious martyr, or, in the purely political realm, there are other deaths for the sake of the common good which might be considered equally brave, like that of the spy Or consider the case Aristotle mentions later, of the man whose family is in the hands of a tyrant. Macduff, in Shakespeare's *Macbeth*, made a far

greater sacrifice in leaving his family in the power of the tyrant than anyone could have made on the field of battle.

31 *Commentary*, pars 537, 538, 539.

32. *NE* 1129$^b$15.

33. *Ibid* 1129$^b$20.

34 *Ibid.* 1135$^a$4, cf *Politics* 1281$^a$36 "But what if the law itself be democratical or oligarchical?"

35 *NE* 1129$^b$12 "Evidently all lawful acts are *in a sense* just acts." Thomas takes especial note of this qualification in the comments on this passage. Every law, he says, is relative to a given polity. But not every polity is simply just but is just relative to its own conception of justice. In a democracy this is relative to the notion of liberty, which treats the citizens as equal in all respects because they are equal in freedom But this is not simple justice, but relative justice (par. 901). Thomas' interpretation of this passage in Book v agrees with our interpretation here. This, we believe, emphasizes the correctness of our criticism of Thomas, because he fails to apply the consequences of this interpretation to the analysis of courage

36. Cf Plato's *Republic* 1. 351D, also Chaucer, *The Canterbury Tales*, "The Pardoner's Tale."

37. We do not mean that a man may not be above the requirements of common bravery, even if he is only an average citizen in a good community, or that he may not be critical of the goodness of his community The point is that, even if he is critical of his community, he is not for that reason *braver* than the soldiers of the bad community American soldiers were undoubtedly more critical of their government than Hitler's soldiers were of theirs. They were not, however, for that reason braver

38. *NE* 1115$^a$14, cf. *Politics* 1256$^a$35, where Aristotle treats brigandage as one of the natural modes of acquisition.

39 This low order of moral requirement on the level of ordinary citizenship is well expressed by Shakespeare, in *King Henry V*, Act IV, scene 1

KING HENRY (*in disguise*) "I could not die anywhere so contented as in the King's company, his cause being just and his quarrel honorable."

WILLIAMS "That's more than we know."

BATES "Ay, or more than we should seek after, for we know enough, if we know we are the King's subjects; if his cause be wrong, our obedience to the King wipes the crime of it out of us."

The courage of the king is higher than that of the subjects because the former involves responsibility for the justness of the cause.

40 The element of paradox in this position is fully exploited by Plato Cf above, n 35, but note also *Republic* x. 619B–E, where it is implied that the morally virtuous in good and just communities are potential tyrants.

41. *NE* 1144$^b$ ff.

42. This common-sense view of courage is presented by Plato (who seems to reject it) in the *Protagoras* (349D) The eminent Sophist is the speaker "Well Socrates," he replied, "I say that all these are parts of virtue, and that while four of them are fairly on a par with each other, courage is something vastly different from the rest. You may perceive the truth of what I say from this you will find many people extremely unjust, unholy, dissolute, and ignorant, and yet pre-eminently brave " Compare Plato *Laws* 963E.

43. Cf. *NE* 1103$^b$26–28

44 *Ibid* 1117$^b$9–12

45 Pars 596, 597

46 *NE* 1100$^a$1–5

47. *Commentary*, par. 589. We may note that our interpretation of the preceding paragraph of the text follows the line of Thomas' comments at this point.

48 Cf above, pp. 54, 55

49. *NE* 1117$^b$13.

50 To take note of the "perhaps" is not without the authority of Thomas himself. See the *Commentary*, par. 414 "And he [Aristotle] uses the adverb of doubt [i e., perhaps], as he does in many other places in this book, because of the lack of certainty in the subject matter of morality " Thus Thomas attributes the ubiquity of the *adverbium dubitandi* in the *Ethics* to the *incertitudo moralis materiae*, which Aristotle so frequently warns against in Book 1 But, although Thomas thus interprets the weight of the *adverbium dubitandi* in the *Ethics* as a whole, he does not interpret its specific weight in the different contexts in which it appears. But it is only following his own principles for the interpretation of the *Ethics* to inquire into the nature of the reservations demanded by the uncertainty of the subject matter in each individual case This is what we are inquiring into here, and such inquiry, we hope to show, would have demanded of Thomas a revision of the general plan of his whole critique

51 *NE* 1117$^b$17.

52. Cf. Macaulay's judgment of Halifax as a man of action, in his *History of England* ("The Student's Macaulay" [New York Hurd & Houghton, 1874], Vol IV), chap xi, p 208 "He was slow from very quickness For he saw so many arguments for and against every possible course that he was longer in making up his mind than a dull man would have been. Instead of acquiescing in his first thoughts, he replied on himself, rejoined on himself, and surrejoined on himself Those who heard him talk owned that he talked like an angel but too often, when he had exhausted all that could be said, and came to act, the time for action was over." This, of course, is a humorous exaggeration of the point we wished to make above, but the valid observation can be seen in the exaggeration.

53. That is, as a virtue relative to certain kinds of action, the lower kind of virtue would be "higher," as a duller man would have been a better minister than Halifax (n 52, above).

54 Above, pp 71, 72

55. Above, p 83

56. *NE* 1144$^{b}$25-1145$^{a}$1

57 "Oportet autem parum transcendere" (*Commentary*, Lectio XI, Book vi).

58 *NE* 1145$^{b}$1-7, see above, pp. 20 ff , cf *NE* 1098$^{b}$9 ff , in which Aristotle shows how his opinion "harmonizes" those of the wise, the many, and the gentlemen.

59 *NE* 1144$^{b}$1.

60 Above, pp 53 ff.

61. *NE* 1144$^{b}$13

62. *Ibid.* 1144$^{b}$35.

63 *Ibid* 1144$^{b}$9

64 *Ibid* 1151$^{a}$18

65. We say "evidently" because Aristotle has spoken only of the virtue produced by habituation up to this point Cf. beginning of Book ii "Moral virtue comes about as a result of habit." Moreover, as stated above, he explicitly distinguishes "true" courage (produced by habituation), which is nonetheless common bravery (as it is not strict virtue), from that produced by passion or ignorance (cf. 1116$^{b}$23 ff. and 1117$^{a}$22 ff.)

66 Cf above, p 73.

67 *NE* 1105$^{b}$1

68. *Ibid.* 1103$^{a}$15-20

69 Cf. above, n. 65.

70. *Laches* 194D.
71. *Ibid* 196E.
72. *Ibid* 199 ff.
73. *Ibid.* 191D.
74 *NE* 1169ᵃ17 ff.
75 See Table 2  2‴ "Determinat modum operationis ipsius."
76 *NE* 1115ᵇ6–14.
77. *Commentary*, pars. 545–48.
78 Above, p 75
79. *Commentary*, par 544
80 *NE* 1115ᵇ1–5.
81. *Commentary*, par 544
82. *NE* 1115ᵇ26.
83. Cf *ibid.* 1117ᵇ12

84  In par. 393 of the *Commentary*, Thomas says that no one sustains an evil except for the sake of a good that outweighs it  Compare also the *Supplement* to Part III of the *Summa theologica* (not by Thomas himself, but supposedly compiled from his other writings), Qu. 47, Art. 2  The question there is whether the compelling quality of fear affects the constant (i e , resolute or brave) man  The second objection quotes Aristotle's statement that death is the most terrible of all things but that fear of death does not affect the brave man  However, the objection continues, if this is true, then no fear affects the brave or constant man. The reply to the objection states that *peccata*, i e , "sins" (or vicious actions), are the greatest evils and hence, by implication, the most terrible things to the good or brave man  It follows, then, as the body of the article states, that the brave man may be driven by fear of a greater evil to sustain a lesser, but, of course, he would not be driven by fear of a lesser evil to avoid a greater (which would be irrational)  In substance, this is identical with Thomas' position in the *Commentary*· that the brave man follows the dictates of reason in all circumstances  But it also avoids the question as to whether, e g , a man might justifiably commit murder or adultery as a way of preventing the betrayal of his country or, rather, whether he would be *obliged* to do so, following the dictates of reason and choosing the lesser evil.

85  Cf *NE* 1115ᵃ10–15, esp. "for to fear some things is even right and noble, and it is base not to fear them." It is clear that, although, according to Aristotle, courage is concerned primarily only with fears which we should overcome, he is not unaware that there are circumstances in which it may be necessary to overcome fear (or

abhorrence) of doing what is base for the sake of what is noble Cf. 1110ª20 "Men are sometimes even praised when they endure something base or painful in return for noble objects gained." Cf Abraham Lincoln "Much as I hate slavery, I would consent to the extension of it rather than see the Union dissolved, just as I would consent to any GREAT evil, to avoid a GREATER one" (*Abraham Lincoln· His Speeches and Writings*, ed Roy P. Basler [Cleveland World Publishing Co , 1946], p 308) It is clear that it is painful for a virtuous man to consent to great evils. For Lincoln, who hated slavery, it would certainly have been extremely painful to consent to the extension of slavery or to enforce the laws securing slavery, e g , the fugitive slave laws, which he certainly considered unjust. Yet he would have done these things, as a moral duty, to avoid the greater evil (as he thought) of the dissolution of the Union Thomas does not seem to grasp the "super-terrible" character of the moral demands when in conflict with one another.

86 *Commentary*, par. 545

87 *NE* 1098$^b$11.

88. *Ibid.* 1110ª4

89 *Ibid.* 1110ª24.

90 *Commentary*, par. 394

91. *NE* 1110ª26.

92 This, of course, is contrary to Thomas' own general assumption concerning the *Ethics*, namely, that it is deliberate and intentional in its smallest details

93 See n 50, above

94 The action which Aristotle blames—that of Alcmaeon—was not done under extreme terror, he calls it "absurd " This example is, in a way, odd and certainly gives an emphasis contrary to that of Thomas in the *Commentary* For, if Aristotle wished to illustrate his point directly, he ought, one would expect, to have given an illustration of someone suffering extreme torture rather than submit to some baseness Or he ought to have shown, as blameworthy, someone under the extremest pressure, committing a baseness so terrible that no circumstance could extenuate it Perhaps, however, this "oddity" in Aristotle's example can be explained from the *incertitudo materiae moralis* and the fact that such examples would imply much more definiteness than he thinks valid in a general statement It is certainly revealing that Thomas has no such hesitancy in the selection of his examples  he explains the passage by the example of a religious martyr who suffers death by fire rather than commit

ıdolatry. Apart from the question whether the martyr, firm ın hıs conviction of eternal blıss, can be brave ın the Arıstotelıan sense, ıt ıs remarkable how thıs example contrasts with Arıstotle's

95 Cf. *Eudemıan Ethıcs* 1229<sup>b</sup>19 ("Oxford English Aristotle") "For ȷust as thıngs hot and cold and certaın other powers are too strong for us and the condıtıons of the human body, so ıt may be with regard to the emotıons of the soul "

96. *NE* 1114<sup>a</sup>1–30.

97 *Ibid* 1114<sup>a</sup>24

98. The Arıstotelıan character of thıs reasonıng may be ındıcated by the well-known passage ın the *Polıtıcs* (1253<sup>a</sup>19) asserting that the cıty ıs by nature prıor to the ındıvıdual, since the whole ıs, of necessıty, prıor to the part A hand or foot, Aristotle says there, will not be a hand or foot, except in an equıvocal sense, ıf the body be destroyed Sımılarly, we cannot know what a hand or foot ıs unless we know what the body ıs, as hand and foot have functions relatıve to the body as a whole. The same would be true of any whole, e g , a house, as we would not know what a door or roof was unless we knew first what a house was

In view of thıs dıctum, ıt is surprising to find a contrary assertıon by Thomas ın hıs comments on a passage ın Book vııı  We do not belıeve that thıs contrary assertıon has any real basıs, eıther ın Arıstotle or ın Thomas' customary mode of arguıng  The passage ıs "Between man and wıfe friendshıp seems to exıst by nature, for man ıs naturally ınclıned to form couples—even more than to form cıtıes, ınasmuch as the household is earlıer and more necessary than the cıty, and reproductıon ıs more common to man with the anımals" (*NE* 1162<sup>a</sup>16–18)  Thıs mıght at first glance seem to contradıct the passage ın *Polıtıcs* 1, but it is clear that what Arıstotle means by "prıor by nature" ıs dıstınguıshed from what ıs prıor ın the order of generatıon (Thomas hımself notes thıs ın hıs comment on thıs passage in the *Commentary on the Polıtıcs*). The famıly ıs a necessary condıtıon for the exıstence of cıtıes, but not vıce versa  It ıs clear, however, that the essentıal character of the famıly, as relatıve to man's perfectıon and not merely hıs survıval, can be seen only when the nature of the cıty has been seen  Yet Thomas, ın the *Commentary* (par 1720), states that those thıngs whıch are prıor and necessary pertaın more to nature—and domestıc socıety, to which pertains the unıon of man and wıfe, ıs prıor to cıvıl socıety  To thıs poınt ıt mıght be thought that Thomas was only tryıng to explaın "prıor," and hence "natural," from the point of vıew of "order of generation " But there follows the assertion that the *part is prior to the whole;* and this is without the qualification "in order of generation " It is noteworthy that this passage in the eighth book of the *Ethics* is cited as authority in answer to the question as to whether the family is natural, in Qu 41, Art. 1, of the *Supplement* to Part III of the *Summa theologica* (not, as noted above, by Thomas himself) It is thus made to serve the Catholic doctrine that the family has a status in nature that gives it a natural right to independence from control by the state On this whole question, see below, pp 183, 184

99. This, of course, agrees with what was said above (p. 78), namely, that Thomas' conception of the "ultimate" of courage was a formal argument, and independent of the empirical perception cited by Aristotle in the actual context of the exposition of courage in iii. 6

100  *NE* 1114ᵃ29

101. Cf Aristotle's method for ascertaining the right number of citizens for the best city, *Politics* 1326ᵃ5 ff.

102. *NE* 1109ᵇ17

103  Above, p. 73.

104. See below, pp. 171 ff

105  *NE* 1145ᵃ24 The word "excess" is literally "superexcellence," i e , above or beyond virtue, i e , the highest virtue is a virtue beyond virtue and is the object of a praise beyond praise This is, of course, as true of Christians as of pagans Leaving aside the saints, we need witness only the deification of Lincoln, in his private temple, after the manner of the ancients, for evidence of the universal character of the opinion (or instinct, or impulse) that makes a quasi-divinity of those considered to be characterized by an amount of virtue that places them "above" humanity. Compare the legends of Frederick Barbarossa, Napoleon, or Lenin. Heroes sleep, but they never die.

106  Cf *NE* 1107ᵃ17–25, esp. the following  "But as there is no excess and deficiency of temperance and courage because what is intermediate is in a sense an extreme." That is, there can be no excess of virtue because virtue *is* an extreme.

## CHAPTER VI

1. *NE* 1123ᵇ20 I have throughout substituted the Latin derivative "magnanimity," which renders the Greek original literally, for the "pride" of Ross's translation (except when quoting the Ross translation directly)

2. *Ibid* 1101$^b$10

3 *Ibid.* 1101$^b$18.

4 Cf. chap vii, n 49, concerning Aristotle's use of the singular and plural for the deity, and Thomas' technique in commenting on it

5 *NE* 1178$^b$7 ff., cf *Metaphysics* 1074$^b$15–35 A comparison of these passages would show that the really basic absurdity, from Aristotle's standpoint, is the notion of particular providence. To call God just (whether analogically or univocally) is absurd, according to Aristotle, because the divine nature cannot be aware of particular and contingent beings.

6 Cf. 1129$^b$5 "Now men pray for and pursue these things    ," in which the objects of prayer are equated with the objects of desire

7. See n. 5 above

8 Cf *Eudemian Ethics* 1249$^b$12

9 In *Summa theologica* 1 19, Arts 1 and 2, Thomas argues that God has will, and wills things other than himself It is outside the scope of the present study to analyze the merits of these arguments, but it seems clear to us that Aristotle asserts the contrary Of course, Aristotle may have been wrong. We are here trying to state Aristotle's position and assay the validity of Thomas' interpretation.

10. *NE* 1124$^a$1

11. *Ibid* 1124$^b$10 ff

12. *Ibid* 1124$^b$15

13 *Ibid* 1178$^b$21.

14 An exception to this statement could be made on the basis of 1100$^b$20, taken in the context of 1100$^b$10–30 We do not say that the magnanimous man may not be a philosopher, only that, qua magnanimous man, he is not a philosopher Whether the philosopher is not *ipso facto* magnanimous is a different question. It may be argued that the magnanimity of the philosopher is higher than that of the nonphilosopher and hence that the perfection of magnanimity implies philosophic wisdom Even if this were ultimately true, it would remain the case that in Book iv the magnanimity which Aristotle discusses is that which appears within the moral-political horizon (see below, pp 140, 141).

15 Heroes, of course, achieve the immortality accorded those of pre-eminent practical or moral virtue, i e., the immortality of fame (cf. above, chap v, n 105).

16. *NE* 1177$^b$6–15

17. *Ibid.* 1140$^b$8

18  According to Plato, the philosophers would never voluntarily be rulers  They would have to be compelled (cf  *Republic* 517E and 518D-E).

19. *NE* 1123ᵃ22–24.

20. *Ibid* 1124ᵇ23.

21. *Ibid.* 1123ᵃ34.

22. *Ibid.* 1124ᵃ1.

23. Cf above, pp 120, 121, for the implicit reservation, however.

24. *NE* 1123ᵇ30

25. *Ibid* 1123ᵇ15–20.

26. *Ibid.* 1115ᵇ20.

27. *Ibid.* 1169ᵇ9

28. *Ibid.* 1124ᵃ16–19.

29  *Ibid* 1124ᵇ30.

30  *Ibid* 1124ᵃ9.

31  *Ibid.* 1168ᵃ27–1169ᵇ3.

32. *Ibid* 1171ᵇ32.

33. *Ibid.* 1177ᵃ29.

34  *Ibid* 1172ᵃ1–5.

35  *Ibid.* 1124ᵇ9 ff

36  *Ibid* 1169ᵃ33  Even in this "solution" there is not perfect reciprocity between friends  in each action one always gets more—in some sense—than the other.

37. Shakespeare, *King Henry V*, Act IV, scene 3, ll 20 ff.

38. *De cive*, chap. i, par. 2

39  *NE* 1159ᵇ30

40. The dependence of the man of practical wisdom, for the actualization of his virtue, upon situations for which he would never wish is particularly acutely shown by the career of Lincoln  Consider the following, from his last speech in the campaign of 1858 (Roy P. Basler [ed.], *Abraham Lincoln  His Speeches and Writings* [Cleveland  World Publishing Co, 1946], p 481)  "Ambition has been ascribed to me  God knows how sincerely I prayed from the first that this field of ambition might not be opened  I claim no insensibility to political honors, but today could the Missouri restriction be restored, and the whole slavery question replaced on the old ground of 'toleration' by necessity where it exists, with unyielding hostility to the spread of it, on principle, I would, in consideration, gladly agree, that Judge Douglas should never be out, and I never in, an office, so long as we both or either, live "  But consider the sequel, e g, as implied in the famous peroration of the annual message to

Congress of 1862 (*ibid*, p 688) "Fellow-citizens, we cannot escape history . The fiery trial through which we pass, will light us down, in honor or dishonor, to the latest generation."

41 *NE* 1177ᵇ15

42 *Ibid* 1095ᵇ23-30

43. Cf *ibid* 1115ᵃ31 "These [deaths in battle] take place in the greatest and noblest danger." "Greatest and noblest" is translated *maximum et optimum* in Thomas' Latin text, and in his paraphrase, par 538 It would not follow that every great danger would have to be a noble danger (e g , any foolhardy danger), but a noble danger would have to be a great one *Optimum* therefore conveys more than *maximum*

44 *NE* 1123ᵇ6.

45. *Ibid* 1178ᵃ1

46 *Ibid* 1168ᵇ28 ff.

47. *Ibid* 1096ᵃ11

48 This is because *philosophia* is a transliteration from the Greek, although *amicitia*, "friendship," is not Thomas, of course, knew the literal meaning of *philo-sophia* and hence the etymological connections in the original.

49. "For, while both are dear, piety requires us to honor truth above our friends" (1096ᵃ16) This is, I believe, the only mention of piety in the *Nicomachean Ethics* The only other suggestion that piety might be a virtue is in the discussion of magnificence—the virtue connected with the expenditure of great wealth—as it is said that the magnificent man spends chiefly for public objects, such as temples

50 *Ibid* 1141ᵃ23, 29

51 *Ibid.* 1177ᵃ27.

52 *Ibid* 1154ᵇ27

53. Cf *ibid* 1141ᵇ4, 1180ᵇ15, 23.

54 Cf *Phaedo* 68 ff

55 *NE* 1177ᵇ33.

56 *Ibid* 1126ᵃ11

57 II 2 23. 1

58 It is true that there is a close formal similarity between Thomas' definition of charity, as a "certain friendship of man towards God " That is, according to Aristotle, man's highest end is to know the truth, which he should prefer to any human friendship For Aristotle, too, to know God and to know truth would be the same But God, according to Aristotle, is in no sense a person. And hence the

personal relationship implied in Aristotle's notion of friendship involves only human beings.

59  *NE* 1095$^b$22.

60  *Ibid.* 1129$^b$25 ff.

61  *Ibid* 1123$^b$33.

62. *Commentary*, par. 747.

63  *NE* 1124$^a$5 ff.

64. *Commentary*, par. 751

65  *Ibid.*, par 755.

66  *Ibid*, par 777

67  *NE* 1125$^a$15

68  *Commentary*, par. 782.

69  *NE* 1116$^a$15.

70  *Ibid* 1123$^b$30–31.

71. *Ibid* 1124$^b$7.

72  *Ibid.* 1124$^b$29.

73  *Commentary*, par. 774.

74  *NE* 1115$^b$20

75  *Ibid* 1124$^b$12.

76  *Commentary*, par. 764.

77  *Ibid*, par. 774.

78  Cf above, pp. 8, 9.

79  *NE* 1124$^b$25.

80  Consider Thomas' comments on Aristotle's remarks to the effect that pusillanimity, or undue humility, is more opposed to magnanimity than to vainglory  Thomas says (par 790) that the pusillanimous man omits doing the good things which he could do, which is worse than attempting to do more than he is capable of doing, and, further, that, as we become good by doing good actions and bad by doing bad or omitting to do good, the pusillanimous man tends more than the other to become worse  Thomas thus shifts the emphasis from the man's attitude toward himself, which is the focal point of Aristotle's analysis, to his attitude toward virtuous actions  The vain man, we should say, thinking himself worthy of great things, has *that* in common with the magnanimous man, the difference being that the latter is worthy of them  The pusillanimous man, on the other hand, has nothing in common with the magnanimous man  he does not regard himself as worthy, and *ipso facto* he is unworthy  Of course, there is a connection between a man's attitude toward himself and his attitude toward virtuous actions, as Aristotle emphasizes  "For each class of people aims at what corresponds to its

worth, and these people stand back from noble actions and under-
takings, deeming themselves unworthy" (1125ª25). It will be noted
that, in the context, Aristotle makes the man's attitude toward himself the condition of his aiming, or not aiming, at noble actions

## CHAPTER VII

1 *NE* 1129^b25 ff.

2 Above, pp. 91 ff.

3 In fact, this is not unambiguously true, even of Thomas As
noted above (p. 31), Thomas admits that, on the basis of natural
reason alone, man's highest perfection is attainable without moral
virtue But if human happiness is something intrinsically rational
and morality is at best a *conditio sine qua non* of happiness (like life,
health, etc ), then morality is not intrinsically rational. The problem
this presents to Thomistic natural law is discussed below, pp 169–71,
esp n 10 (p 222).

4 *Diogenes Laertius*, trans. R. D. Hicks ("Loeb Classical Library")

5 *NE* 1128^b23.

6 *Ibid* 1101^b4.

7 *Commentary*, par. 203.

8. *Ibid*, par. 211.

9 *Ibid*, par. 212

10 This is not to say that there is anything wrong with *obiter
dicta* in a commentary, so long as they are delivered as such and
are distinguished from interpretation.

11 Above, p 75.

12 Cf *NE* 1095ª14–29.

13 *Ibid* 1111^b21.

14 *Commentary*, par 444

15. *NE* 1115ª27.

16 *Commentary*, par. 536.

17. *NE* 1100ª12

18 *Commentary*, par 180.

19 *NE* 1117^b11.

20 *Commentary*, par 180.

21 *Ibid*, par 113

22 Other passages in which Thomas' reservation in favor of personal immortality occur in the *Commentary* include the following
pars 129, 202, 590, 1912, 2136.

23 *NE* 1101ª14–20.

24  *Commentary*, par 202.

25  Cf *Summa contra Gentiles* iii 48 for this reasoning with *Commentary*, par 129  After Aristotle has given the "outline" of his definition of happiness ($1098^{a}1–18$), that it is activity of the soul in accordance with perfect virtue, he adds the qualification "in a complete [i e, perfect] life " Thomas comments  There is required for felicity *continuity and perpetuity* as far as possible  For the desire of one having intellect involves the apprehension not only of the *now* perceived by the senses, but also of being simply  For, as being is in itself desirable, it follows that, just as an animal by its senses perceives that it is now, and hence desires to be now, so man, by intellect apprehending being simply, desires to be simply and always, and not only now  And on that account perfect felicity is continuous and perpetual, which cannot be in this life  Whence in the present life there cannot be perfect felicity  But that desire for "being," which Thomas admits is identical with desire for truth, is not and cannot be identical with desire for personal immortality, cf above, pp 132 ff, and below, pp. 150 ff.

26  *NE* $1177^{b}27$

27  Cf *ibid* $1129^{a}25–30$, on the subject of ambiguity.

28.  *Ibid* $1102^{b}32$

29.  *Ibid* $1139^{a}5–15$

30  *Ibid* $1145^{a}7$ ff, cf *Eudemian Ethics* $1249^{b}10–16$

31  *NE* $1178^{a}2$.

32.  *Ibid* $1154^{b}26–30$, $1177^{a}15$, 20 ff

33  The distinction between man's composite and noncomposite natures is one that Thomas explicitly recognizes in his comments on the passages in Book x, where Aristotle distinctly speaks of the moral life as only in a secondary sense happy ($1178^{a}9$ ff, *Commentary*, pars 2115, 2116). Thomas here distinctly notes that the life which is called the "active life," which is the life in accordance with prudence and moral virtue, is human, in the sense of composite  And it follows, he says, that the happiness which is in this life is human  But, he continues, the life and the happiness which is speculative, which is proper to the intellect, is separate and divine  This is more fully explained, Thomas says, in the third book of *De anima*, where it is shown that the intellect is separate  But it is clear, he concludes, that the felicity of speculation is greater than that of action, as what is separate and divine is greater than what is composite and human. Now in this passage Thomas does not clearly imply that the life which is not the human life of here and now is, temporally,

only after the dissolution of our composite human selves  Indeed, if Thomas did mean that the happiness of man's highest perfection came only after death, it would make complete nonsense of the *Nicomachean Ethics*. For that would mean that the quintessence of happiness came only after this life, but that (as Thomas himself admits) Aristotle does not speak of a life after this life because it would not be germane to the subject of ethics. Thus Thomas must have had in mind, in this passage at least, a distinctively human happiness and a divine happiness, existing side by side, *in this life*, as potentialities of human nature  In view of this, it is surprising that he confounds the two kinds of happiness elsewhere. Cf, in particular, below, pp. 158 ff

34  *NE* 1177ᵃ11 ff

35  Cf *Summa contra Gentiles* iii  48, where Thomas says that, according to Aristotle, perfect happiness (*felicitas, secundum suam perfectam rationem*) is not possible to men. But the authoritative statement we have quoted, that the operation of wisdom is *perfect* happiness, should deprive this interpretation of any authority

36  *NE* 1111ᵇ22.

37  *Commentary*, par 2083

38  *Ibid*, par. 2084.

39  I realize that, from a purely verbal viewpoint, one could deny that Thomas has actually imputed this view to Aristotle  Thomas could be said to mean that Aristotle held intellect to be part of the soul and that what follows is implicit in this view, whether or not Aristotle drew the full and accurate consequences. Nevertheless, the least one would have to say is that this is, according to Thomas, a true consequence of Aristotelian principles.

40.  *Commentary*, par. 2106.

41  *NE* 1177ᵇ31.

42  *Commentary*, par 2107.

43  Of course, here as elsewhere, the reader may ask  Is Thomas correcting Aristotle or interpreting him? I assume throughout, for practical purposes, that he is interpreting, i e, bringing out Aristotle's intended meaning (which in a loose sense may be taken sometimes to include the consequences of Aristotle's statements, whether or not Thomas thought Aristotle always to be fully aware of those consequences)  I have assumed this for "practical purposes" because no other assumption, it seems to me, warrants taking Thomas as an interpreter of Aristotle seriously (cf  above, p  27).

44  *NE* 1099ᵇ9 ff.

45. *Ibid* 1178$^b$7 ff.

46. *Ibid* 1099$^b$19.

47 *Commentary*, par. 170.

48 *NE* 1179$^a$23.

49. In Book 1, Thomas had said "if happiness is not sent *imme-diately*," thus only indirectly ascribing to, or hinting at, a notion of particular divine providence in Aristotle In the present passage he makes such an authoritative statement that it is difficult to say what, if any, connection with the *NE* it is intended to have. It may be noted that whenever Aristotle speaks of the divine nature in a way which reflects the popular notions of the gods, he always (so far as a check of the *NE* reveals) uses the plural "gods." When he speaks in a philosophic sense, he uses the singular A clear instance of this is in the passage in Book x refuting the popular notion imputing moral virtue to the divine nature He begins by using the plural, e g , "Will not the gods seem absurd if they" do the things that pop-ular religion actually imputes to them As soon as Aristotle leaves off the negative references, what the gods do not do, and says what they really do, he then speaks of the activity of "God " It is signif-icant that when Aristotle refers to divine providence (e g , 1099$^b$10, cf also 1179$^a$24) he speaks of "gods," plural. Similarly, when he speaks of a friendship of "gods" for men, he uses the plural (1179$^a$24). When he says friendship of man and God is impossible (1159$^a$5), he uses the singular. It is needless to multiply instances Although Thomas' Latin text is not always so scrupulous as it usually is, in the matter of rendering the plural instead of the singular vis-à-vis deity, there are a number of cases in which Thomas paraphrases "gods" with "God" (cf. esp pars. 169, 2133, 2134) It is not that Thomas objects to the plural, as he explains that the ancients called the "separate substances" gods and that Aristotle sometimes speaks in the vulgar manner (e g , par 1634) What is curious is how Thomas tacitly corrects Aristotle's "vulgar manner" when Aristotle tacitly disparages divine providence, or the notion of a personal deity.

50. *Commentary*, par. 2133

51 *NE* 1178$^b$25, 23.

52 *Commentary*, par. 2134.

53. Thomas' Latin text has *sapiens*, i e , "wise man," not *philo-sopher*. This is a correct translation of the Greek *sophos*

54 *Ibid* , pars 2135, 2136

55 *NE* 1177$^a$16.

56 *Ibid.* 1096$^a$4, 1117$^a$17.

57. The theme of Aristotle's chapter is supplied by Solon's saying But compare the story of Solon and Croesus in Book 1 of Herodotus, which so strongly emphasizes this point We are not shown a man like *Solon* thus suffering Still more, compare Maimonides' interpretation of Job (*Guide for the Perplexed*, Part III, chap xxii) "It is remarkable in this account that wisdom is not ascribed to Job The text does not say he was an intelligent, wise, or clever man, but virtues and uprightness, especially in actions [as distinct from thoughts] are ascribed to him "

58. *NE* 1139$^b$25, 1141$^b$3

59 Again, cf. *Summa contra Gentiles* iii 48, where Thomas applies this same Aristotelian qualification on happiness, drawn from Book i, to the happiness first described in Book x.

60 Above, pp 15 ff.

61. Cf *Summa theologica* i 1. 6

62 *NE* 1122$^b$18

63. *Commentary*, par 719

64 *NE* 1178$^a$9

65. In par. 170 Thomas speaks of the Averroist notion of happiness as consisting *in illa continuitate ad intelligentiam separatam*, and in par 2135 as *in continuitate ad intelligentiam agentem* The agent intellect (here, apparently, called "intelligence," instead of "intellect") is, of course, only part of the separate intellect, which includes the passive part Thomas may be speaking only loosely here, or there may be a defect in the text It is no part of my present intention to enter the infinite complexities of Aristotelian-Scholastic psychology, except in those broad (and, I believe, not truly controversial) respects that have to do with the interpretation of the *Ethics*

66 *NE* 1139$^b$23.

67 *On the Soul* 420$^a$30

68 *Ibid* 429$^b$5

69 *NE* 1177$^b$26–1178$^a$1.

70. *Ibid* 1178$^a$7

## CHAPTER VIII

1 Above, p 5

2 *Summa theologica* i 2 91. 2, O t c

3 It is true that, in the unequivocal meaning of "end" indicated by the expression "last end," man has but one end, according to Thomas Nonetheless, Thomas speaks of *beatitudo imperfecta*, which is possible in this life and which can be acquired by man *per sua naturalia*

(*Sum theol* 1 2 5 5). I think it therefore not improper to speak of the imperfect end acquired by natural means as man's natural end

4. A criticism of a doctrine arrived at by unassisted natural reason, by principles "informed" by faith, would not, properly speaking, be a criticism of its philosophic adequacy. That the criticism may be intended to indicate the inadequacy of unassisted natural reason is another matter. The philosophic adequacy of a doctrine can be determined only by reference to principles intrinsic to unassisted natural reason.

5 Cf. Thomas' procedure in the *Commentary*, pars 1119-23

6. Of course, it is clear that the natural law contains the principles of the habits whose object is the *jus* The law commands the acts of all the virtues, and legal justice is the habit whereby we do the right or just things (cf *NE* 1129ᵇ19 ff ) But precisely because Aristotle distinguishes the legally from the naturally just—and the law which commands the acts of all the virtues is positive law—there is a problem in the very expression "natural law" which requires thematic discussion.

7 1373ᵇ1 ff

8. *Summa theologica* 1 2. 90 4.

9. Cf *ibid* 1. 2 90 4 "Therefore, in order that a law obtain a binding force which is proper to a law, it must needs be applied to the men who have to be ruled by it But such application is made by its being made known to them by promulgation." It seems hardly possible to say that a law can be made known by promulgation, without being known to be promulgated. In this same article Thomas says that a law is imposed "on others," which would dispose of the objection that the good man, obeying the natural law, simply obeys the dictates of his own reason. He must, on the basis of Thomas' conception of law, recognize the dictate as emanating from the ruler of the community. Thomas also says, in the same article (reply to obj 1), that "the natural law is promulgated by the very fact that God instilled it into man's mind so as to be known by him naturally." But, to repeat, it would not be natural knowledge of law *as* law, by Thomas' own principles, unless at the same time it included the knowledge that God had promulgated it It is not possible to satisfy this requirement by referring to the belief in divine providence which is common to most men In the first place, the laws which are specifically believed to be of divine origin are usually, if not always, of the character of divine positive laws (see the beginning of Plato's *Laws*). Secondly, as our analysis has shown, Aris-

totle regarded the common opinion ascribing to the gods a concern
for the moral order as being an untrue opinion, required to make
morality intelligible to the nonphilosophic multitude whose lives do
not transcend the moral order, and whose happiness depends on
moral virtue.

10 The weakness of this rejoinder is further indicated by the
passages in the *Summa theologica* referred to above (pp 31, 169-
71), where Thomas admitted that, on the basis of natural reason
alone, wisdom (*sapientia*) is possible without moral virtue. But, on
the basis of natural reason, happiness is an operation of wisdom, and
hence happiness is possible without moral virtue. Therefore, to fail
to be morally virtuous does not necessarily mean to fail to be happy
But, if one can be happy without moral virtue, whence arises the obligation to moral virtue, according to natural reason? There is no
reward for virtue beyond happiness, in this life, according to natural
reason—as Thomas, following Aristotle, admits Clearly, then,
Thomas must suppose a God who punishes and rewards in another
life, in order to enforce the demands of moral virtue, according to
Thomas' conception of the *natural* law. Unless one admits a natural
knowledge of such a God and such an afterlife, I do not see how one
can call such a doctrine "natural law." If, in fact, there is no such
natural knowledge, what is called "natural law" is only a species of
divine law "natural divine law" as contrasted with positive divine
law

11 *NE* 1096$^b$18
12 *Ibid.* 1129$^a$12 ff.
13. *Metaphysics* 930$^a$1 ff.
14 *Summa theologica* i. 2. 94. 1.
15. *NE* 1103$^a$14-25.
16. *Ibid.* 1103$^a$29.

17 From the passages quoted it is not clear whether Thomas regarded synderesis as a second natural habit, distinct from intuitive
reason, or only the name for the one natural habit, when regarded
*sub specie boni.* I am inclined to believe that the latter is the case.
This, however, makes no difference for the present argument. The
point is that Thomas considered that, by the operation of a wholly
natural habit, we are informed of the principles of morality, as regards both its content and its obligatory character This, incidentally,
does not imply that Thomas regarded the principles of morality as
innate They are no more innate than the principles of theoretical
reason He certainly followed Aristotle in regarding the mind as,

a priori, a *tabula rasa* (*On the Soul* 430ᵃ1). But they would be necessary consequences of the human experience of moral phenomena

18 1 79. 12.

19. *NE* 1134ᵇ17–1135ᵃ4

20. *Commentary*, par. 1017, *ad finem*.

21. *Ibid*, par. 1018, *in principium*.

22. *Ibid*, par 1018, *ad finem* Cf par. 1277, "naturaliter indita sint prima principia operabilium humanorum, puta nulli esse nocendum, et similia", and par 1733, "quod non est scriptum, sed rationi inditum, quod supra nominavit justum naturale" From both these passages, particularly the latter, it is clear that Thomas is ascribing his notion concerning natural knowledge of morality to Aristotle.

23 "In this context" is meant to indicate emphatically that no comprehensive account of Thomas' natural law doctrine is here intended I am well aware that Thomas never worked out any such Euclidean system of natural law and that, therefore, he stands in marked contrast to the eighteenth-century natural law teachers Nevertheless, it is contended here that, on the basis of this passage in the *Commentary* and parallel passages in the *Summa,* one could properly infer the possibility of such a system. That Thomas never worked out such a system can only mean, then, either that he did not mean what he actually says here (which I do not think a proper assumption to make concerning a writer of Thomas' stamp) or that he meant it, but thought it prudent to leave the working-out of the principles proximate to actual practice to those who would actually supervise conduct Another possibility is that he never worked out his notion of natural law to the point of clarity where the "Euclidean" element could be developed in harmony with the other elements.

24. Cf above, n. 10.

25. *NE* 1095ᵇ20.

26. *Ibid.* 1179ᵇ11–16.

27. *Commentary*, par. 1023.

28 *Ibid*, par 1024.

29 *Ibid*, par. 1025.

30 *Ibid*, par 1028.

31. *NE* 1129ᵇ13.

32. *Ibid.* 1128ᵇ22

33 *Politics* 1301ᵃ40.

34. *NE* 1179ᵇ22.

35. *Politics* 1337ᵃ10.

36 If it be said that the family's rights over against the state in the matter of education derive from the fact that the persons who make up the family have an end that transcends the natural order (in which the state is supreme), the reply would have to be made (as far as Aristotelian natural right is concerned) that this "fact" is not known to unassisted natural reason, and no natural rights can be inferred from any facts not so known.

37 *Politics* 1335$^b$22 ff

38 Above, p 177 (cf. n. 18)

39 1277$^b$25

40. Even this is not unequivocally true There is, in fact, a tension between *phronesis* and *sophia*, in Aristotle's doctrine, which, for reasons of obvious prudence, is never emphasized As noted above, Thomas, who is absolved both of the tension and of the dictate of prudence by the dispensation of theological wisdom (cf above, p. 31 and n 15, p. 199), clearly says that wisdom (*sophia*) is possible without prudence (*phronesis*) As we have explained (cf above, pp 143 ff ), the philosopher would certainly choose to do virtuous acts, so far as the necessity of living in a human community constrained him to live within the moral-political dimension (cf *NE* 1178$^b$5). The difficulty is that he would not live on this level except in so far as necessity constrained him. To take the Platonic and supreme example, he would never choose to rule Yet, as Aristotle says in the *Politics* (1278$^b$1-5), the good man in the strict sense (1 e., morally good) is the man who rules in a good city The full development of moral goodness then requires as a motive the untrue opinion that happiness is to be found in moral excellence Strictly speaking, the philosopher would never be a good man, in the sense in which Aristotle uses that expression in the third book of the *Politics* Sophia is the virtue, par excellence, of private life, but *phronesis*, like justice, which it directs, reaches its highest perfection when in relation with "others " In other words, practical wisdom reaches its peak when it obtains the common good, but philosophic wisdom obtains a good that is enjoyed only by the philosopher, and perhaps his very few friends

41 Above, pp. 142, 143

42 Above, n. 13 Cf *NE* 1170$^a$15 ff "Now life is defined in the case of animals by the power of perception, in that of man by the power of perception or thought, and a power is defined by reference to the corresponding activity, which is the essential thing, therefore life seems to be essentially the act of perceiving or think-

ing. And life is among the things that are good and pleasant in themselves, since it is determinate and the determinate is of the nature of the good ..." Ross's note to this passage (in the "Student's Oxford Aristotle") quotes Burnet's analysis of the argument. The first two syllogisms, contained in the above passages, are presented as follows

I Capacity is defined by reference to activity.
  Human life is defined by the capacity of perception or thought
  . Human life is defined by the activity of perception or thought.
II The determinate is good by nature.
  Life is determinate.
  . . Life is good by nature.

43 Above, pp. 18, 19.

44 It is true that Thomas might consider some, if not all, of these as knowable by natural reason But the fact that they were not known by Aristotle—as we believe has been shown—would certainly suggest that their value as principles of *unassisted* human reason, from Thomas' own point of view, would be negligible.

45. Above, pp. 20 ff. and 34, especially.

## POSTSCRIPT

1 Frederick Copleston, *A History of Philosophy*, Vol. II  *Mediaeval Philosophy  Augustine to Scotus* (Westminster, Md  Newman Press, 1950), p  400.

2. *Ibid*, p  398

3. *Ibid*, p  386

4. Cf above, pp  164, 165

5. Cf above, pp  149 ff  and n. 25, p. 217.

6. Copleston, *op  cit*, p. 405.

7. *Ibid*, p  402.

8 *Ibid.*, pp. 410–11.

9. *Summa theologica* i  2  104  1, repl obj  3.

10 *Reason and Revelation in the Middle Ages* (New York, 1938), p  79

11. Cf. above, pp  1–4

12. Winston Churchill, address at the Mid-century Convocation of the Massachusetts Institute of Technology, *New York Times*, April 1, 1949.

# BIBLIOGRAPHY

A PRINCIPAL SOURCES

Aquinas, Thomas *Summa contra Gentiles* Ed. Leonina manualis. Turin Marietti, 1946
—— *Summa theologica* Cum textu ex recensione Leonina Turin· Marietti, 1948
—— *In Aristotelis librum De anima Commentarium.* Ed. II Cura A Pirotta O P. Turin, 1948
——. *In X Libros ethicorum Aristotelis ad Nicomachum expositio* Cura A. Pirotta O P. Turin, 1934.
——. *In Metaphysicam Aristotelis commentaria.* Ed. III Cura R Cathala O P 1935
—— *In VIII libros Politicorum Aristotelis expositio* Éditions de l'Université Laval Quebec, 1936.
Aristotle *The Works of Aristotle* Translated into English under the editorship of W D. Ross (Text identical with the "Student's Oxford Aristotle ") London Oxford University Press, 1942.

B REFERENCES

Adams, Henry *Mont St Michel and Chartres* New York Houghton Mifflin Co., 1905.
Aristotle *Nicomachean Ethics.* Translation and notes by Rackham "Loeb Classical Library."
Chaucer *The Canterbury Tales,* "The Pardoner's Tale."
Diogenes Laertius. *Lives of the Philosophers.* "Loeb Classical Library."
Frank, Philipp *Foundations of Physics* Chicago· University of Chicago Press, 1946.
Gibbon, Edward *Decline and Fall of the Roman Empire.* "Modern Library" ed
Herodotus *History of the Persian Wars* "Modern Library" ed
Kant, Immanuel *Foundations of the Metaphysics of Morals.* Translated by L W. Beck Chicago University of Chicago Press, 1949.
King James Bible, The New Testament.
Lincoln, Abraham *Abraham Lincoln· His Speeches and Writings.*

Edited by Roy P. Basler Cleveland World Publishing Co , 1946.

Macaulay, Thomas B. *History of England*

Maimonides *The Eight Chapters of Maimonides on Ethics* Translated by Joseph I. Gorfinkle. New York Columbia University Press, 1912

——. *The Guide for the Perplexed*. Translated by M. Friedlander London George Routledge, 1947.

Plato *Epistles* Translated by R C Bury. "Loeb Classical Library."

——. *Republic*. Translated by Paul Shorey. "Loeb Classical Library."

——. *Laws*. Translated by R. G Bury "Loeb Classical Library."

——. *Crito, Phaedo, Phaedrus*. Translated by H. L. Fowler "Loeb Classical Library."

——. *Laches, Protagoras* Translated by W R. M Lamb "Loeb Classical Library."

——. *Symposium*. Translated by W R. M Lamb. "Loeb Classical Library."

Plutarch *Lives*. Translated by John Dryden "Modern Library" ed.

Ross, W D *Aristotle* London Oxford University Press, 1926

Rousseau *The Social Contract*. Translated by G. D. H Cole. "Everyman's" ed

Shakespeare. *King Henry V, Macbeth*.

Xenophon. *Memorabilia* Translated by H. C. Dakyns New York Macmillan Co., 1897.

# INDEX